Undoing Depression

including depiction

Undoing Depression

*What Therapy Doesn't Teach You and
Medication Can't Give You*

RICHARD O'CONNOR,
Ph.D.

LITTLE, BROWN AND COMPANY

Boston New York Toronto London

First Edition

The author is grateful for permission to include the following previously copyrighted material:

"Daily Record of Dysfunctional Thoughts" from *Cognitive Therapy of Depression* by Aaron T. Beck, A. J. Rush, B. F. Shaw, and G. Emery. Copyright © 1979. Reprinted by permission of Guilford Press.

The figure on page 223 is based on "Why the Complexity of Consciousness . . ." (adapted) from *Flow: The Psychology of Optimal Experience* by Mihaly Csikszentmihalyi. Copyright © 1990 by Mihaly Csikszentmihalyi. Reprinted by permission of HarperCollins Publishers, Inc.

The Wakefield Self-Report Questionnaire (Appendix B) is from R. P. Snaith, S. N. Ahmed, S. Mehta, and Max Hamilton. "Assessment of the Severity of Primary Depressive Illness: Wakefield Self-Assessment Depression Inventory." *Psychological Medicine* 1(2): pp. 143–147 (1971). Reprinted by permission of Dr. Snaith and Cambridge University Press.

"There's a certain Slant of light," Poem #258 by Emily Dickinson, reprinted by permission of the publishers and the Trustees of Amherst College from *The Poems of Emily Dickinson,* Thomas H. Johnson, ed. Cambridge, Mass.: The Belknap Press of Harvard University Press. Copyright © 1951, 1955, 1979, 1983 by the President and Fellows of Harvard College.

Library of Congress Cataloging-in-Publication Data

O'Connor, Richard, Ph.D.
    Undoing depression : what therapy doesn't teach you and medication can't give you / Richard O'Connor. — 1st ed.
        p. cm.
    Includes bibliographical references and index.
    ISBN 0-316-62643-0
    1. Depression, Mental. 2. Depressed persons — Life skills guides.
I. Title.
    RC537.0326 1997
    616.85'27 — dc 21   96-50214

10 9 8 7 6 5 4 3 2 1

MV-NY

Published simultaneously in Canada by Little, Brown & Company (Canada) Limited
Printed in the United States of America

Contents

Author's Note

TWO PARTICULAR PROBLEMS with language occur throughout this book. One is the difficulty of what to call someone with depression. In different contexts, this person may be called a patient, a client, a victim, a sufferer, or a consumer. Each term says more about the assumptions of the person applying the label than the recipient. The only descriptive term I know of, which is to call someone with depression a "depressive," will suggest to some the concept of a "depressive character," which is a loaded concept suggesting that there is something in the personality that causes depression. I disagree with the implication that there is a depressive character, yet I argue that depression does affect one's character and personality, so I opt for the term depressive as descriptive of what can become a way of life. Since I count myself among this number, I can plead the right to use the term without its implicit value judgment.

The second problem is the use of "he" or "she" to refer to a person when gender really doesn't matter. In this book in particular, since depression is much more commonly diagnosed among women, and since that phenomenon is a subject of some heated debate in gender politics, the issue becomes ticklish. For a male writer to refer to depressed individuals as "she" may appear to perpetuate what, to some, is an artifact of male-dominated science and culture. For me to refer to depressed individuals as "he" exclusively, however, may appear to gloss over the apparent greater suffering of women. For me to write "he or she" and "himself/herself" every time just becomes too awkward. I have, therefore, decided to try to intersperse male and female pronouns in instances when gender really doesn't matter, but there are times when this becomes labored, and I revert to using "he" to refer to an individual of either sex.

Acknowledgments

WRITING THIS BOOK has been a wonderful exercise in remembering experiences and people who have helped me over the years. Any attempt to acknowledge them all is bound to be incomplete, but there are some teachers and colleagues who stand out: Bill Reid, Laura Epstein, Bernece Simon, Mary Gyarfas, Joe Palombo, Frank Lachmann, Susan Buckman, Florence Forshey, Rob Mardirossian, Kathy Fox, Ann Schreiner, Irwin Hoffman.

I also owe a tremendous debt to Arthur Rosenthal, for his wise advice, and to Sally Ellsworth, for her friendship and unwavering support. My agent, Jim Levine, and Jennifer Josephy at Little, Brown have both been instrumental in turning this into a readable book. Two friends and colleagues, Jeanne Russo and Helen Bray-Garretson, were kind enough to read early drafts and make encouraging and helpful suggestions.

A therapist learns most from his patients, and I've been lucky to know some brave and inspiring people. I hope I've been able to portray them here with the affection and admiration I feel for them. I particularly want to thank my current Tuesday group for all the support they've provided, as well as serving as a catalyst while some of these ideas were in the process of development.

ACKNOWLEDGMENTS

My father came through with a special gift at an important time. My children, Sarah and Michael, have not only put up with my moods over the years but have come out of it as pretty admirable human beings, which warms my heart. Most of all, my wife, Robin, has always lent me her confidence and given me her love and support. I know I wouldn't be writing this today if I hadn't been able to lean on her when I needed to.

Undoing Depression

Introduction

THE ESSENTIAL QUESTION that patients and therapists ask themselves over and over is: why is it so hard to get better? Once we understand the hidden meanings and motives behind our behavior, once we understand that what we're doing is essentially self-destructive, that these repetitive patterns prevent us from feeling good about ourselves and getting to where we want in life, *why don't we just stop?* Once we have the right medication to prevent us from sinking back into the blackest depths, once we can start feeling a little more optimistic about the future and ourselves, why do we remain shy, passive, and withdrawn? Why do people persist in self-destructive behavior when they can see that it does them no good? Freud had to invent theories as elaborate and arcane as the death instinct to answer this question—the idea that as a counterpart to a desire to create, enjoy, and live we have an equally strong desire to destroy, suffer, and die. All my experience tells me that there is a much simpler answer: people persist in self-destructive behavior because they don't know how to do anything else.

I'm convinced that the major reason why people with depression stay depressed despite therapy, medication, and support from loved ones is that we are simply unable to imagine an alternative. We know how to do depression. We are experts at it. Our feelings about ourselves and the way we see the world have forced us over the years to develop a very special set of skills. We become like those who are blind from birth. They become very attuned to sounds, smells, and other senses that sighted persons take for granted. They can read Braille as well as anyone else can read printed matter. They get very good at memorization. But asking them to imagine a sunset, or a flower, or a Van Gogh is pointless—they have no reference; it's beyond their experience. Expecting us to stop being depressed is like expecting a blind person to suddenly see the light of day—with one important difference: eventually, we can do it.

Depression becomes for us a set of habits, behaviors, thought processes, assumptions, and feelings that seems very much like our core self; you can't give those up without something to replace them and without expecting some anxiety along the way. Recovery from depression is like recovery from heart disease or alcoholism. The good heart patient knows that medication isn't enough, that lifelong habits of diet and exercise and how one deals with stress must change. The recovering alcoholic knows that abstinence is not enough; ways of thinking, relating to others, and dealing with emotions have to change. We depressives become shaped by our disease as well; the skills that we develop with depression in a vain effort to save ourselves pain—skills like emotional control, isolation, putting others first, being overresponsible—prevent our recovery. We have to give up the depressed habits that keep us down and make us vulnerable to relapse.

This book presents a "program" for depression. People in AA know that not drinking is only the beginning; they have to "live the program." Like alcoholism, depression is a lifelong condition that can be cured only by a deliberate effort to change our selves. Later chapters explain how in five key elements of our personality—feelings, thoughts, behavior, relationships, and the self—

depression has taught us certain skills that have come to feel natural, a part of who we are. But in fact we have to unlearn those skills and replace them with new habits—which are explained in detail—for real recovery to take place. Practicing the exercises described later can be a way for people with depression to "live the program"—and live a vital, rich existence again.

I believe very strongly that people can recover from depression but that medication and/or conventional psychotherapy don't go far enough. People need new tools, and practice in using them, in order to make a full recovery. In putting these techniques together I've had the benefit of being able to draw on a great deal of research and clinical experience developed over the last twenty years, which have suggested new ways of thinking, acting, relating, and feeling to replace the old ways of being that have never worked and often made things worse. I've also had the benefit of working in clinics in the real world to help me understand how these methods can be applied in everyday life. Further, my own experience with depression and recovery has helped me learn firsthand what's helpful and what's not.

This is an unorthodox theory of change and recovery. I remember how for decades the analytic community debated whether true "structural change," as opposed to mere "symptom relief," could ever come from anything other than full-blown psychoanalysis. Now prominent scientists argue that recovery can come only from medication. These dogmatic positions are appeals to magic, not reason. I believe that people can make substantial changes in how they live their emotional lives, in their personalities, even in their brain chemistry, by making changes in their behavior. This is despite the fact that there certainly are unconscious forces at work that oppose change. But rather than postulate that these unconscious forces can be overcome only through the psychoanalytic method, or by use of medication, it seems to make perfect sense to suppose that the need for these defenses and resistances can be removed. People learn and grow through experience, but the depressed person, out of fear, avoids the curative experience. I think that by practicing, by taking big challenges in small steps, by learning gradually that fears can't kill you and impulses don't overwhelm you, the depressed person learns alternatives to depressed behavior; and enough non-depressed behavior means you're not depressed anymore.

This book is meant both for the interested professional and for the lay reader, especially those who suffer from depression. Because it's meant for both audiences, I'm asking both to read things they aren't ordinarily asked to read. There is a lot more how-to-do-it, more self-help, than mental health professionals are ordinarily exposed to. But I urge the professional to read these sections carefully and to ask yourself what effect it would have on your patients—whatever theoretical frame of reference you operate from—if they actually practiced these skills. I think you might find they would be helped, perhaps substantially changed. And the lay person is being asked to read much more theory than most self-help books require. This is partly because I feel the theory helps organize a way of thinking, gives you something intuitive to hold on to, rather than just learning a list of behavioral techniques. But it is here more because I find the theory comforting and ultimately hopeful. The basic assumption is that we need to find ways to express ourselves and to connect with others as we go through life. Despite what depression tells us, no one is inherently bad, no one is worth more than anyone else, each of us can help each other, everyone can achieve this goal, to express the self and to make connections with other people.

When I was fifteen I came home from school one day to find that my mother had committed suicide in the basement. She had bolted the doors and taped a note to the window saying she was out shopping and I should wait at a neighbor's. I knew something was wrong and was climbing in a window when my father came driving in after work. We discovered her body together.

She had put a plastic bag over her head and sat down at the table where I played with my chemistry set. She ran the gas line from my Bunsen burner into the plastic bag and turned on the gas. Later we learned that she had also taken a lethal dose of a sleeping pill that my father sold in his job as a pharmaceutical representative. Her body was cold, so she must have started to set things up soon after we had left the house in the morning. This was not any cry for help; she went to a great deal of trouble to make sure she would end her life.

Until two years before, my mother had seemed happy, confident, and outgoing. I remember her joy getting ready to go out to a party, or singing forties songs with my father on evening car rides. When I look back at the course of my life, I realize now how much it has been shaped by my need to understand what happened to her.

To understand also what was happening to me, because I've had my own depression to contend with. I didn't recognize it for a long time, though I'm a reasonably well-trained and experienced psychotherapist. I've been a patient myself several times, but I never put a label on my problems; I always told myself I sought help for personal growth. This was despite the fact that there were long periods in my life when I drank too much, when I alienated everyone close to me, when I could just barely get to work, when I would wake up each morning hating the thought of facing the day and my life. There were many times I thought of suicide, but if I couldn't forgive my mother, I couldn't forgive myself, either. And I have children and family, patients, and colleagues I couldn't bear to do that to. But for many long periods life seemed so miserable, hopeless, and joyless that I wished for a way out. Everyone who has ever been depressed knows it's impossible to be sure, but I think those days are finally behind me now. I don't hit the deepest depths, but I live with the after-effects. I still struggle with the emotional habits of depression. But accepting the fact that it's going to be a long struggle has made me more able to deal with the short-term ups and downs.

I've worked in mental health for twenty years, as a therapist, supervisor, and agency director. I've studied psychoanalytic, family systems, biochemical, cognitive, you name it, ways of understanding people. I've worked with some wonderful teachers and had some wonderful patients. I won't pretend to have all the answers on depression, but you won't find many people with more experience, both personal and professional.

I believe now that depression can never be fully grasped by mental health professionals who have not experienced it. I've repeatedly seen "comprehensive" theories of depression develop, flourish, and dominate the field for a time, then be rejected because new, contradictory evidence is found. These are all theories that try to explain depression from a single point of reference—the unconscious, the brain and its chemistry, cognitive processes, family interaction. Many psychologists and psychiatrists seem to have a fatal predilection for theory-building—for making their experiences fit with some preexisting theory or for destroying someone else's theory or for developing a new theory that will explain it all—rather than trying to figure out practical ways to help their patients. They get too far away from experience. I realize now that no simple, single-factor theory of depression will ever work. Depression is partly in our genes, partly in our childhood experience, partly in our way of thinking, partly in our brains, partly in our ways of handling emotions. It affects our whole being.

Imagine if we were in the state of science where we could reliably diagnose heart disease but knew nothing about the effects of exercise, cholesterol, salt and fat, stress, and fatigue. Patients who were diagnosed would be grasping at all kinds of straws that might help them recover. Some would stop all exercise, some would exercise furiously. Some would withdraw from stressful situations. Some would take medication to reduce blood pressure without knowing that their unhealthy diet undoes any beneficial effect of medication. Many would die prematurely; some would get better accidentally; without good controlled scientific studies, medicine would not learn what was causing some to die, some to recover.

This is where we are with depression. We get all kinds of advice, some of it helpful, some of it not, most of it unproven. The depressed patient is in the dark about what exactly he or she needs to do to help recovery. But in fact a great deal is known about how people recover from depression. It doesn't all fit into a neat theoretical package, so it's hard to pull together; but the knowledge is there to be used.

Depression is a complex condition that blurs our Western boundaries between mind and body, nature and nurture, self and others. Many people with depression seem to have been primed for it by loss of loved ones in childhood. Most people with depression describe difficulties in their childhood or later in life that have contributed to low self-esteem and a sensitivity to rejection, an uncertainty about the self and an inability to enjoy life. But these observations are not true for everyone with depression: some people who have no history of stress, who appear very stable and well integrated, develop it suddenly, unexpectedly, in response to a life change. There is clearly a biochemical component to depression, and medication can be very helpful for most people, but it is not sufficient treatment for very many. The truth is that whether the roots of depression are in the past in childhood, or in the present in the brain, recovery can only come about through a continuous act of will, a self-discipline applied to emotions, behavior, and relationships in the here and now. This is a hard truth, because no one deserves to feel this way, and it doesn't seem fair that the blameless have to help themselves. Besides, the depressed are always being told to snap out of it, pull themselves together, don't give in to weakness, and it's the cruelest, most unfeeling advice they can be given. What I want to do here is to give guidance and support along with advice, to help the depressive find the resources he or she needs for recovery.

People who are depressed are in over their heads and don't know how to swim. They work very hard at living, at trying to solve their problems, but their efforts are unproductive because they lack the skills necessary to support themselves in deep water. The real battle of depression is between parts of the self. Depressed people are pulled under by shadows, ghosts, pieces of themselves that they can't integrate and can't let go. The harder they work, the more they do what they know how to do, the worse things get. When their loved ones try to help in the usual ways, the commonsense ways that only seem natural expressions of caring and concern, they get rejected. The depressed person then feels more guilty and out of control.

People with depression have to learn new ways of living with themselves and others—new emotional skills. These skills take practice, coordination, and flexibility. Instead of flailing at the water in panic, they have to learn emotional habits that are much more like swimming—smooth, rhythmic, learning to float, learning to be comfortable in the water. Depressed people are great strugglers, but to struggle is to drown. Better to learn how to let the water hold you up.

The families of people with depression also have to learn new skills. Many of their usual patterns of family interaction are related to the depression, rewarding it or blaming the victim. With the best intentions, family members sometimes make things worse for the depressive. They have to learn how to mix confrontation and support, caring and limits. In the process of changing, some family members will come to grips with distressing truths about themselves—but the truth is nothing to be afraid of.

Chapter 1 describes the nature, impact, and pervasiveness of depression. Chapter 2 reviews the different kinds of depression that current science delineates, and describes briefly some of the controversy involved in diagnosis. Chapter 3, "Why Don't We Have a Theory?" reviews some of the reasons why mental health professionals have difficulty agreeing on what depression is, and then presents a way of understanding it—as a response to pain or loss that unfortunately has taken some unnecessary twists because of the way the individual experiences the world. The concepts of self psychology and of defense mechanisms are introduced, two points of view that greatly help us understand how depression works. Chapter 4 elaborates on the "skills of depression"—how we become very good at doing certain things that, tragically, only perpetuate our depression. Two cases are discussed in detail that illustrate how these depressive skills are used, and how they backfire on the user.

Part 2 reviews the major functional areas in which depression affects us—feelings, behavior, thought processes, relationships, and the self. Habits that we take for granted, assumptions that we unconsciously make about people, ways of working and communicating that seem to make perfect sense to us—these all must be questioned and examined for real recovery to take place. Not that everything we do is wrong; but too much of it only perpetuates a depressive cycle that goes on continuously, outside our awareness. The first chapter in this section focuses on changing emotional habits, because those changes must come first. Once we begin to change how we experience and express our feelings, our emotional life becomes a more reliable guide to differentiate between healthy and unhealthy behavior. There are some very specific exercises in these sections, which I urge the reader to practice—just reading about them doesn't help. A last chapter in this section reviews how psychotherapy and medication can help, and how a better understanding of their effects contributes to a complete understanding of what depression is.

Part 3 takes this new knowledge and extends it further, into the world of work, marriage, divorce, the family, and the community. In an age when depression is epidemic, we have to use our knowledge out in the real world to help keep ourselves, our children, and our communities healthy. In the last section, some specific principles for maintaining recovery are described. Then twin themes—of the development of the self, and of the self's interaction with the world as understood by the theory of psychological defenses—are brought together in a discussion of creativity.

Obviously this is an intensely personal book for me. I want to keep would-be suicides alive, I want to spare people the useless pain of depression. There is a great deal more that can be done now than was available for my mother or for myself when I was younger. Medication and psychotherapy offer hope to everyone. Learning techniques of self-control, skills of communication and self-expression, challenging one's assumptions about the self and the world, can give people who literally don't know anything other than depression the chance for a rewarding life.

Something that touches me deeply at our clinic is the large number of people who don't know they are depressed. People are usually prompted to call for help not because of subjective feelings of depression, but because something is going wrong in their lives; their children won't listen, there is a marital problem, they are having trouble at work. But it often doesn't take much digging to find that the caller has been depressed for some time;

the family problem, the job problem, is a manifestation, not a cause, of the depression. This is a person who feels almost no joy in life, who has no hope, no ambition, who feels stuck, powerless, and perennially sad—*and who thinks this is the normal way to feel.* It's not.

Part 1

What We Know About Depression

1

Understanding Depression

WE ARE LIVING in an epidemic of depression. Every indication suggests that more people are depressed, more of the time, more severely, and starting earlier in their lives, than ever before. Depression is not going to go away, no matter how much we ignore it, scorn it, or neglect it. If we're smart, we'll attend to it. But doing so goes against our grain; the idea of depression frightens us, and we think of a descent into madness. We have a natural wish to forget about depression, to hope that we are immune. Can you make yourself remember the sensation of pain? Most people react to the question with a cringe but really can't describe pain or evoke the sensation in their memory. We repress it, push it away, so that most of the time we don't think about it and we can get on with life. But when we hear the dentist's drill, we suddenly remember exactly what it's going to feel like. We do the same mental trick with depression. We've all felt it, but we believe we have to shut out the memory. We want to think of depression as something that happens to somebody else.

But it strikes closer to home now, because the incidence is increasing. People born after World War II are more likely to develop depression, and more likely to develop it at a younger age, than the previous generation.[1] "Baby boomers" seem to be at particular risk. And this is not merely a phenomenon of a new pill generating new awareness of its disease, but a true growth in hard numbers.[2] Nor is it only a phenomenon of American, or even Western, culture. A recent study comparing incidence of depression in Taiwan, Puerto Rico, and Lebanon, among other countries, found that for each successive generation, depression was likely to begin at earlier ages, and that over the course of a lifetime, the risk of depression kept increasing.[3]

Clinical depression is a serious, often fatal illness that is so common it's hard to recognize. Researchers estimate that almost 20 percent of the population meet the criteria for some form of depression at any given time—and that does not mean people who are temporarily feeling the blues and will be better next week, but people who are having real difficulty functioning in life.[4] In terms of overall economic burden to our society, depression is the second most costly disease there is. The cost, in terms of direct treatment, unnecessary medical care, lost productivity, and shortened life span, is estimated at $44 billion a year.[5] It's second only to cancer in terms of economic impact, approximately the same as the cost of heart disease and AIDS—and the number of deaths from suicide each year is approximately the same as the number of deaths from AIDS.

Approximately 20 million Americans will experience an episode of major depression in their lifetimes. There is no question that major depression is a serious illness. If you have it, most likely you have real trouble getting through your daily routine, you can't connect to other people, you have distressing physical symptoms, you can't concentrate, you feel guilty, worthless, and hopeless, and you think about suicide. Twenty million means one in ten Americans. Take the phone book and start with the letter *A.* Go on through the end of the *E*'s. That's how many people from your community will have a very serious episode of depression. Children, teens, adults, and seniors, men and women; depression is not choosy.

Depression is amazingly underdiagnosed. Many people don't realize they have it. At our office, a community mental health center in rural Connecticut, we see two or three new people every week who have trouble sleeping and have other physical symptoms, feel anxious and overwhelmed, have lost ambition and hope, feel alone and alienated, are tormented by guilt or obsessional thoughts, may even have thoughts of suicide—but they don't say they're depressed. They just feel that life stinks and there's nothing they can do about it. They go to their doctors for aches and pains, sleeplessness, lack of energy, and they get a useless prescription or medical procedure or get dismissed as hypochondriacs. They may medicate themselves with alcohol and drugs. Their families don't know how to help; neither sympathy nor moralizing seems to have any effect. The depressed person is caught up in a vicious circle from which there seems to be no escape.

The real tragedy is that in mental health, where there is so much we can't help, depression is one thing that can usually be treated effectively and efficiently. Estimates are that when people are treated promptly, 90 percent of them will recover. New medications are quite helpful, with few side effects. Psychotherapy and medication together have been reliably demonstrated to be more effective than either alone.

Janet was admitted to a psychiatric hospital in an acute state of depression. She was extremely upset and confused, could not organize her thoughts, could not drive to the store or take care of her children. She was obsessed with thoughts and impulses of suicide, though she did not consciously desire to kill herself. She could not sleep, felt hopeless and helpless, and had lost all interest in ordinary activities. She was convinced she was losing her mind.

This all seemed to start when Janet found out her husband had had an affair. Although he seemed ashamed of himself and assured her it would never happen again, her world seemed to collapse. Within a few weeks, her ability to function had deteriorated dramatically. Her husband brought her to the family doctor, and together they arranged for emergency admission.

After a week in the hospital, with the help of medication and the support of the staff, Janet felt much better. Just before she was ready to be discharged, she went home on a weekend pass. Her visit went smoothly until Janet discovered a letter her husband's girlfriend had recently written to him. Again he tried to reassure Janet that the affair was over. But her condition took a dramatic turn for the worse, and she spent several more weeks in the hospital.

Depression is a fascinating condition. There is a great deal of value in thinking of it as a disease. For one thing, it responds very well to medication. Seventy percent of patients who take medication for depression report feeling better. Further supporting the disease idea is the finding that the brain chemistry of depressed people is different from that of other people; and it is possible to find the same biochemical differences in the brains of animals who appear "depressed." On a human level, helping people who are depressed understand that they have a disease can free them from much of the guilt and self-blame that accompanies depression. They can learn different ways of reacting to stress and learn to intervene more quickly with medication so that the danger of future episodes is greatly reduced.

But if it's a disease, how do we contract it? If Janet's husband hadn't had his affair, would she ever have come down with depression? There was nothing to suggest it about her before she got sick. Janet now thinks she has had a "breakdown," she now thinks of herself as a mental patient—but isn't this because her husband is a jerk? Is the depression in Janet or in her marriage? If it's in her marriage, how can the pills Janet takes help her feel more competent and capable? If it's in Janet, is it the part of herself that sees the truth more clearly than she and her husband can admit to?

Most people who have had a true experience with depression have no trouble at all believing that something biochemical in nature has happened to them. The change in mood, in how the self and the world are perceived, seems so profound and over-whelming that it makes intuitive sense to feel that the self has been invaded by something alien. We do not feel like our selves. Something very powerful, something from outside us, has invaded and changed us.

But most people with depression also recognize that this feeling that seems so foreign is also very familiar. They remember many times from their childhood and adolescence when they felt the same way. They felt alone, helpless, and friendless. They may remember their parents as kind and loving, but they wonder why they felt so unloved. They may have believed that they had to be perfect, and they may have tried very hard, but failed, and felt again the futility of their efforts. As adults, they may have thought they'd grown out of it, but here it is again. Winston Churchill referred to his depression as the "black dog"—the familiar beast that quietly pads in in the evening and settles down at your feet.

Depression is a disease both of the mind and of the body, the present and the past. In psychiatry now we have pitched battles going on between opposing camps, those who want to treat the brain and those who want to treat the mind. Both sides have powerful motives for pushing their own theories, some of which are idealistic and some of which are ignoble. Unfortunately, the patient is caught in the middle. The family doctor, supported by the pharmaceutical industry, is likely to say, "Take this pill"—but when it doesn't work, the patient just has another in a long line of failures to add to his baggage. The mental health professional is likely to say, "Let's talk about it"—and the patient is likely to feel patronized, misunderstood, because how can simply talking cure such terrible pain?

It's not an either-or question. Both ways of thinking are true.[6] Both points of view have much to contribute to helping the depressed patient and his family. Both also have a lot to teach people who simply want to raise emotionally resilient children in a difficult world. *There is a biochemical process in depression, but the individual has been made susceptible to depression through life experiences. The current episode may be precipitated by an external event, but the event has set in motion a change in the way the brain functions.*

When he was in his thirties, Robert went to bed for fourteen months. He was not sick in any physical sense, but profoundly depressed. A highly intellectual man, his mind was preoccupied with questions about the meaning of life. Unable to find a reason for living, he saw no reason to get up. He didn't consciously feel depressed, he just felt empty. His wife begged, pleaded, and threatened in an effort to get him out of bed. She brought in doctors, family members, appealed to his duty to their child. It became a power struggle between them. Finally, one day long after his wife had given up, Robert decided to get up and go back to work.

I got to know Robert fifteen years later. He had had a few more episodes in which he took to his bed for weeks, but never for so long. He and his wife had separated a few years previously, when she finally tired of his coldness. Their only child had been killed in a terrible accident two years earlier.

Robert came in for treatment because he feared slipping back into his old ways. He lived alone now, in a house literally crammed with junk. There were days when he just couldn't get out of bed. When he did, he procrastinated and couldn't accom-

plish anything. He was troubled by his wife, who seemed bent on a nasty divorce battle. He had received a small inheritance from his family, and he didn't want her to get it. He still saw absolutely no purpose in living, but he wanted to resolve the divorce. He was dead-set against medication of any kind, and since he never went into a major depressive episode while we worked together, I didn't push it.

Robert was a very intelligent man with an odd, dry sense of humor, an acute observer of life with absolutely no understanding of feelings. When his son died, he read several books on the grief process and self-consciously forced himself to pay attention to his feelings as he went through the described stages. Though I had my doubts, after knowing him for some time I was forced to conclude that he had really "successfully" mourned for his son, as much as anyone can.

He had exactly the family background that is so common among depressed men: a critical, distant, hostile father and a shallow, narcissistic mother. He felt he couldn't satisfy his father or interest his mother. Because children can't see their parents objectively, they make the way their parents treat them part of themselves; if you are treated like dirt long enough, you begin to feel like dirt. Instead of understanding that father is too critical, the child experiences himself as inadequate; instead of understanding that mother is cold, the child experiences himself as unlovable. These feelings persist into adulthood as the basis for a characterological depression, an existence without hope or joy.

Robert had tried therapy, analysis, and psychiatric hospitalization before, never with much success. The last time, the therapist had sent him to get a "New Age" treatment to help him get in touch with his feelings. That experience was so invasive for this brittle man that he fled in a panic. I decided to try to go with his strengths: his intelligence, his intellectualized curiosity about the meaning of life, and his recognition that the world of feelings was foreign territory.

I suggested Robert do some reading so that he could better understand his own condition. He was fascinated with Alice Miller's book Prisoners of Childhood,[7] *understanding that she was describing his parents and childhood with perfect accuracy. He learned that depression is not a feeling, but the inability to feel. He began to learn that when he felt like taking to his bed, it was in response to some interpersonal event. He wanted to learn better ways of responding.*

In one of those coincidences that make psychoanalysts say there are no coincidences, Robert's neighbors' marriage was breaking up. The wife, Betty, who had nursed Robert through previous depressions after his own marriage fell apart, began spending more and more time with Robert. Eventually he confessed shamefacedly to me that they had begun an affair. I wondered if she was just using him for temporary comfort, but their relationship developed. And Betty helped educate Robert about feelings. When he got mad at her, she wouldn't let him withdraw. She teased and joked him out of his coldness. For his part, he was so moved by her evident love for him that he wouldn't let himself act like the aloof, self-absorbed iceberg he used to be. Instead of ruminating about the meaning of life, for the first time he began to enjoy living.

The crisis in therapy came after a few months. Betty decided to leave her husband and move. She had family in another state who would help her make a new start. Robert could come too. But he got caught up in obsessional thinking. His divorce would be heard within a few months. Shouldn't he stick around until it was over? How could he leave his house? He was terrified his wife would break in and steal something he didn't want her to have. He and I examined these worries carefully; it wasn't hard for Robert to see that they were really trivial in proportion to the opportunity he had. With his new understanding of depression, he could see that he was displacing his anxiety about change and commitment to seemingly simpler things.

I saw Robert recently, three years after he moved away with Betty. He was in town for another hearing on his divorce, which still drags on. He and Betty are living together, he's working, and he's happy. For three years, there has been no sign at all of his depression.

What cured Robert? Was it the therapy, his relationship with Betty, or something else? Aging is a factor—many mental illnesses become less severe as we grow older. What about the effects of his son's death—catastrophe can bring out the best in people, and Robert certainly seemed to respond well. How destructive was his marriage? His withdrawal into bed was at least partly a retreat from his wife's nagging. Would medication have helped him sooner, or helped him even more effectively?

To understand depression we should ask ourselves, what was it about Robert and Janet that made them respond to the vicissitudes of life in the way they did? This is what sets them apart from other people. Many wives in Janet's situation would have questioned their marriage, not themselves. Others might have shrugged off a husband's affair. What made Janet so vulnerable? How could Robert become immobilized by relatively minor stresses during his marriage, then pull himself together when his son died? To what extent did his coldness, his inability to feel, which seemed so much a part of him, contribute to his depression?

William Styron, the author of *Sophie's Choice* and winner of the National Book Award, wrote *Darkness Visible* to describe his own bout with depression. He referred to his experience as "madness," feeling that the word "depression" is simply an inadequate expression of the experience—"a true wimp of a word for such a major illness. . . . Told that someone's mood disorder has evolved into a storm—a veritable howling tempest in the brain, which is indeed what a clinical depression resembles like nothing else—even the uninformed layman might display sympathy rather than the standard reaction that 'depression' evokes, something akin to 'So what?' or 'You'll pull out of it' or 'We all have bad days.'"[8]

Styron is exactly right. People feel ashamed of being depressed, they feel they should snap out of it, they feel weak and inadequate. Of course, these feelings are symptoms of the disease. *Depression is a grave and life-threatening illness, much more common than we recognize.* As far as the depressive being weak or inadequate, let me drop some names of famous depressives: Abraham Lincoln; Winston Churchill; Eleanor Roosevelt; Sigmund Freud.

According to the U.S. Department of Health, up to one in eight individuals may require treatment for depression during their lifetime.[9] This rate seems to be increasing dramatically in the United States at the end of the twentieth century. A lifetime study of 9,500 adults found that people born earlier in the century were significantly less likely to develop depression than those born later.[10] Another study of people with depressed relatives found the same thing—the later in the century you were born, the more likely you were to develop depression.[11] This also means that depression strikes at a younger age. If you were born in the thirties, your own first depressive episode was likely to strike between the ages of thirty and thirty-five. But if you were born in 1956, your first episode was likely to strike between twenty and twenty-five. There is more than sufficient reason to call depression an epidemic. Of all people with major depression, 15 percent will end their lives by suicide.

Depression accounts for 20 percent of the caseload in most community mental health clinics. At ours, we see a big difference between self-report and diagnosis; only 12 percent of people when they first call us state that depression is their primary problem, but 45 percent of our patients currently have a diagnosis of some form of depressive disorder. People usually call, not because they are aware they are depressed, but because they see that something is going wrong in their lives—the children won't listen, they can't get along with their spouse, they are having trouble at work. But we see someone who looks sad, tired, and defeated, can't sleep, is irritable, hopeless, and blames himself for the situation. Depression often grows in us so slowly that neither we nor those close to us notice the change, while an objective observer detects it right away.

Depression most often strikes young adults, but 10 percent of all children suffer an episode before age twelve, and 20 percent of the elderly report depressive symptoms. Both children and the elderly are amazingly undertreated. Estimates are that 6 million elderly persons suffer from some form of depression, but that three-quarters of those cases are undiagnosed and untreated, despite regular routine medical care. Depression in the elderly tends to get dismissed as inevitable, but in fact it is caused more by poor health and poor sleep than grief, loss, and isolation. Among the elderly who commit suicide, almost three-quarters visit a doctor within a week before their death; but only in 25 percent of those cases does the physician recognize a depression.[12]

Twenty-five percent of all women and 11.5 percent of all men will have a depressive episode at one time in their lives. But this reported lower incidence among men may really be a mistake arising from the way we diagnose. Men are socially prohibited from expressing or even experiencing the feelings associated with depression. Instead, they act them out through substance abuse, violence, and self-destructive behavior. In Amish culture, where macho acting out is not socially rewarded, the incidence of depression is the same for both sexes.[13]

Suicide, the "worst case" outcome of depression, is the eighth most common cause of death in America.[14] There are 55,000 documented suicides annually, but the true incidence is more like 100,000. One out of every two hundred people will eventually commit suicide. And although I personally think that suicide

27

can be a conscious, rational choice for people who are in intractable pain or facing great disability, the controversy around these issues means that coroners distort their reports so that we have no reliable data on how many suicides are people who are really depressed, how many are "rational." My experience is that far, far more suicides are truly depressed. The suicide rate among adolescents has quadrupled in the past twenty-five years. A few years ago in a small city near where I work, there were eight suicides among young people in one year. These were usually by young men just out of school, often while they were intoxicated, usually with no "warning signals" beforehand. An angry, bitter kid who has an unexpected disappointment, gets drunk, and has a gun close at hand is a disaster waiting to happen.

When I still lived in Chicago, I worked with Jane, whose twenty-year-old son had shot himself while she slept in the next room. This was a young man no one would have described as depressed; rather he was a troublemaker. With a history of arrests for minor offenses as a juvenile, he had been sent to a "reform school" when he was fifteen. Since being discharged, he had lived off and on with Jane and with friends. He worked occasionally, drank a lot, and got into fights.

On the night he took his life, Jimmy had two pieces of bad luck that probably put him over the edge. First he met his ex-girlfriend at a local hangout; she went out of her way to be snotty to him. Then he ran into his father at another bar. A true town drunk, the father barely recognized his son; when he did, it was to ask him for money.

Jimmy came home about midnight. His mother woke, got up and spoke to him, asking him if he needed anything. He was drinking a beer and reading a magazine, and as far as Jane could see, he was his usual self. She went back to bed. Jimmy went to his room and wrote a brief note, more a will than a suicide note. He wanted his brother to have his motorcycle, snake, and hunting rifle. Then he shot himself with the hunting rifle.

Jane kept asking me why. I couldn't tell her what I thought was the true answer to that question, because I thought it was too cruel; but in my opinion she and her son were as much victims of chance as anything else. If you take any sample of impulsive, alcoholic youth whose lives are going nowhere, get them drunk, expose them to rejection, and leave them alone with a gun, some of them will shoot themselves. Which ones take their lives on any given night is just the law of averages. Are they depressed? They sure are, but they can't admit it or show it.

Jane is like most survivors of suicide I've known. You certainly don't get over it, but you learn to live with it. She was depressed herself for over a year, had terrible headaches (a psychosomatic symptom mimicking her son's injury), was unable to work, became overwhelmed with stress, and went from doctor to doctor seeking relief from her pain. Antidepressant medications didn't help; all I could do was listen while she grieved. Eventually her headaches became less frequent and she began to have a little more energy to put into her life. I think of her every time I hear of an adolescent suicide.

The Experience of Depression

Everyone knows what depression feels like. Everyone feels the blues at times. Sadness, disappointment, fatigue are normal parts of life. There is a connection between the blues and clinical depression, but the difference is like the difference between the sniffles and pneumonia.

Depressive disorders are "whole person" illnesses; they affect the body, feelings, thoughts, and behavior. The depression itself can make us feel it's useless to seek help. The good news is that 80 to 90 percent of people with depression can be treated effectively, but the bad news is that only one sufferer in three seeks treatment. More bad news is that almost half the American public views depression as a character defect, rather than an illness or emotional disorder.[15] Still more bad news is that only half of all cases of depression are accurately diagnosed, and only half of those receive adequate treatment.

We confuse depression, sadness, and grief. But the opposite of depression is not happiness, but vitality—the ability to experience a full range of emotion, including happiness, excitement, sadness, and grief. Depression is not an emotion itself. It's not sadness or grief, it's an illness. When we feel our worst, sad, self-absorbed, and helpless, we are experiencing what people with depression experience, but they don't recover from those moods without help.

The hallmark of depression is a persistent sad or "empty" mood, sometimes experienced as tension or anxiety. Life lacks pleasure. People with mild depressions may go through the motions of eating, sex, work, or play, but the activities seem hollow; people with more severe depressions withdraw from these activities, feeling too tired, tense, or bitter to participate. There is often a nagging fatigue, a sense of being unable to focus, a feeling of being unproductive.

People with depression usually experience a lowered self-esteem. In a depression, you may feel that you are a helpless victim of fate, but you also feel that you don't deserve any better. Feelings of guilt, shame, and hopelessness are common.

There are often a host of physical symptoms, of which sleep disturbances are key. People may have difficulty falling asleep, may awaken early without feeling refreshed. Others may sleep excessively, again without feeling rested. Appetite may increase or decrease. There may be difficulty in sexual functioning. There may be nagging aches and pains that don't respond to medical treatment. But there are physical illnesses that cause symptoms like depression—Lyme disease, diabetes, thyroid conditions, anemia—and depressions can cause physical symptoms that look

like other diseases. If you are feeling depressed, it is important
to be sure that an underlying health problem does not exist, and
you should see your physician for a checkup. At the same time,
if you know you have a health problem and are feeling depressed, don't assume you will feel better once the health problem is under control. See chapter 10 for some advice about
getting good medical care.

Suicidal thoughts and impulses are often present, and suicide
may be a real risk. Some people are repeatedly tormented by
these impulses, which they experience as frightening and painful, while others have them appear as if out of the blue, detached
from emotions. The impulse to spin the wheel and drive suddenly into oncoming traffic is horribly common.

Alcohol and other drugs may be used to give relief from the
depression. But the relief is only temporary, at best, and usually
the person just hates himself more for giving in to temptation.
Alcohol itself is a depressant, and long-term alcohol abuse may
lead to chronic depression—it certainly doesn't help you make
the right decisions in life, and that is enough to be depressed
about.

From all these symptoms, it might seem that a depressed person
is easy to recognize. It is often easy when the person recognizes
it himself—when it's a change from a more normal state of mind,
the depression is experienced as something foreign to the self,
something to be overcome. But very often, depression has become part of the self: the person has felt this way for as long as
he or she can remember, and can't imagine anything else. These
people come to the attention of health professionals through
some other crisis, not seeking help with depression, but the
depression emerges as a big emptiness in the background.

There is a sequential process in the recognition of depression.[16] First is a stage of confused pain in which the sufferer
knows he suffers, but doesn't know why. People often blame

circumstances. Adolescents blame their home lives, married people their spouses, employees blame their bosses. But there is a recognition that the pain is not normal. The second stage is a recognition that something is wrong with *me*. It may be that external circumstances have changed but the pain continues, or it may be a gradual recognition that the suffering is so extreme that circumstances can't be blamed. This is a painful recognition that often takes years. It is an acceptance of a damaged self. But because of the nature of depression, the self-blame and guilt that are manifestations of the disease, this acceptance does not always lead to seeking help. People then may move to the third stage, a crisis that usually leads to professional intervention and diagnosis. It is often a suicide attempt or psychiatric hospitalization. The diagnosis often provides hope, that treatment or a cure is possible, and explanation, a way to understand what has only been confusion before, but the fact is that this is a diagnosis of a mental illness, with all the shame and stigma that that entails. The fourth stage involves acceptance of an illness identity. Depression comes to be seen as an outside agent invading the self, rather than as a manifestation of the self.

It's essential that anyone suffering from depression get good help from a competent, qualified professional. These are the warning signals: if you or someone you love experiences four or more of the following symptoms for more than a few weeks, you should seek competent help as soon as possible.

1. Sad, depressed, or "empty" mood
2. Loss of interest or pleasure in ordinary activities
3. Eating disturbances (appetite and/or weight loss or gain)
4. Sleep disturbances (insomnia, early-morning waking, oversleeping)
5. Activity level slows down or increases
6. Decreased energy, fatigue
7. Feelings of pessimism, guilt, worthlessness, helplessness, hopelessness

8. Diminished ability to think, concentrate, or make decisions

9. Thoughts of death or suicide, suicide attempts

If you're reading this book and recognize that you are seriously depressed, but hope that I can tell you how to recover without help, abandon that idea. You're only indulging in more depressed, self-defeating behavior. Read chapter 11 about finding a good therapist and/or psychiatrist, then make the call before you go on reading. If you're not sure whether you're depressed or not, you might want to take the Wakefield depression inventory, which appears as Appendix B (page 330). It's meant to be a screening tool only, and it's certainly not a substitute for a professional diagnostic evaluation, but it may be helpful. But let me urge you to be open to the idea of therapy. If you think you see yourself in my stories, or if you recognize the symptoms in yourself, go get good help now.

Diagnosing Depression

RECOGNIZING AN emotional problem and giving it a psychiatric diagnosis are very different processes. At what point does the depressed mood that everyone experiences from time to time become an illness that requires intervention?

Diagnosis in psychiatry is currently based on the *Diagnostic and Statistical Manual of Mental Disorders,* Fourth Edition, commonly known as DSM-IV.[1] The process of arriving at a standard nomenclature for emotional conditions and mental disorders has been complex, partly because so many of the conditions are themselves controversial topics in contemporary culture: Is alcoholism a disease, a habit, or a weakness? Is bulimia a disease, or a symptom of oppression? Is homosexuality a disease, or a lifestyle? Why do Vietnam vets apparently suffer from Post-Traumatic Stress Disorder at such higher rates than soldiers in previous wars? Should rebellious adolescents be hospitalized against their will because they can't get along with their parents? Should people with chronic substance abuse problems be considered disabled, and thus entitled to Social Security benefits? These questions require answers that make us question our deepest values—do we have the ability to make our own decisions in life, or are our decisions programmed by our heredity, nervous system, or early childhood experience? If our decisions are determined, what happens to the social contract, guilt, crime, and punishment?

Depression as a diagnosis has not pushed quite so many of society's hot buttons, but it is subject to the same controversies. For instance, until the third DSM came out in the seventies, many psychiatric diagnoses were strongly influenced by Freudian theory. Because the theory held that depression was caused primarily by a harsh, strict superego, and because a superego was not thought to be developed until the resolution of the Oedipal conflict, it was assumed that children could not be depressed. DSM-III addressed that, and many other blind spots in the diagnosis business, by taking a phenomenological approach that DSM-IV has followed: if a symptom cluster was observed commonly enough to be a problem perhaps worth addressing, and if observers with the same training could reliably identify the same symptom cluster with the same patients, that symptom cluster was given a name. There might or might not be a good explanation, a theory, for why that particular group of symptoms seemed to occur reliably together. Certainly it was the hope of the compilers of the new DSM that a reliable classification system, in which we could all be sure we were counting and observing the same things, might lead to better explanations for the underlying mechanisms beneath the symptoms, and improvements in treatment.

But this approach has also had its drawbacks. It has certainly contributed to the medicalization of complex emotional/behavioral states, like alcoholism, depression, or Post-Traumatic Stress Disorder. It led insurance companies to go along with the idea that an expensive course of hospital-based treatment was appropriate for these conditions, contributing to our current backlash of attempts to overcontrol behavioral health care costs. It has led to absurd legal strategies by defendants who eschew responsibility for their actions. It can lead to patients hoping that the cure for their condition will come about from a new pill, and that until the pill comes along there is nothing they can do to help themselves.

In the case of depression, the phenomenological approach has led to some hair-splitting in diagnosis that emphasizes artificial and unimportant distinctions, minimizing commonalities and contributing to the trivialization of research. Currently, the DSM-IV recognizes several distinct depression-related diagnoses, which we will describe together with their reported epidemiological data. The caveat is that the formal requirements for a diagnosis are often rather arbitrary and the distinctions between the diagnoses may be more apparent than real. The most important of these diagnoses are Major Depression, Dysthymic Disorder, and Bipolar Disorder.

Major Depression

Major depression is a very serious condition. Usually the patient and family recognize that something is gravely wrong, but exactly what it is is not so easy to tell. In the simplest case, the patient feels, looks, and acts depressed, and tells people about it.

Nancy has major depression. Although she is able to hold down a responsible job and has raised a family successfully, most of the time she is miserable. She looks tense and sad. She is thin, shy, and worried. She's hesitant to say what's on her mind, though she is caring and intelligent. She constantly puts herself down. She believes she can't handle any stress; in fact, she copes very well, but constantly fears that she's messing up. She has recurrent migraines that force her to bed several times a month. She has to take a medication for these that costs $80 a dose, and her antidepressant medication costs $8 a day. Her family is on a tight budget, and her insurance doesn't pay for *medication, so she blames herself for having to spend so much money on treatment.*

Nancy describes her depression as a well. When it's at its worst, she is stuck down in the mud at the bottom of the well. The mud is full of worms and rats, and it's all she can do to keep from being eaten alive. When she's feeling good, she's out of the well, able to look around at life and see opportunities and joy. Most of the time, she's partway down the well. Her view of life is restricted; she can see it's there, and she remembers what it's like to feel good, but she can't quite reach it.

The formal criteria for a diagnosis of major depression include a depressed mood or a loss of interest or pleasure in ordinary activities for at least two weeks, accompanied by at least four of the following symptoms:

1. Significant weight loss when not dieting, or weight gain, or change in appetite
2. Insomnia or hypersomnia (sleeping too much) nearly every day
3. Psychomotor retardation or agitation (activity level slows down or increases)
4. Fatigue or loss of energy
5. Feelings of worthlessness or excessive guilt
6. Diminished ability to think, concentrate, or make decisions
7. Recurrent thoughts of death or suicide, or suicidal ideation, or a suicidal plan or attempt

The symptoms must not be due to the direct effects of medications, drugs, or a physical condition, and must not be better accounted for by a grief reaction. The depressed mood is usually self-reported as a feeling of sadness, hopelessness, or discouragement, although it is sometimes denied and may be elicited by a professional interview (the therapist says "You sound sad," and the patient starts to cry), or inferred from facial expression or body language. Some people emphasize physical complaints or report irritability more than sadness.

One way scientists measure the epidemiology of a disease is "point prevalence," referring to the proportion of people at any one time who are found to be suffering from the disease. The point prevalence of major depression in Western countries is 2.3 to 3.2 percent for men, 4.5 to 9.3 percent for women. The lifetime risk (the chance that any one person will develop the condition at some point in his or her life) is 7 to 12 percent for men, 20 to 25 percent for women.[2] Risk is not affected by race, education, income, or marital status. The reported higher incidence among women raises questions of a gender bias in the diagnosis, since men are generally considered to be socially prohibited from self-reporting feelings of sadness, worthlessness, or hopelessness, a primary criterion for the diagnosis. Conversely, it may be true that women have more to be depressed about than men. Or that male-dominated science tends to label "sick" behavior that is more innately feminine than masculine. These issues are explored in greater depth in chapter 19.

There is good statistical evidence that recent stress may precipitate the first and/or second bouts of major depression, but that later episodes may not be precipitated by external events. This observation agrees with clinical experience, where it is often easy for the patient to pinpoint what made him depressed the first time, not so easy for the current episode.

Dysthymic Disorder

Dysthymic Disorder is the term for what used to be called depressive neurosis; "neurosis," with its roots in psychoanalysis, has been dropped altogether from the DSM. The essential criterion for diagnosis of dysthymia is a depressed mood for most of the day, for more days than not, for at least two years (!). In addition, there must be at least two of the following symptoms while feeling depressed:

1. Poor appetite or overeating
2. Insomnia or hypersomnia
3. Low energy or fatigue
4. Low self-esteem
5. Poor concentration or difficulty making decisions
6. Feelings of hopelessness

Note that the secondary symptoms are very similar to those for major depression, except that psychomotor agitation/retardation and thoughts of death or suicide are not listed, and low self-esteem is. Clearly the distinction between major depression and dysthymia is rather arbitrary, a matter of degree rather than kind. Yet since the distinction is made, we have researchers testing interventions on one population or the other, with no attention paid to the possibility of error or overlap in the diagnosis. When Prozac or interpersonal psychotherapy is reported to be successful with 70 percent of patients with major depression but only 50 percent of patients with dysthymia, it's quite likely that many patients who didn't improve were misdiagnosed. Perhaps a treatment or medication is effective with almost all patients who are correctly diagnosed; perhaps it is no better than a placebo. But research tends to gloss over the ambiguities of diagnosis and report its results as facts.

Chris fits the picture of dysthymia. A bright, intelligent woman with a forceful manner and a terrific sense of humor, she has been unhappy most of her life. Raised by an alcoholic mother and a critical father, as a child she tried to make them both happy—an impossible task. She rebelled in adolescence, getting in all kinds of trouble. Her first marriage was to a man who was alcoholic and abusive. Having found a lot of strength through Al-Anon, Chris is determined to get her life together.

But she and her present husband can't communicate. Chris is very quick to anger and her husband withdraws. She struggles constantly with her sense of having a grievance against life—she knows this, along with her angry expression, drives people away, but she can't control herself.

Chris speaks of her depression as a big soft comforter. It's not really comforting, but it's safe and familiar. Sometimes she feels as if she's entitled to be depressed, to quit struggling, to snuggle down and watch old movies and feel sorry for herself.

The point prevalence for dysthymic disorder is estimated at 3 percent, while the lifetime risk is estimated at 6 percent. Again, female gender is associated with higher risk, but race, education, and income are independent.

People with dysthymia are sometimes dismissed as the "worried well," but nothing could be further from the truth. Imagine spending the better part of two years feeling depressed, having trouble functioning, unable to enjoy life, feeling lousy about yourself, sleeping poorly, and feeling powerless to do anything about it. These people are more accurately described as "walking wounded." They get through life, but life tends to be nasty, brutish, and short. They are not the Woody Allen stereotype of the self-absorbed neurotic, but rather long-suffering and self-sacrificing.

We often see the effects on children of having a mother who functions like this. Frequently, the children are anxious, tense, and have difficulty getting along with their peers and keeping up with schoolwork. They know all too well that something scary is going on with mom, and they feel that they should be able to do something about it. These children often adapt and become "pseudoadults," who appear tough and independent. They may actually take care of mom by assuming adult responsibilities—meals, housecleaning, baby-sitting the younger siblings. Often when mom recovers, there is a backlash. With a functioning mother again, the child is able to feel the anger he has suppressed at having been emotionally abandoned. He becomes rebellious and tests mom to see if she can really be relied on. Mom, still vulnerable, has difficulty understanding why her child isn't grateful to see her functioning again and may revert to her depressed stance. Depression becomes a vicious circle in the family.

Depressive Disorder Not Otherwise Specified

Someone who self-reports feeling depressed, has suicidal impulses, has lost pleasure in life, and is not sleeping well, is seriously depressed, but because he does not have four of the secondary criteria cannot be diagnosed as having "major" depression. Likewise someone who suffers all the symptoms of dysthymia, but for a period which has not lasted two years. Such people are usually classified as Depressive Disorder Not Otherwise Specified (DDNOS), a catchall term that may include some people who are quite seriously depressed, others who aren't.

This grouping is used for all patients who show some symptoms of depression but do not meet the criteria for one of the more restrictive diagnoses. Their symptoms may be less severe, or of shorter duration, or they may meet most of the criteria, but not all, for major depression or dysthymia. This category also includes women suffering from depression associated with the menstrual cycle and people with schizophrenia or other psychotic disorder with an associated depression. But it still excludes people who are grieving, who are depressed as a result of a loss or change in their lives, who are dealing with a medical problem and depressed as a result. In other words, the diagnosis includes a wide variety of people who suffer from depression that has no clear external cause, but is serious enough to interfere with their ability to function.

Estimates are that, at any given time, 11 percent of the population meets the criteria for DDNOS. This is truly an astounding number, making DDNOS easily the single most common disease in the United States. The combined incidence of major depression, dysthymia, and DDNOS approaches 20 percent at any given time. This does not mean that 20 percent of the population will have depression at some time in their lives, but that 20 percent have it *right now*. One in five of your friends, family members, coworkers. There is just no other disease that approaches this kind of prevalence.

Bipolar Disorder

Bipolar disorders typically feature episodes of major depression interspersed with periods of mania or hypomania (an abnormally elevated or expansive mood that does not impair reality testing). A manic episode must meet the following criteria:

A. A discrete period of abnormal, persistently elevated, expansive, or irritable mood

B. At least three of the following in the same period:
1. Inflated self-esteem/grandiosity
2. Marked decrease in need for sleep
3. Pressured speech
4. Flight of ideas (racing thoughts)
5. Marked distractibility
6. Increased goal-directed activity or psychomotor agitation
7. Excessive involvement in pleasurable activities without regard for negative consequences

C. Symptoms must be severe enough to cause marked impairment in functioning or place self or others in danger

D. Not caused by schizophrenia or substance abuse

Walt has bipolar disorder. A big man, a truck driver, who seems pleasant and good-natured in his normal state, Walt has had trouble holding down a job for the past few years because of his erratic behavior. Sometimes he becomes sexually obsessed. He can't get sex off his mind. If an attractive woman is anywhere near, he can't concentrate on anything but his sexual fantasies. Sometimes he loses touch with reality enough to start believing that she returns his fantasies. When he's in this state, he'll spend money he doesn't have on prostitutes, on gambling junkets, on anything to impress women. He believes he's attractive, power-ful, and charmed, and he feels he can do no wrong. Nothing bothers him. He can stay up for days, talking nonstop.

But at other times, Walt is severely depressed. He doesn't believe he's capable of anything. He hardly has the energy to get out of bed. He tries to go to work, but his lack of confidence makes his employers distrust him. He develops obsessive anxiety symptoms—going back into the house ten times to make sure the coffee pot is unplugged. He's constantly apologizing for himself.

The mean age of onset for bipolar disorder is the early twen-ties. It affects men and women equally; over the course of their lifetime, between 0.4 and 1.2 percent of men and women will develop bipolar disorder. At any given time, between 0.1 and 0.6 percent of the population are suffering from an episode. There is a high genetic correlation; first-degree relatives of bipolar patients have a 12 percent lifetime incidence, while another 12 percent will experience major depression.

Untreated, a manic episode will last an average of six months, and a major depressive episode eight to ten months. The interval between episodes decreases as time goes on. There is a high mortality rate, due to suicide (15 percent of untreated patients), accidental death due to risky behavior, and concurrent illness.

Many people with untreated bipolar disorder will die from alcoholism, lung cancer, accidents, or sexually transmitted disease; feeling so invulnerable during an episode, they simply do not take the precautions that most of us have come to accept as part of a sensible lifestyle.

Bipolar disorder seems to be a different kettle of fish from other kinds of depression, though the depressive episodes may look and feel the same as major depression. Bipolar disorder has such a high degree of genetic transmission, the manic episodes are so distinctive and limited to the disease, and the disease itself has such a unique response to a specific medication (lithium) that it makes sense to think of it as primarily a biogenetic disease that causes a chemical imbalance in the brain. This is not to say that the bipolar patient also doesn't have to change his lifestyle to help his recovery.

Time *magazine's Man of the Year in 1992, Ted Turner, may be the first to come out of the closet regarding his psychiatric treatment. His story is fascinating reading for those who are interested in the problems men have with success and intimacy, and for those who are interested in the mix of genetics, biochemistry, and family dynamics that underlies depression.*

Turner's fifty-third birthday, celebrated in November 1991, was a milestone in that Turner outlived his father. Turner's father had killed himself before he reached fifty-three, and for years Turner was troubled by the obsessive thought that he would not live longer than his father had. He talked of suicide rather often, and drove himself mercilessly to succeed in joyless pursuits. After all the time he put in sailing, including winning the America's Cup, he told a friend repeatedly that he never enjoyed the sport. "I got cold and I got wet." His eye was always on the finish line, always looking for some achievement that would finally be enough to make him feel good about himself.

Turner's father, Ed, by all accounts was a tortured man who inflicted psychological torture on his son. Young Turner was beaten with a coat hanger when he let his father down; when Ted did something really bad, his father had Ted beat him with a razor strap. When Ed served in the navy during World War II, he had his wife and daughter move from base to base with him but left Ted, only six, behind at a boarding school. From fifth grade on, Ted was sent to military academies. No grade he ever got was good enough, no achievement great enough, to please his father. Ed shot himself when Ted was in his early twenties, leaving Ted to rescue the family billboard business, which had sunk into debt. By working feverishly and gambling recklessly, he not only rebuilt the business, he began the communications empire that became CNN.

But with his father dead, Turner had no yardstick to measure his success against. He drank, womanized, alternately neglected and bullied his own children, and apparently was sheer hell as a boss. Finally, in 1985, he sought help, and began to work with a psychiatrist in Atlanta.

The psychiatrist first put Turner on lithium. Lithium is appropriate primarily for only the small number of patients who suffer from bipolar disorder. Because in this disorder patients may have great self-confidence and energy, may go without sleep, may believe they are capable of great achievements, may enjoy taking risks, for someone like Turner it can be hard to tell where disease ends and personality begins. It can also be hard to get the patient to accept treatment for symptoms that in many ways have worked well. But Turner was a cooperative patient.

As Turner began to be stabilized by the lithium in his system, therapy helped him deal with the shadow of his father. Like most men with critical, emotionally rejecting fathers, Turner had developed no internal mechanism for feeling good about himself. Like most family members of suicide victims, he was haunted by the idea that the suicide had the truly accurate perspective on life: that it's not worth the trouble. Time could not get the psychiatrist to talk about the details of Turner's case, but it's clear that Turner had to work hard to make peace with his own children and with the women in his life.

Turner is a classic example of the observation that achievement doesn't mean happiness; instead, it's how we live rather than what we do that leads to peace.[3]

Adjustment Disorder

Adjustment disorder with depressed mood or with mixed anxiety and depressed mood is diagnosed when the depression is clearly a response to an external stress. This is not the same as grief. Grief is a state that looks and feels a lot like depression, but people normally recover from grief without formal help. There is also some question of degree. Most people who are grieving are still able to feel that life will go on and hold some future rewards for them, and are able to experience enjoyment when the occasion merits. They don't feel decreased self-esteem or irrational guilt. But people with an adjustment disorder with depression are in worse shape than this. They feel hopeless and helpless, empty and joyless. They can point to exactly what made them feel this way—a setback, a loss, an illness, a narcissistic injury of some sort—and they don't yet meet the criteria for dysthymia or major depression. This may be the first episode in what will turn out to be a lifetime struggle with depression, but many people recover from an adjustment disorder with no permanent effects.

The diagnostic criteria for adjustment disorder are:

A. The development of emotional or behavioral symptoms in response to an identifiable stressor, within three months of the onset of the stressor

B. Symptoms are clinically significant:

    1. there is marked distress that is in excess of what would be expected from exposure to the stressor, or

2. there is significant impairment in social, occupational, or academic functioning

C. The symptoms do not meet the criteria for another psychiatric diagnosis and are not merely an exacerbation of a preexisting condition

D. The symptoms do not represent bereavement

E. The symptoms do not persist for more than six months once the stressor or its consequences have terminated

Mood Disorder Due to a General Medical Condition

This disorder consists of a prominent and persistent disturbance in mood that is judged to be due to the direct physiological effects of a general medical condition. A number of conditions, like Parkinson's, thyroid disease, hepatitis, multiple sclerosis, and stroke, are generally recognized to cause disturbance in mood directly; but this category also refers to patients with severe, painful, or terminal conditions who experience a depression in response to their pain, loss of functioning, or loss of hope.

Seasonal Affective Disorder

Seasonal Affective Disorder is a new diagnosis, describing people who regularly become depressed in response to changes in daylight. The DSM compilers feel enough confidence to say that there are people who become depressed regularly (usually in winter) and recover in the spring, and that this is not related to lack of exercise or opportunity to socialize or to stimulus deprivation, but appears to be related to absence of sunlight. In the depressive phase, patients feel lethargic, sleep too long, gain weight, and crave carbohydrates. They become sad, anxious, irritable, and socially withdrawn. Four times as many women as men are affected; over half the women complain of premenstrual mood problems as well. Symptoms often improve if the patient moves nearer to the equator during winter. Phototherapy, or light therapy, has sometimes been found to be effective. In phototherapy, the patient is seated three feet from a bright full-spectrum fluorescent light and asked to glance at it for a few seconds once a minute. Patients who respond usually begin to feel better after doing this several hours a day for two to four days. The treatment must be continued throughout winter. Apparently the light has its curative effect through vision, not skin exposure. Theories of how it works relate to either altering secretions by the pineal gland (melatonin), which seems to relate to hibernation in many species, or to repairing a disruption in the body's circadian rhythm caused by the shorter periods of winter daylight.

People have long recognized that winter makes depression worse.

> *There's a certain Slant of light,*
> *Winter Afternoons—*
> *That oppresses, like the Heft*
> *Of Cathedral Tunes—*
> *Heavenly Hurt, it gives us—*
> *We can find no scar,*
> *But internal difference,*
> *Where the Meanings, are . . .*
> *'Tis the Seal Despair—*
> *An imperial affliction*
> *Sent us of the Air—*
> —EMILY DICKINSON

"Internal difference,/Where the Meanings, are." One of my great joys of middle age has been perennial gardening. I freely admit to have no conception whatever of garden design. I buy one of any plant I like and stick it in where I have room, with just a little thought to color combinations and space. As a result my

garden from afar looks like a crazy quilt. But I like to look at it from up close, to see the growth of individual plants that interest me, how their leaves and stems spring up from the earth, how they blossom and flourish in the summer heat. There is something about the rebirth of the world in spring, the cycle through summer and even into the fall, when I can see the plants preparing themselves for the winter to come, that I find deeply satisfying. It seems to me to have to do with the cycle of death and rebirth, something about how I experience my own body aging but my children coming into full maturity, that gives me a sense of continuity and some degree of acceptance of my own mortality. And it's more than just a state of mind. I get up early in the morning and go out to see what I can see new in the garden. I come home from work and can't wait to go weeding or transplanting. I feel energy throughout my body.

But I hate winter. *The Zen-like peace that I find in the garden only lasts through the last days of fall. When winter comes, I'm bored, grouchy, sorry for myself, withdrawn, a bear who can't get to sleep. The intensity of the change certainly feels to me as if it comes from something more than being deprived of my favorite leisure activity. It feels qualitatively different. There are plenty of other things I can do besides gardening, but I don't want to do them; and I have trouble enjoying the other things I normally enjoy. I can usually force myself out of this mood, but it requires a deliberate act of will.*

How much of all this is the result of lack of sunlight, how much a function of the lack of opportunity for favorite activities, of being cooped up inside breathing stale air, how much the fact that everything is more difficult and time-consuming in winter, is an open question. Man is the only animal that seems to believe he can control nature. Perhaps if I could accept the desire to hibernate in winter as a natural phenomenon, I wouldn't confuse it with the onset of depression. Instead of labeling it depression, I could just consider it normal winter functioning.

Why Don't We Have a Theory?

FOR THE PAST thirty years or so, ever since Thomas Kuhn wrote *The Structure of Scientific Revolutions*,[1] it seems that every new development in science has been described as a "paradigm shift." Kuhn used that term to describe the kind of change in perspective that comes about when an old theory is replaced by a new one. Typically the old theory has become creaky and unwieldy, as new information has come to light that contradicts its basic assumptions. The new information has to be explained away or else hammered into agreement with the old theory by some very convoluted thinking. The new theory is simpler, leaner, more elegant; it explains all the new information more parsimoniously and even predicts future observations, lending itself validity. The classic example is the replacement of the Ptolemaic, Earth-centered solar system theory by the helio-centric theory of Copernicus; once people could give up their emotional or religious attachment to the idea of Earth being the center of the universe, the Copernican theory was obviously, intuitively correct. And it became impossible to put ourselves in the mind-set of the Ptolemaic astronomer, who thought he could explain why the planets viewed from Earth seem to reverse direction in their orbits by means of a Rube Goldberg–like contraption of spheres rotating within themselves. Once people understood Copernicus, they literally lost the ability to understand the Ptolemaic system. That way was lost forever; a "paradigm shift" had occurred.

Not that these things happen overnight. The new way of seeing and the old one battle it out for a while. A more cynical observer said, "Science advances one funeral at a time," as minds change more slowly than the population of scientists replaces itself.

Now most new ideas are being touted as paradigm-shifters. The concept is in danger of losing its meaning by being trivialized. But the fact is that the Freudian theory of human functioning has been on its last legs for some time, and we wait for a new theory, a new paradigm, to replace it. Most of our advances lately have been in understanding the brain, not the mind. New medications have helped literally millions of people, and understanding certain problems as physiologically rather than psychologically based has changed somewhat how we think of ourselves. But although there is a wish to achieve a biochemical theory of human behavior, our current knowledge leaves us far from it; and if we had it, it would not answer our most interesting human questions.

Although the sciences of mental health lack a paradigm, there is so much ferment that it certainly feels as though big things are happening. Much of Freudian psychology is withering away; concepts such as id, ego, and superego, drive and libido, are increasingly irrelevant to the kinds of patients and problems we deal with. Those are terms associated with the elaborated Freudian theory of human behavior and motivation that will fall by the wayside. However, I don't think that means psychoanalysis or analytically informed therapy is useless or irrelevant, or that less abstract Freudian concepts will be abandoned. As much as those who treat alcoholism have against Freudian therapists for treating drinking as the symptom, not the problem, they should remember that the concept of "denial" that they have popularized is a Freudian construction. So are all the rest of the familiar defense mechanisms, many of which have entered our everyday vocabulary. These concepts and others that are at a relatively low level of abstraction—resistance, transference, the understanding of metaphor, dreams, symbols, and slips—I think will be with us for a long time, because they will continue to be useful.

In other words, an adapted Freudian method for working directly with patients, and the ideas that make it work, will survive, with modifications, while the Freudian metapsychology will fall apart. Yet we don't have a new encompassing theory of what motivates people, what makes them tick, to replace it with. However, it is possible to describe some of the features of what's coming. I think there will be an increasing acceptance of some basic assumptions from self psychology, that a person's conception of himself is a useful organizing concept, that regulation of self-esteem explains a lot about interpersonal relations, productive activity, growth, and aging, and that these concepts are very useful in understanding why today's patients suffer in the ways they do, instead of in the ways Freud's patients did. I think there will be an increasing understanding of the effects of trauma on the individual; that some types of trauma—for instance, childhood sexual abuse—are much more common than we've ever recognized; and that they have effects that explain adult symptoms and pain. Other types of trauma—separation and loss, fear and suffering—will be better understood as well. (Attention to what is called Post-Traumatic Stress Disorder is one of the few good things to come out of Vietnam.) I think there will be a better and better understanding of the differences we have in how we integrate information and of the effects those differences have on how we construct our world and our self-image.

Finally I also think there will eventually be an integration with a biochemical, neurological understanding of the physical side of the brain and the effects of psychotropic medication. These four strands—the self and others, the effects of trauma, the ways we learn, and brain biochemistry—will eventually come together in some way. For instance, to me it makes perfect sense to hypothesize that a traumatic event or a series of minitraumas in the relationship with a parent will set up a biochemical pathway in the brain that will be experienced by the child as depression; that the creation of this depression pathway lowers a threshold in the brain so that the same feelings will be experienced over and over in reaction to less traumatic stimuli; that some of us are born more vulnerable to this process than others; and finally that what is a trauma for me is not necessarily a trauma for you, based on differences in how we process information, how our selves are constructed, and how the people and the world around us make us feel about ourselves. Thus one of us becomes an adult with what is diagnosed as a cyclic major depression and the other doesn't; and while medication can intervene in the bio-chemical pathway that leads to experiences of depression, that doesn't mean that a physiological theory "explains" depression.

But of course while paradigms are shifting, there is a lot of conflict and turmoil. I think one of the dangers right now is the creation of division by those who would draw a sharp line between mental health and mental illness, as some state legisla-tures have done and as some privately written health insurance plans do, by designating "biologically based mental illnesses" (schizophrenia, manic depression, major depression) and distin-guishing them from mere "problems in living." The hope is that by designating them as biologically based, we remove the stigma of self-blame and create the possibility of cure through medica-tion only. I can destroy that illusion just by mentioning three names from the news—Vincent Foster, Susan Smith, and Sol Wachtler.[2] If there is such a sharp line between mental health and mental illness, how could those three people, and thousands of others like them every day who seem perfectly "normal" to

WHAT WE KNOW ABOUT DEPRESSION

all outward appearances, suddenly step over into the twilight zone?

We have a long way to go before we understand how people work, and the answer won't be just biochemical. Of course there is something amiss with the brain when people are extremely depressed or anxious or schizophrenic. You can't experience these states and not believe that something beyond normal experience is taking place. All symptoms have to have a bio-chemical mechanism. Everything is biochemically mediated, but that doesn't make it biochemically caused. Of course we will find better and better medications that will relieve the symptoms, and for many people this will be enough to restore them to a satisfying life. But the medications won't tell us how to raise healthy children, won't help us make difficult decisions, won't help us find meaning in our lives.

Alice is a woman in her forties who came to our office complaining of anxiety, difficulty sleeping, and hopelessness. She says she has felt depressed since adolescence, and remembers her father as depressed. When she was a teen, she closed herself off in her room, withdrew from friends and family, and became bitter and angry. Eventually she ran away from home. Resourceful and responsible, she continued her education and developed a good career.

In her twenties Alice began to have episodes of severe depression. She became so immobilized that it broke up her marriage. She had lots of psychotherapy and always managed to work and care for herself, but never felt good. She was constantly angry at herself, her work, and her life.

After a few months of counseling, the therapist talked Alice into trying Prozac. Alice was very reluctant. Distrustful of everything, hypersensitive to all medications, and perennially pessimistic, Alice had heard too many horror stories about Prozac to believe it would do her any good at all. But three weeks later, Alice woke up one morning and realized she felt different. She didn't hate herself. For the first time in her life, she looked forward to the day ahead.

Now Alice no longer needs psychotherapy and is on a maintenance dose of Prozac. She says that this past spring was the first one she can remember when she really experienced the optimism of the season. Her attitude is now, "Okay, I may never be rich and famous, but in the meantime I may actually enjoy living."

Science is subject to the same forces that shape most human events—pride, politics, and self-interest—and the effect of these forces when there are competing theories in any field is to make the debate a battle instead of an opportunity to learn. Most regrettably, it seems that researchers and therapists who work with depression are choosing up sides in this battle, with patients and families caught in the middle. A little background is necessary to understand why this is such a controversial issue.

Discussion of the causes of any mental illness increasingly brings with it a painful, polarized debate. The focus always seems to come down to nature-nurture factions, with neither faction able to listen to the other. The fact that there are special-interest groups active in the debate makes things worse. The National Alliance for the Mentally Ill is an increasingly powerful lobbying group composed primarily of parents of children with schizophrenia. NAMI argues very forcefully that all severe mental illnesses, including major depression, are biologically based, as opposed to other conditions, which are referred to as "problems in living." One obvious and quite justifiable advantage to this argument is to maintain health insurance coverage for difficult, often chronic, problems by putting them on the same playing field as heart disease, cancer, and other illnesses that we think of as exclusively physical. But NAMI parents have been so beaten up by the psychiatric establishment for so long—blamed for their children's mental illnesses—that it is not hard to understand why they also would lean toward a biologically based theory for emotional reasons. If depression and other mental illnesses are in the genes, then parents clearly don't have to feel that the times when they lost their temper, failed to understand, or made other expectable mistakes of parenting somehow contributed to their child's condition.

Similarly, the American Medical Association has always had an uncomfortable relationship with psychotherapy; most psychiatrists (MDs) who practice psychotherapy are not considered true colleagues by other MDs. But psychiatrists who prescribe medication and see a special role for medicine in treatment of emotional disorders are more welcome in the medical establishment. Institutional medicine clearly has a vested interest in reducing complex emotional states to entities that can be treated only by medically trained practitioners.

Again, the National Institute of Mental Health, whose research is partly supported by large grants from pharmaceutical manufacturers, reversed direction in the 1980s, rejecting all the research of previous decades that focused on social causes of emotional disturbance like poverty, discrimination, or family functioning. Instead, the new NIMH focuses research exclusively on genetic and chemical theories of causation of mental illness. Such thinking can be very constructive; it has led us to promising new medications and other advances in research. But it can also support the idea that there is nothing to be done until the right pill comes along. This can lead to passive patients and an uneasy social conscience. Homelessness, for instance, can be rationalized as something "in" the homeless person that makes him reject all the perfectly wonderful options society offers him, rather than a social problem having to do with poverty, discrimination, or lack of public housing.[3]

These are some of the forces currently in ascendancy, which tilt toward a biochemical/genetic explanation of mental illness rather than a trauma/social explanation. Yet there has always been a pendulum swinging in psychiatry that points first one way, then the other. American psychiatry has long been a battle-ground between therapists, who at first adopted Freudian, later other "nurture" explanations, and hospital superintendents/sci-entists, who hospitalized the disturbed and studied them, treat-ing them with medication, shock, and lobotomy. From the thirties through the seventies, the Freudians and other nurture factions were clearly in the driver's seat. All mental disturbance was seen as inherently the same—a reaction to anxiety—with patients manifesting differences in severity and symptoms based on their ego strength, which in turn was based largely on early childhood experiences. This is one manifestation of the spec-trum theory of mental illness. In the spectrum theory, mental illness is like a rainbow; it's very hard to say just when red fades into yellow. Biologically, the opposite of a spectrum theory is a classification system like the Linnaean nomenclature for species. A red-throated warbler is a different species from a yellow-throated warbler. They don't interbreed and produce orange-throated warblers. Spectrum theories are more friendly to multicausal explanations, taking into account factors that may vary in intensity—like trauma—than are classification theories, which are sympathetic to explanations that are either present or absent, such as genetic malfunction.

Although the spectrum theory has some very attractive quali-ties, notably its egalitarianism, a simplistic reliance on it led down some wrong pathways. For instance, there seems to be no doubt now that schizophrenia is best thought of as a disease of the brain, to be treated aggressively with medication, social support, and intensive therapy, rather than as only an extreme of neurosis, to be treated passively with only interpretive psy-chotherapy. So a more "nature" oriented theory of emotional disturbance is a better[4] explanation for some conditions than a "nurture" theory; but that doesn't discredit all explanations that consider the effects of trauma or the environment. And in depression, both nature and nurture are important.

David Karp's *Speaking of Sadness* is a thoughtful and moving sociological study of the effects of depression. A psychiatrist reviewing it commented:

> The profession's mistake is not that it emphasizes biological research and the use of helpful drugs to treat, for example, major depression, but that it is gradually reducing the accepted understanding of what depression *is* exclusively to biological and pharmacological elements. . . . Many forms of depression will one day be found to have common biological signatures (for example, reduced serotonin levels in certain brain cortical areas). But I do believe that this is only a "sign" of depression and not a "meaning."[5]

We have already seen that there is a spectrum among depressed patients. There is too much error and overlap in our diagnostic system for us to be confident that most people who are diagnosed with "major depression" are different in any way other than degree from those who are diagnosed with "dysthymia."[6] We have a few people we can be sure are the equivalent of yellow-throated warblers, and a few we can confidently call red-throated warblers, but the majority of patients with depression are shades of orange.

Too much time and energy is spent arguing about whether depression is "caused" by early childhood experiences or neurochemical imbalances. Whatever the cause in the past, the patient and his family have to recover in the present. From the standpoint of effective treatment, pursuing these questions is not terribly relevant. Depression, like agoraphobia—another disorder that we now know how to treat—develops a "functional autonomy." Once begun, it continues even after the immediate cause is removed. The patient can have all the insight in the world, but the symptoms have a life of their own. In agoraphobia, you provide medication and the anxiety goes away, but the patient still doesn't leave the house. You use a metaphorical crowbar or dynamite to get the patient out of the house, the patient experiences the outdoors without experiencing the symptoms, and the disorder is "cured." In depression, you use medication to help alleviate the pain and suffering, but the patient may still feel a lack of confidence, be painfully shy, lack assertive skills, have a distorted self-image, ruminate and procrastinate, abuse alcohol, be stuck in a loveless marriage or a dead-end job. The patient must address these kinds of issues—in psychotherapy or, as this book proposes, through a deliberate skill-building program—or else he may suffer less but still not be part of life.

Monkey Depression

Both nature and nurture play a part in the development of depression; both the mind as a mental apparatus and the brain as organ of the mind are involved.[7] Many people probably remember Harlow's experiments with rhesus monkeys in the fifties and sixties.[8] He was trying to understand how monkeys learn to be monkeys. He took infant monkeys and gave them a choice between two surrogate mothers—one of wire, with a nursing bottle to give food; one of cloth, with a hot water bottle for warmth. The baby monkeys would cling to the warm, soft mother and only leave it to go to the other for food. The conclusion was that primate infants have an innate need for security, comfort, and attachment to a mother figure as well as a need for food.

Scientists have been studying Harlow's monkeys ever since. Rhesus monkeys are interesting because they share 95 percent of human DNA and because they live in social groups. Their ability to function, as with humans, is less "hard-wired" than that of lower animals; they depend on what they learn as children in order to get by. Monkeys separated from their mothers at birth and reared by humans appear very disturbed as adults. They don't know how to socialize, they are overly aggressive, they are likely to be neglectful or abusive mothers.

Other monkeys who are separated from their mothers for more limited periods show more complex patterns of behavior. They fit more easily into monkey society and in general are hard to distinguish from other monkeys. But if these monkeys with a history of trauma in childhood are then subjected to stress—social isolation—as adults, they behave differently from normal monkeys. They act as if they are depressed—they are more passive, they cry, they rock themselves—and anxious—they engage in excessive self-grooming and other self-stimulating behaviors. If they are repeatedly subjected to the same stress annually, their behavior continues to deteriorate when compared to normal monkeys.

There are also changes in the brain. The deprived monkeys, when isolated at six months, show changes in levels of cortisol and norepinephrine significantly different from those of normal monkeys under stress. At eighteen months, these changes are stronger, and serotonin levels are also significantly different.

These monkeys appear to be a good analogue for depression in humans. Under normal circumstances, they look the same as other monkeys. When something goes wrong, however, they can't respond to the stress as well. With repeated stress, their ability to respond deteriorates. It's hard to escape the conclusion that it was the early childhood experience of deprivation that has led to stereotypical troubled patterns of behavior in adult life that look like depression, and to changes in brain functioning that are similar to the brain functioning of depressed humans.[9]

Conversely, high-status monkeys, those who are the natural leaders of the troop, are very high in serotonin blood levels. But then if you take these monkeys and isolate them from the troop, deprive them of the opportunity to be dominant, their serotonin level decreases.[10] Without the opportunity or need to be effective leaders, their bodies apparently slow down production of the chemical that seems to be associated with competence and self-esteem.

These observations certainly raise interesting questions about the origins of depression: how much in humans is the result of early childhood experience, how much the result of current stress, how much is a biological given. Therapists and researchers tend to hang their hats on a theory that stresses one of the three at the expense of the other two. But just as it doesn't make sense to try to understand world history from an exclusively religious, economic, or political perspective, it doesn't get us very far to be reductionistic in thinking about depression. Rather we must think of multiple causal factors.

Every patient I've ever known who was depressed had a difficult childhood. Sometimes it was a very critical, demanding father, sometimes a cold, narcissistic mother, sometimes both, sometimes variations on these themes. Death of a parent at an early age or loss of the parental relationship through divorce or separation certainly seems to make people susceptible.

On the other hand, I can't find such evidence in my mother's story. I remember her parents as warm and loving. She was the youngest of three daughters, younger than the middle daughter by ten years, so she was the baby of the family. My grandfather was a factory worker and they were not well off, but the family seemed happy and stable. Photographs show a happy child and adolescent. She was successful and popular in school.

When we left West Virginia for Chicago, her troubles seemed to start. I was an only child. My growing up deprived her of what had been her major function in life. She had trouble making friends. She tried working but didn't stick with any-

thing. She and my father fought bitterly. She started to drink and abuse prescription drugs. She would spend hours watching television, dressed in her nightgown and slippers. The model of the rhesus monkey in isolation, self-stimulating and self-soothing, makes intuitive sense to me.

But I know that the grandchild's perception of grandparents, who may be warm, loving, and indulgent with a child who is not their primary responsibility, may be very different from that of the therapist listening to his patient describe her childhood, tuning into cues of rejection and parental narcissism. It may ultimately be that my mother experienced her childhood as difficult or depriving for reasons that other people may not be able to understand. It may be that she was genetically predisposed to be unable to respond effectively to stress and isolation.

My case is similar. It may well be that I've inherited some genetic predisposition to depression. I certainly worry about it in my kids. I also know that my childhood experiences, and my mother's death and its aftermath, left me angry at the world, suspicious and reserved, wanting very much to be loved but afraid to trust—a sure setup for depression.

Human Depression

While all the research on brain chemistry has been attracting most of the attention in mental health over the past few years, major changes have been taking place in the practice of psychotherapy as well. When I was in graduate school, I had classes taught by Freudians, behaviorists, and family therapists. Freudians wore suits and ties, behaviorists lab coats, and family therapists wore sportswear. The Freudians and behaviorists could barely disguise their contempt for each other—it was interesting to watch them when they had to pretend to be colleagues, for example, at faculty cocktail parties. The family therapists were polite but condescending to each camp, trying to apply their point of view to campus politics, while the Freudians and the behaviorists largely ignored them. From the viewpoint of the advancement of science, it was extremely unfortunate. The different camps didn't even talk to each other, let alone read each other's literature. You would find interesting and potentially helpful articles and books on subjects like depression or empathy that didn't even agree on definitions. There was no way for one point of view to inform another.

What's happened since that time is a withdrawal from those extreme doctrinaire positions. Effective therapists today will use an amalgam of methods that have their roots in different theories, but their combination makes for effective, humane psychotherapy, often short-term in nature. We don't assume that the patient is in ignorance about the true nature of his problems, but instead that the patient's expressed pain and needs are the natural focus of treatment. The therapist does not have to be a silent presence behind the couch or a rat-runner in a lab coat, but instead can be a human person with some special expertise whose understanding and advice are freely given. Patients are much better off for the change.

But missing in this emerging eclecticism is an underlying theory of human behavior that logically and coherently explains why people come to grief. This is what the structure of Freudian theory had promised, though in fact the theory itself was constantly under revision during Freud's lifetime. After Freud's death, his disciples, less willing to revise the basic theory than the master himself had been, got stuck in more and more fine detail, being led away from the practicalities of patient care. Freudian psychoanalysis, at least in America, had developed a way of thinking about people that saw all human behavior as motivated only by aggressive or sexual drives, and emphasized competition, self-expression, and a kind of rugged independence as the ultimate ends of life. Relationships with other people, including spouses, children, and other loved ones, were seen through a lens that emphasized them as opportunities for expressing sexual or aggressive needs—never a need for love or creativity or self-esteem.

Partly in reaction to this reductionistic way of thinking, a newer way of understanding people came about through the development of what is referred to as *self psychology*. Self psychology emphasizes the interdependence of human beings; that we all, always, need some degree of support and reassurance from important people in our lives. Relationships with others, starting with our need for our parents as infants but continuing into adulthood, help us sustain our sense of ourselves as capable of doing well and deserving of love. These needs are not seen as something to be overcome to achieve true autonomy. True autonomy comes from learning how to express the self in relation to other people. And no relationship is entirely free from expression of our own needs; the closest we come is the unselfish, unquestioning love of parent for child. Though no single theory will ever explain all of human behavior, self psychology offers a point of view that is comprehensive, practical, intuitive, and potentially open to correction from other fields.

A self psychology view of depression is that it is as if depressed people have a leak in the part of the self that contains a positive, nurturing self-image. Instead of having a good opinion of themselves—a reservoir of self-esteem—that can be sustained through the vicissitudes of life, they are overly dependent on love, respect, and approval from significant people in their lives. Sometimes they are not so visibly dependent on others, but on the symbols of love, respect, and approval—financial success, control, power. Therefore a loss or threat to these relationships or symbols can precipitate a depression in people who have been functioning quite well when these relationships were stable, and can make a depression much worse in people who have had some depressive symptomatology.

A useful analogy is the oil system in a car's engine. In a well-running engine, oil is a lubricant; by reducing friction between moving parts, it helps the engine run smoothly and efficiently. We need to change the oil periodically, because it accumulates dirt, but for the most part when the engine works well, the oil system requires little maintenance. But if there is a leak in the system, like a cracked oil pan, the oil runs out or burns up, and we have to keep putting in new oil. The depression-resistant person has a good tight oil system; he or she can function well in life with only periodic maintenance of self-esteem and isn't thrown for a loop by loss or reversal. But the depression-prone person has a "crack in the pan"—a leaky oil system—and needs more or less continual success, love, or reassurance to function unless something is done to repair the system.

This explains why the loss of a loved one is the most common precipitant for a depressive episode—the death of a parent, a divorce, the independence of a child. The loss may be real or only threatened. The reaction may be immediate or delayed for days, weeks, or years. What the individual fears is not the loss of emotional involvement that the nondepressive must deal with—for the depressive, the loss is of something essential to life, a threat to continued functioning.

Other threats to self-confidence can also precipitate depression—failing a test, losing a job. The depression-prone individual is dependent on continued positive feedback about himself from his environment. When this is disrupted, depression increases. This factor is also tied in with loss of the love object—the fear is that, if I'm not a success, the people who are so important to me won't love me anymore.

Paradoxically, success can also precipitate depression. The person usually fears that he doesn't truly deserve the recognition he's been given, that the new responsibilities will point out his inadequacy, that rivals will be angered by his success and will be out to get him. Because he has such a poor opinion of himself, he feels guilty about any assertive behavior. More simply, success for depressives represents one of those "magical solutions" which, it is hoped, will take away the bad feeling and replace it with a kind of invulnerable euphoria. The depression-prone individual has hoped that success will mean never having to feel depressed again. When this turns out not to be the case, depression may strike harder than ever.

A powerful, evocative exposition of the childhood of the future depressive, similar to that of self psychology, was presented by Alice Miller in *Prisoners of Childhood,* the book that Robert and I used. To Miller, depression is "a sign of the loss of the self and consists of a denial of one's own emotional reactions and feelings."[11] She believes that the cause of depression is a distorted relationship between the child and parent, especially the primary caretaker, in the first three years of life. She notes that the infant needs mirroring from the parent in order to develop a healthy self-feeling. The infant needs to look at his parent's face and find himself mirrored there, which he can do only if the parent "is really looking at the unique, small, helpless being and not projecting her own introjects, expectations, fears, [or] plans."

The parent who looks at the child's face and sees only aspects of himself or herself there—his own wishes, needs, and emotions—has a *narcissistic* relationship with the child. The child is used by the parent as a container for his or her own problems. The child adapts to this situation. It is in his vital interest to do what the parent wants; to achieve, to minister, to protect from his worries. He learns that feelings like anger, anxiety, jealousy, and despair, and impulses like playing in the dirt, fighting, or crying are not what the parent wants. In fact, the parent can't accept these things. However the parent may respond on a behavioral level, the child experiences a momentary loss of the connection with the parent that is vital to a positive self-feeling.

WHY DON'T WE HAVE A THEORY?

Gradually, the child begins to feel that such emotions or impulses are alien to the self, so they are not felt anymore. *The ability to feel is lost.*

Ralph and Jean were an extreme example of a very familiar type of couple, the obsessive male and the hysterical female. He is aloof, controlled, and intellectualized. She is loud, emotional, and demanding. When we began to see them, their marriage was already falling apart. Ralph was "gaslighting" Jean—"I can't live with you because you're crazy. You're so crazy your judgment and perception are all wrong. You can't be trusted to take care of the children." It was true that Jean was unstable and had disturbing symptoms. The house was a terrible mess because she was unable to focus her attention. She had regular terrifying nightmares.

Ralph had taken a job far away and was interested in another woman. Jean was left with their two girls, barely able to contain herself. Although she had told Ralph many times to leave, when he did she couldn't forgive him for abandoning her. Their divorce became a terrible battle over custody of the children, but the real struggle was over who was to blame, with Jean's sanity literally on the line.

The girls suffered. When Ralph picked them up for visits, he would ask questions about their mother's functioning. Was she cooking, cleaning? Did she still have nightmares? Were the girls scared? While he thus chipped away at the girls' trust in their mother, Jean was more direct. Though she knew the girls needed a father, she couldn't contain herself: he only was using them to get at her. It was he who was sick, the sadistic bastard. He was incapable of love. The older girl, who bore a striking physical resemblance to her father, became a target. "You're just like your father—get out of my sight."

When parents can't refrain from using children to fight their battles, children conclude that they themselves are not really very important to the parents. Though the parents may tell children that they are loved, that they are special and wonderful, the children always wonder if they're not being manipulated. Children have an unerring sensitivity for deceit. At six and eight, things don't look good for the girls. The older one is in a self-contained classroom because she can't interact with other children without becoming violent. The younger has been diagnosed as learning disabled, with severely low self-esteem.

The aspects of the self—like the ability to feel certain feelings—that are lost due to a faulty relationship with the parent remain unavailable in mature relationships. The same ways of gaining access to "narcissistic supplies"—reinforcement of a good feeling about oneself—that were learned in the relationship with the parent continue to be manifested in other relationships. The grandiose man seeks admiration everywhere. He was his parents' "special son," the one who carried their hopes and admiration, the one who relieved their depression by his success. At the same time, he learned to conceal his weaknesses and shames because to reveal them would mean loss of the admiration that came to serve as a substitute for healthy parental love; and he learned the terrible fear of failure that comes from feeling that he is loved not for himself, but for what he can do.

Depression can be felt when grandiosity fails, due to real or imagined loss of love or inability to keep on achieving at the same high level. Depression also can be projected outward; the grandiose adult can choose a depressed spouse whom he can care for, make dependent and admiring, and thus create a constant prop for his shaky self-esteem. Or depression and grandiosity can alternate in the same person, in response to real or imagined achievements and fluctuations in the amount of admiration forthcoming from the external support system.

Depression is an atrophy of parts of the self. Miller's paradigm of depression is a look to the parent to see if he/she is attentive to the child's needs; disappointment or rage when the child perceives that the parent is still out of touch; and consequent depression. Rage must be denied out of fear of loss of the opportunity for love. Depressed children never give up on their parents, never burn their bridges and face the fact that the parent doesn't have what the child needs. Rather, the child feels that he is at fault somehow, swallows the disappointment, and tries harder next time. The feelings that the parent couldn't respond to are split off and gradually no longer experienced. The child has learned that what self-esteem he has is dependent on continually pleasing others, protecting them from aspects of himself that he has pushed outside conscious awareness. Pleasing others temporarily adds some nutrients to the self, but the hunger remains. The only conscious manifestation may be a sense of emptiness or futility.

Many readers may object at this point. What am I doing if not laying out what I have already said doesn't work—a simple, single-cause theory of depression? Not only that, but this theory seems to put the blame right at the feet of parents. Yes, Miller espouses a single-cause theory. I think she worked with a small sample of patients who had indeed experienced narcissistic parenting and erroneously generalized from them to all depression. Many other depressed patients report similar disturbances in their relationships with parents, but that doesn't make childhood experience the cause of depression, any more than we can say that rejection sensitivity, too-rapid serotonin uptake, or distorted thought processes are the cause. I have gone into detail on this point of view because I think it captures and explains depressed patients' feelings about themselves and self-defeating relationships with others in an elegant and evocative way, but that doesn't mean that all the assumptions behind the theory are true.

The experience of a child with a parent is much more complex than most psychological theorists would like to admit. No parents can offer a consistently positive experience to their child, and most likely no parents offer a consistently negative experience, either. Heinz Kohut, the founder of self psychology, points out that there are adults who, despite traumatic backgrounds and relatively severe pathology, experience life as a joyful challenge; while to others, life is continually stale, flat, and distasteful even though their lives are outwardly rewarding and they are not aware of developmental trauma. His later followers have talked about the innate differences in temperament, activity level, response to being held, and so on, in infants, and the potential for minor trauma—colic, a separation from the parents, illnesses that parents can't comfort—in young children to snowball into very difficult-to-manage problems that may strongly affect the child's sense of self. It is recognized now more and more that what matters is the "fit" between the child's temperament and the primary caretaker's parenting capacities.[12] Someone who is a terrific mother with a docile, easy baby may not be able to respond adequately to a fussy, demanding child. And parenting capacities are not etched in stone, either. A mother who can handle two fussy, active children may not be able to handle three. A mother who can handle one when there is a husband working and she can devote full attention to the child may be pushed over the edge when she has to go to work as well as be the primary caretaker. A father who may dote on and indulge his little girl may somehow experience his son's behavior as a challenge; the girl ends up spoiled, the boy feels picked on and resentful of all authority.

4

Being Good at Depression

CONSIDERABLE RESEARCH has shown that people with depression differ from others in how we perceive the world and ourselves, how we interpret and express our feelings, and how we communicate with other people, particularly loved ones and people in authority. We think of ourselves as unable to live up to our own standards, we see the world as hostile or withholding, and we are pessimistic about things ever changing. In our relationships with others we have unrealistic expectations, are unable to communicate our own needs, misinterpret disagreement as rejection, and are self-defeating in our presentation. Finally, we are in the dark about human emotions. We don't know what it's like to feel normal. We fear that honest feelings will tear us apart or cause others to reject us. We need to learn to live with real feelings.

I have divided the effects of depression into five main areas.

Feelings—how we deal with our emotional lives

Behavior—how we conduct ourselves, our use of time and energy, our habits

Thinking—the assumptions we make about how the world works

Relationships—how we act with other people, what we want and expect of them

The self—our self-image and self-esteem

Part 2 will describe how depression affects us in each of these areas, but, more important, will also prescribe some things we can do about it. The thesis is that we can repair and restore ourselves through learning new ways of thinking, feeling, and doing—self-constructive behavior. What at first seems forced and artificial becomes with time a habit, part of ourselves, replacing our old ways of being with new skills.

First, though, I want to explain what I mean when I say we get "good at depression."

Why Depression Is Self-Defeating

We have a right to be furious with people who tell us there is a simple answer to depression. Whether they see the answer coming from a pill, from psychotherapy, from self-help, or from somewhere else, by minimizing its complexity they dismiss our struggle. Like it or not, if we want to get better we have to change ourselves, and to suggest that it can be done simply and easily is insulting. Recovery from depression is hard work, but at least depressed people are used to that.

Depressed people work harder at living than anyone else, although there is little payoff for our effort. But in the course of our hard work, we become very good at certain skills. We are like weight lifters who concentrate exclusively on upper-body strength—massive muscles in the arms and trunk but little spindly legs underneath—easy to knock down. Depression permeates every aspect of ourselves, but we can free ourselves by consciously deciding to do things differently. People get good at depression—they overadapt and develop skills that, at best, just keep them going, and often make things worse. What we as sufferers can do to recover is apply our energy, talents, and dedication in more appropriate directions. With practice, we can undo the effects of depression, the hypertrophy of self-defeating skills, by replacing them with healthier, more adaptive skills.

Many people who have had severe depressions report that they suffered for years, sometimes for decades, before they told anyone. They felt so isolated and so self-blaming that they assumed there was nothing to be done, nothing that anyone else would understand. Meanwhile they "passed"—they went right ahead with life, putting on a happy face and achieving success in school, in careers, in the family. Often the meaning of a suicide attempt, a "nervous breakdown," or a psychiatric hospitalization is "Look. I can't keep up this charade. I'm sick and I need help." It becomes a transforming experience, an adoption of the sick role, a clear message to the self and others that there is terrible distress below the appearance of competence and good cheer.

Depressed people tend to be overly dependent on external factors—continual feedback from others and/or a relentless quest for accomplishment—for a good feeling about the self. Because there is really little we can do in life to influence the behavior of others or to change events, the depressive's self-esteem is always in danger. Self psychology uses the term *self-object* to describe relationships that help us sustain our sense of ourselves as doing well and deserving love. Parents and spouses are self-objects for us, but so are our friends, coworkers, neighbors, and other people we interact with regularly. Our work, our recreation, and our daily routines serve self-object functions for us. Everyone needs self-object relationships throughout life; they are like water to a fish. We swim in a sea of self-objects that invisibly holds us up and provides us with nutrients. But the depressive's need for self-objects is more desperate, sometimes more distorted or disguised. It is as if the depressive has lead weights on his ankles, dragging him under; or as if the depressive has never learned how to swim effectively or float effortlessly. Instead, all he can manage is an exhausting, desperate flailing and gasping. The sea of self-objects that provides others with nurture and support doesn't give the depressive any buoyancy.

In self psychology theory, the depressive is understood as relying on others in his life in order to make up for deficits in the self. These deficits may come about as a result of a number of causes, but the best understood is the absence or inability of parents to provide the child with functions he or she needs in order to grow. A maturing child needs certain qualities in the parents to acquire and maintain a healthy sense of self-esteem. Heinz Kohut[1] refers to the need for the "idealizing" and the "grandiose" functions to lay the foundation for a strong, reliable sense of the self.

The *idealizing* aspect of the self means that part that needs to look up to parental figures as powerful, confident sources of comfort and models for identification. It lays the groundwork for mature forms of idealization, such as identification with values or religion—a sense that in being part of something larger or more important than ourselves, we are enriched and our lives are given meaning. As the child's immature grandiosity—his fantasy of being invulnerable and omnipotent—diminishes in response to his growing ability to perceive reality, idealization partly replaces it. The child may no longer feel that he alone is omnipotent, but through merger with a strong, comforting parent or other adult is protected from feeling helplessness and loss. Failure of parents to provide a sense of strength and support— often because of their own depression—leaves the child feeling alone and vulnerable. He may grow into an adult who sees himself as weak, seeks others to model himself after, and remains dependent on a connection with other people for a sense of self-esteem.

The *grandiose* aspect of the self refers to the need of the young child to feel himself as powerful, omnipotent, the center of the world, the object of unquestioned love and adoration. Failure of the parents to respond empathically to these feelings of the child, to respond with some delight as they get in touch with these childish aspects of themselves, can lead to a sense of worthlessness, rejection, and a hunger for response. Such people are described as "mirror-hungry"—they constantly look to others for affirmation of themselves as potent, worthwhile, and worthy of love.

Depression is the loss of parts of the self, the gradual numbing of feelings and experiences that the child learns are unacceptable and banishes from experience. Cure comes from recovery of the missing pieces. Depressive moods in everyday life come from suppression of impulses or unwanted emotions. *"The true opposite of depression is not gaiety or absence of pain, but vitality: the freedom to experience spontaneous feelings."*[2] As patients learn from their experience in psychotherapy that the breakthrough of suppressed emotions, however painful or upsetting, can be counted on to lift depression, they begin to change how they handle feelings. Specifically, painful or upsetting feelings are no longer avoided, but experienced. This leads to a reconnection with the lost parts of the self.

Experienced therapists are familiar with the frustrations of working with depressed patients. Many make the therapist feel depressed; caring, advice, concern, medication, anything the therapist provides is not good enough. This type of patient puts the therapist in the role the patient held in the family. If the therapist offers advice, the patient rejects it; if the therapist doesn't offer advice, the patient feels rejected—just as the patient's successes were never enough for the family, and his failures precipitated a loss of love. The therapist needs to point out this process and interpret that the patient has felt the same way in his own family—frustrated, inadequate, depressed. The therapist offers a new solution for the patient by modeling autonomy yet helping the patient accept, understand, and finally detoxify these feelings.

John is a man in his forties who came to therapy complaining of obsessive thoughts and difficulties with his family. He was desperate to be a good father, but the harder he tried to connect with his children, the worse mess he made of things.

John's childhood seemed strangely cold and frightening. His mother worried constantly about thunderstorms, the rent, John's health. His father rarely spoke at all. With a mother who could not insulate a child from the normal anxieties of childhood because of her own terrors, and a father who seemed to withdraw actively if not cower from other people, the young John was completely on his own in learning how to live. Somehow he did a very good job.

Coming from a working-class family, John put himself through college and eventually rose to a very high position in his profession. Although he felt confident about his skills at work, he felt completely inadequate to the task of being a father and husband.

The therapist talked to John about being a self-made man who had learned the rules in the working world but didn't know the rules about family life. Together they set about assembling a manual, a metaphorical how-to book for a father's role in a family. John's idealization of the therapist was obvious from speculative comments he made about how well the therapist's family must function. The therapist did not challenge this but let John feel that he had a strong, capable friend to rely on. Whenever they would discover one of the rules of family life, John was very pleased. He felt a sense of shared accomplishment which he was then able to use as his children grew and mastered their developmental tasks. Instead of constantly trying to control his children—a response which was, in essence, a reaction to his anxieties about fatherhood—he developed empathy for them. Seeing the world from their point of view, he was much better able to respond to their needs.

John's need to control his children was what set him up for failure. Though children always need limits, John could not get in touch with their joy and exuberance and help them redirect their energy when they went too far. He couldn't tell the difference between high spirits and out-of-control behavior, so he was always trying to control. Helping John feel that he understood the "manual" enabled him to get out from under the horrible anxiety that his children's normal behavior caused him. Without the anxiety, he became a much more effective parent—able to enter into his children's play and then step out of it into a parental role when it was time. As he developed the capacity to experience joy, his depression—which was never the focus of treatment—was greatly relieved.

Ideal-Hungry Depression

One of my best teachers used a bicycle analogy to describe how the child absorbs a healthy sense of self-esteem from the parent. At first, the young child learning to ride a two-wheeler needs a parent literally to hold her up. When the training wheels come off, the parent continues to provide support and direction, running along beside the little bicyclist, at first with a hand on the handlebars to steer and another on the seat to hold the bike up. Very gradually, as the child develops a better sense of balance and understands—unconsciously—the principles of momentum, velocity, and gyroscopic stability, the parent needs to provide less and less support. The parent and child engage in a very complex and unspoken transfer of knowledge and control from one to the other. Can you imagine trying to teach the physics of bicycling didactically to a child? The needed skills are transferred through shared experience, not through explanation. Eventually the parent lets go of the handlebars, keeping the other hand on the seat but with a light touch, running along beside and encouraging the child with words and emotions. At some point the parent lets go of the seat. The empathic parent doesn't stop now and say, "You're on your own"—the startled child will look back and fall down. Instead, the parent runs along, perhaps with arms outstretched to catch the child in case of accident. The child hears the parent's footsteps and does not even realize, at first, that she is now in control. The parent's knowledge, judgment, and confidence have become a part of the child.[3]

Now you can take this analogy and make it work with depression. The fearful parent teaches the child that the street is unsafe. The parent lacking confidence teaches the child that bicycling is too difficult. The angry, resentful parent teaches the child that she's not worth teaching.

But depression is not that simple at all. What complicates it is that people have any number of ways of dealing with psychological needs like protection from fear or lack of self-worth, other than seeking them directly. Many of the methods that we have for protection from these needs have been described as psychological "defense mechanisms." *Defense mechanisms* are ways we learn to not feel unpleasant emotions or unacceptable impulses. Denial, projection, intellectualization, sublimation, somatization are some of the defense mechanisms that alone, or in combination, protect us from feeling the true extent of our needs. These defenses, and the secondary habits that their use requires, add up to what I refer to as the "skills of depression." As depressed adults, we don't simply go through life asking for the security and love we need—we make it much more complicated than that.

For instance, many adolescents who appear to be "conduct disordered"—rebellious, argumentative, in minor legal trouble—may actually be depressed. They don't look it because they have learned a set of skills—they can stir things up, get everyone mad, keep the emotional pot boiling so that they don't have to feel empty inside. They can *project* (make others feel) responsibility for their own behavior, keeping parents and school engaged in a power struggle, so they don't have to start really facing independence. One theorist observes that with delinquent kids, "at least one of the parents feels rage against some social injustice, which usually involves displaced anger against a powerful authority figure within the family. The child thus assumes the role of avenger for the parent against society, releasing the parent from having to own and assume responsibility for his or her own feelings and actions."[4]

Jason was fifteen when I first got to know him. He was referred by juvenile probation after having been caught in some petty vandalism. He was a strong, handsome young man who could have been a popular football player at his high school if he hadn't felt too alienated from the system to take part in things.

His mother was one of the angriest people I've ever met. She seemed to have a grievance against the world. She and her second husband, Jason's stepfather, fought constantly, mostly about money. The stepfather spent every spare penny on adult toys—boats, snowmobiles—which he would gleefully deny Jason access to. Jason's mother would rant and rave about how unfair this was to Jason but was never able to put her foot down with the stepfather. This was despite the fact that she was the real breadwinner in the family and that her own father had paid for the house they lived in. They were suing their neighbors on either side over petty neighborhood disputes.

Jason was quite depressed, though outwardly functional. He was lethargic, absorbed by small bodily concerns. He slept poorly and abused alcohol. He saw absolutely no purpose in living but was not directly suicidal. He complained about having to come in for treatment but always was on time and talked openly. When his probation was up, he committed another petty offense and got it extended, which I interpreted to mean that he wanted more counseling. He was bright and could have done well in school, but he never studied. He spent his leisure time either making out with his girlfriend or watching television. He wanted to do more; at times he felt a strong desire to make something of himself, but it was as if he didn't know where to start.

Although Jason was a moderate troublemaker at school, he had so many winning qualities that the school authorities never turned against him. His mother was a different story. Several times a week she was on the phone with the guidance department or the principal's office, haranguing them about something Jason or his sister had done or failed to do.

One day Jason told me somewhat sheepishly that, as he was talking to his mother, he'd taken off his sweater and a bag of marijuana had rolled out and fallen at her feet. He laughed as he told me how he'd gotten her to believe that it wasn't his, he was only holding it for a friend.

Incredibly enough, the exact same scene was repeated a few weeks later. This time I could see that Jason wasn't only laughing at his mother's gullibility. When I said that he must have been disappointed that she didn't seem to care enough to see through his story, he started to cry—the first time I'd seen him admit any pain at all. He poured out all his years of resentment at feeling that he was the true grown-up in the family. He told me that he'd been sexually active since the age of eight, always right under his mother's nose; that he knew he was too young to be involved with older girls like this, but that he had the strange feeling his mother knew about it and approved. He had the same feeling about some of the petty theft and vandalism he committed. He didn't get any joy from these acts.

Jason clearly needed people he could respect, who could give him some guidance, but he would push away anyone who attempted to offer it. Someone like him who was less angry and less intelligent would make a good "true believer" in any powerful cause. If Jason continued to grow without better role models, he could easily turn into a cynical, bitter man who achieves outward success but feels empty inside. He could be a smooth and successful drug dealer. If so, he'd be living out his depression—doing something every day that increased his hatred for himself.

Jason used his intelligence, charm, and empathic skills both to seek help for himself and reject it. He could outsmart himself—certainly he had no conscious intention of showing the marijuana to his mother—but then outsmart everyone else by talking his way out of difficult situations. As much as he hated it, he could read his mother's mind—she did not want to hear that he might need her help—so he would tell her what she wanted to hear, denying his anger at her and increasing his self-loathing.

Mirror-Hungry Depression

People like Jason need someone in their lives as a mentor; someone to look up to, who can set a standard for their aspirations and provide guidance and patient understanding on the way. Other people with depression look to others not for ideals, but for a resonance. Experiencing themselves as empty, damaged, or barren, they need people close to them who can respond to deeper feelings, draw them out, and help them experience life.

Peter was in his mid-forties when I first met him. He was troubled by anxiety, depression, and family conflict. He had been taking a number of different psychotropic medications, notably Prozac and tranquilizers, for years. He also used a light box for seasonal depression.

None of it seemed to be helping much. A very intelligent, perceptive man, he appeared tense, nearly exhausted, hypersensitive. He had been in psychotherapy twice before and seemed to have an odd mixture of powerful hope that something could be done for him and a wish to deny that need altogether. Some days he would fence with me, display his erudition, set traps that I couldn't help but fall into; other days he was one of the most direct, honest, courageous patients I've ever worked with.

At first we focused on his family. His two children were somewhat estranged from him. One had recently dropped out of college, entered therapy, and withdrawn from Peter. She said her therapist had told her to put some distance between them for a while. This seemed to obsess and preoccupy Peter. He was continually on the watch for communication from her. When something came, like a simple birthday card, he would spend hours trying to interpret hidden meanings in it. He would work himself into such a state over what he thought was there that he would call his daughter and accuse her of participating in some scenario that existed only in his mind. She would blow up, and they would be further estranged.

In an effort to understand how he got this way, I began to explore his own history. His father was cold, critical, and frightening. His mother was shallow, narcissistic, and competitive. Peter had had a miserable childhood. When he was about twelve, he discovered girls, and had the happiest years of his life in and out of various puppy-love affairs. This ended abruptly when his father sent him away to an all-boys boarding school. Peter was miserable there and ended his first year at the bottom of his class. But he forced himself to work, and by his fourth year he was in the top quarter. He went on to Princeton, the Navy, and the New York financial world without looking back. He always worked hard. I think he liked the structure of these worlds; he learned that if he followed the rules, he would be successful. In material terms, he was a great success.

He married and had children. It was not a happy marriage, and Peter began to think about divorce when the children were in their early teens. Then his wife developed a terminal illness. It was very painful, and she was devastated emotionally by her illness—raging, crying, self-pitying. It was two years until she died, with Peter trying to protect the children from her rage all the time.

Not long after, Peter remarried. He retired from the business world and devoted himself to volunteer work. But he was never happy. He had been in therapy of one sort or another since his twenties. Now he and his second wife had everything they could want—they traveled all over the world, had one of the biggest houses in town—but he looked haunted. Though extremely intuitive about other people—he was a terrific salesman—he was quite lonely.

I suggested, repeatedly and in many different ways, that he was trying to use his relationships with people, including his family, to fill a hole in his self. There seemed to be a yawning emptiness inside him that no one could ever fix. But while this theory made sense to me, there was no confirmation from Peter.

Finally he told me his guilty secret. In his mid-thirties, before his wife became ill, he had failed his own test. There was an opportunity to move up in his firm. It was logical that he should make his move. But no one in higher management gave him a clear signal that he should go ahead, so he didn't apply. It was the first time since childhood that he'd consciously felt fear. To Peter, this meant that he was not who he pretended to be—that, in fact, all he was was pretense. Ever since then, he reflected, he'd been trying to make up for that failure.

I said the usual things—that he had no support or encour-

agement from his wife, his parents, or anyone on the job, that it was a long time ago, that he should forgive himself for one small "failure." Of course this all fell on deaf ears.

As time went on, I understood better what this meant to Peter. He has recovered a great deal, and has forgiven himself; but to him, this event was a turning point in his life. An entire defensive structure was destroyed. After a disastrous childhood, he had learned that if he worked hard and played by the rules, he would be treated well, and he could pretty much ignore the part of him deeper inside that felt lonely and afraid. But the other part was always there and always made him feel that he was only faking being successful and confident. When he was finally faced with something he just couldn't do, he felt that all his old fears were perfectly true; that his "real self" was needy, weak, and afraid.

No wonder he was driven crazy by his daughter's withdrawal. He thought she had found him out, found the "real self" that he tried so hard to hide.

Peter was extremely sensitive and intuitive about people, outwardly successful, a very impressive figure, yet a man who needed constant reassurance from others that he was worthy of love. His own children, who did love and respect him and assumed he would take that as a given, could not imagine how much he needed them, so were irritated and confused by his obsessive attention to their communication. It took a long time in therapy for him to trust me enough to tell me the secret about himself that made him so ashamed, made it so hurtful when people who he loved withdrew from him. But he was not consciously keeping a secret from me—he used the defense of isolation so that he didn't see the connection that I did between his "failure" and his need for continuous positive affirmation.

In all his relationships, Peter used his considerable charm and sensitivity to engage people quickly and deeply. The more they seemed to like him, the better he felt, for a brief while. But he was really outsmarting himself. By presenting to others only a facade—confident, witty, outgoing—he was isolating what he believed to be his real self—weak, frightened, a failure. He felt that he was fooling everyone, that if they knew him the way he knew himself, they would reject him in turn. He used his own skills to put himself in a downward cycle of depression from which there was no escape.

John, Jason, and Peter have all lost parts of their selves—a sense of resilience, a core of aspirations, a feeling of vitality—but they don't seek these missing parts directly. Instead, they put on a false front. They act confident, cocky, tough. Those who love them can't understand why they are so difficult to be with and so unhappy. They have become experts at the skills of depression. They adapt certain psychological defense mechanisms to keep their needs out of consciousness. They know how to fool people, but they don't know how to get their own needs met. Many people with depression are experts at fooling people. They cover their own emotions, they act happy and successful. A career, a cause, an exercise regime, can become an obsession. "If I didn't work, then I'd have to think about how miserable I was and how I didn't have any friends and how no one loved me."[5]

Part 2

Learning New Skills

5

Where to Start

HEART DISEASE is a good analogy to major depression. Heart disease is "caused" by a complex of factors, including a genetic predisposition, emotional factors like how we handle stress, and habits like diet and exercise. You don't catch heart disease from an infection. You develop it gradually, over time, as plaque builds up in your arteries. Once you cross an invisible threshold marked by standards of blood pressure and cholesterol levels, you have heart disease, and you have it for the rest of your life. Yesterday you were normal, today you have heart disease. You don't feel any different, but now you have to change your life. Depression may be a similar threshold disease—genetic and biochemical factors may determine a different level of stress for each of us that, once reached, puts us over the edge into depression. Childhood trauma, stress, and loss may bring us closer to the edge.

Some stress pushes us over into our first real depression. Once over the line, we can't go back. We "have" depression. We can recover from episodes, we can modify our lifestyles to prevent or moderate future episodes, but we "have" depression.

Unfortunately we know a lot more about treatment and prevention of heart disease than we do about depression. You can change your eating habits, your exercise habits, and your stress level and reduce your risk of heart disease. No one seems to know how to reduce your risk of depression. There are many effective medications and some very sexy surgical procedures that can reverse the effects of heart disease, restore you to near-normal functioning, and reliably reduce your incidence of another attack. Although there are medications and treatments that help depression, no one knows whether they effectively reduce the risk of future episodes, and opinion is divided on whether they can return you to normal.

Since no one seems to really understand depression, everyone feels entitled to an opinion. You have no way of knowing if your physician's advice is any better than your wife's, your clergyman's, a mental health professional's, or the guy on the corner's. But the truth is that experienced, open-minded therapists in fact know a great deal about what helps people recover from depression. This "practice wisdom" of therapists rarely filters out to the public, not because it contains trade secrets, but because much of it is tied to theoretical points of view that themselves get in the way of exchanging knowledge and experience.

I want to briefly summarize here how good psychotherapy works with depression to facilitate recovery. The purpose at this point is not to sell psychotherapy, but to use it as a model to explain recovery from depression; how people can learn to stop the self-defeating behavior that seems to them to be the only possible response to their desperate inner state.

One of the essential elements in effective psychotherapy is trust. The patient is open and honest with the therapist in return for an implicit contract that the therapist will use his special knowledge only to help, never to harm, the patient. For many adults, the therapeutic relationship is the only one in which they can let their guard down. Depressed patients are almost always full of guilt and shame. They haven't lived up to their own standards. They feel like failures. They feel that they've let their loved ones down. When the therapist hears the guilty secrets and doesn't run screaming from the room in revulsion, or castigate the patient as the moral leper he thinks he is, healing begins. The acceptance of the patient as a worthwhile individual, even though he's not perfect, is crucial for the patient to overcome his pervasive guilt and shame.

Another essential element is emotional engagement and support. The patient does not usually communicate the depth of his pain and fear to those closest to him. It may be that he wants to protect them, it may be that he fears they will reject him; regardless, he "stuffs" his feelings, to borrow an AA term. He bites back on his feelings and tries to pretend they aren't there. If he shows them at all, he usually gets advice from those around him that is less than helpful. Others are quick to give advice because they, like the patient, are afraid of the need and pain. The good therapist, at this stage, doesn't give advice. He shows by example that the feelings are not to be feared; in fact, he probes and goes deeper. He lets the patient know that depression is a process that has a life of its own, that there is good reason for hope because depression does end, but that feelings are important. Sometimes all the therapist can do is hold the patient's hand, as it were, while they wait together for the medication to work. Often there is no one else in the patient's life who can do this.

Once trust and support are relatively stable, the healing work of psychotherapy can begin. Many aspects of the individual's functioning can change with treatment. I have grouped these into five major areas: how emotions are experienced; patterns of behavior; thought processes; relationships with others; and how the patient feels about himself. Each of these aspects is explored in depth in the coming chapters, but here is a brief overview.

Emotions. People with depression usually have learned ineffective or self-defeating ways of handling emotions. Some, like Robert, seem to be frightened by all emotions, cold, intellectual, and afraid of human contact. When he got better and recognized this, Robert liked to joke about himself as "emotionally chal-lenged." Many depressed people have particular trouble with anger. We feel we should never get angry, so we bite back on it until we can't take any more, and then explode. Those nearby can't understand the explosion because they don't know all the little frustrations that led up to it. The depressive gets even more depressed because he feels he's lost control. In therapy, these emotional patterns must be challenged, and the patient must learn, for instance, that intimacy doesn't lead to being engulfed and that anger doesn't lead to violence. This is often played out in the relationship between therapist and patient, where the patient feels safe enough for the first time to experience trust and anger without running away or being destroyed.

Behavior. The patient often must also change patterns of behavior that lead to a depressed lifestyle. Most depressed peo-ple are perfectionists. We feel that if we don't do a job perfectly, our entire self-esteem is endangered. Often this leads to pro-crastination. The job is never really begun; outright failure is avoided, but the depressive knows he's let himself down. Then again, depressed people want to make ourselves over from the ground up: we want to lose thirty pounds, run five miles a day, quit smoking and drinking, get our work completely reorga-nized, and have time for relaxation and meditation. It seems like there is so much to do that we never start; or we may start one day in a burst of energy that gets dissipated in so many directions that nothing really gets accomplished, and we are again con-firmed in the belief that there's no point trying. We have to learn that attaining more limited, realistic goals is much more satisfy-ing than building castles in the air.

Thought processes. Cognition, the way we think, must be changed. Jerome Frank talked about our "assumptive world,"[1] the set of beliefs that we all have that explain how life works. We get some assumptions from our parents, we develop others as we grow up, and we continue to add to and revise our beliefs about what makes things tick into adulthood and old age. Depressed people tend to have certain assumptions in common, which are self-perpetuating and not corrected by experience. We think that we are responsible for the bad things that happen to us, while the good things are just accidental. We are pessimists, thinking that things left alone will usually go to pieces rather than working out for the best. We think that we have to be in control of things at all times, and if we're not, disaster will happen. These habits of thinking are largely unconscious. They must be brought out into the open, challenged, and changed for the depressive to recover.

Relationships. Relationships with other people are always difficult for the depressive. We walk around with a vast hurt inside and long for someone to heal it, but we're also ashamed of feeling that way, so we don't let anyone know. We care too much about how others feel and think about us, but we're afraid to let them know we care; consequently we're almost always disappointed. Always expecting rejection, we may reject first as a defense. Our boundaries are too permeable, so that we often assume others know how we feel, and that we know how they feel. Despite the fact that we're wrong about this so often, we don't learn from experience and stop making these assumptions. We have to learn specific techniques of communication that will establish boundaries and stop the confusion.

The self. Depressed people don't have inner resources of self-esteem that help them get through trying times. We look to others to replace those resources but know that such wishes are unfair and unrealistic; consequently we are consumed by shame and guilt. We want desperately to be loved, but feel we are unlovable. We haven't been able to determine principles and values for ourselves, nor to guide our lives by rational priorities, because we're so guilt-ridden that every detail seems important; we can't afford any mistakes. We can't feel good when we accomplish a meaningful goal because all goals are the same;

making a lousy dinner feels as if it can undo our pride about graduating from college. We need to learn how to set priorities, to take pleasure in our accomplishments, and to integrate that pride into our selves. We have to cultivate detachment, to learn patience and discrimination.

The next five chapters review how depression affects our functioning and how our altered functioning in turn reinforces depression in each of these five areas of living. By stepping back from ourselves and seeing how we do depression, we can also perhaps see how to undo it. The reader may not need any more from this book than an altered perspective. But most people with depression need more—they need specific advice about how to change, they need specific techniques, skills, or habits that they can learn to replace the self-defeating skills of depression. So I'm providing these as well. I'm going to be concerned that the depressed reader will be overwhelmed by this section, concluding, "Oh God, I have to remake myself from the ground up. I'll never be able to do all this. I'd better just go back to bed." What I want to say is, Relax; take it easy. You don't have to do it all at once. You can start anywhere to undo depression. Any chapter, any suggestion, may be enough to get you started on a self-reinforcing cycle of healthy behavior. But you do have to start.

6

Emotions

ALEX WAS an extremely introverted man. An only child, his parents deceased, he had lived by himself since college. He worked in a job that most people would consider boring. Though he did not appear shy or self-conscious—he had a pleasant smile and talked easily when spoken to—he seemed to avoid most human contact.

He told his therapist how lonely and depressed he was. He was envious of people who had others to be close to. He identified himself as gay, though he had had little sexual experience of any kind. His only outlet was to go to gay bars. There he would always find someone who became his imaginary lover. These affairs in Alex's mind lasted for months. Alex would interpret every look and gesture made by his imaginary lover in the bar as a secret signal to him, confirming their love. During these times, Alex was euphoric. He often missed his therapy appointments, and when he did come in, he was feeling so good that he was hard-pressed to think of things to talk about. Inevitably, however, the imaginary lover would make some gesture that Alex interpreted as a betrayal. Then his bubble would burst, and Alex would be plunged into the depths of *depression, feeling for all the world as if a real lover had rejected him cruelly and thoughtlessly.*

Alex's therapist took pity on him and talked him into trying Prozac. It had a miraculous effect. Within a few weeks, Alex was talking realistically about his life for the first time. He realized he was kidding himself with these imaginary affairs. Also, he saw that he was going nowhere in his career. He and the therapist excitedly began to make plans for how Alex could really meet people. They considered his going back to school, or asking for more responsibility at work. Alex seemed like a changed man, and the therapist was much heartened.

Then Alex dropped out of therapy for a few months. When he called again, it was because he had been spurned by a new lover. Her heart sinking, the therapist realized this was another imaginary affair. She asked Alex if he was still taking his Prozac. "Oh, that," said Alex. "That wasn't good for me. I didn't feel like myself on that. This is me."

When the therapist and I talked about Alex, we found that psychotherapy had many ways of explaining why he'd gone back to his old ways. It was "resistance"—there was a part of him that wanted to get well, and a part that didn't, and the two parts were at war. His old pattern was a "security operation" designed to make him feel safe in a threatening world. Or perhaps he was misdiagnosed—he wasn't really depressed, he was suffering from a "personality disorder of the schizoid type." Perhaps he needed behavioral coaching—the specific ways to act, to talk to people, weren't in his "behavioral repertoire."

Though there may be something helpful for the therapist and patient in all these ways of looking at the problem, I think they miss an important point—*Alex was afraid of feelings he couldn't control.* When the affair was only taking place in his imagination, he wrote the script. Everything that happened, including the final rejection, was a product of his own mind. But if he got close to a real person, he wouldn't be in charge anymore. He placed himself in danger of feeling real feelings. What if someone else really loved him? To be loved is heady stuff. Alex spent his life avoiding extremes of emotion.

In order to learn any new skills that will help overcome and prevent depression, it's essential to start with emotions. *Depressives fear feelings.* Other self-defeating habits that will be explored in the following chapters—in how we think, act, communicate, and view ourselves—are essentially ways we have developed to help us not feel certain things. Unless we understand first that these emotions are not to be feared, we won't be able to change our other habits.

Most people, depressed or not, have some fear of feeling. One of the central insights of psychodynamic therapy is that "anxiety"—the fear of being torn apart, consumed by our emotions—is the underlying problem in most human situations. And one of the central truths is that there is really nothing to fear. It is our fear itself, and the habits we develop to control or avoid it, that leads to most of our suffering. If we stop running and turn around and face the demons, they usually turn out to be no threat at all.

People with depression have a special talent for stuffing feelings. They can pretend to themselves and the world that they don't feel normal human emotions. They are very good at the defenses of repression, isolation, and intellectualization. They raise self-denial and self-sacrifice to the point where the self seems to disappear.

One of Freud's greatest but least-understood contributions is the notion of unconscious guilt. The paradigm is the Oedipal situation: the young boy harbors incestuous desires for his mother and murderous impulses toward his father, but because these desires and impulses are forbidden, the child represses them: they are lost to consciousness. *Yet the child still feels guilty.* This is one of the most fiendish aspects of the human mind: we don't get to imagine the desire, to indulge it in fantasy, to relish the thought of seduction or revenge, but we still get to feel guilty about it.

If the Oedipal child feels remote from your experience, consider Peter (in chapter 4) as his wife was dying. Despite the fact that he had already decided to divorce her, despite the fact that her illness made her a vengeful, raging harridan, Peter didn't let himself feel a wish that she would die—yet he still felt guilty. All his tender ministrations and self-sacrifice during her illness couldn't undo his guilt. Or look ahead to Sharon's story in chapter 14. Sexually abused as a child, she couldn't allow herself to experience normal sexual desires. She had to make the men in her life the sexual aggressors, then feel guilty, dirty, and ashamed for letting herself be seduced again. It is a guiding principle of everyday life, but one we'd like to forget about—we feel guilt about feelings and desires without being aware of the feelings and desires themselves.

Now, people with depression hardly let themselves feel any emotion at all. Instead of the normal fluctuations of happiness, sadness, disappointment, joy, desire, and anger that most people cycle through many times a day, depressed people feel a kind of gray neutrality that translates into subterranean tectonic shifts in mood. But even though they aren't aware of the emotions, they still get to feel guilty about them. When the meek, depressed wife of a bullying husband doesn't consciously feel angry at his treatment, she will still feel guilty about her rage without even experiencing it. If a man is unaware of his attraction to a coworker, but instead treats her badly out of *reaction formation* (a primitive defense in which we do the opposite of our wish— what little boys do to little girls they like), he still feels guilty about unacceptable impulses. If my drinking interferes with my ability to work, even though I'm in denial about my drinking, I can still feel guilty. This is one of the great secrets of depression. The depressive is full of guilt about feelings, desires, and impulses he's not even aware he has. *If you're going to feel guilty anyway, you'd better know what it is that you feel guilty about. If you know, you can do something about it.* The first step in overcoming the guilt is to become aware of the feelings.

Learning to Feel

How do you go about recapturing the ability to experience emotions? First of all, it's necessary to understand that emotions are innate, instinctual responses that are with us from infancy on. When the baby is feeling warm, comfortable, and secure, she experiences an emotion we can call contentment or happiness. When she experiences something that pleases her, like a new puppy, she experiences joy or delight. When something startles her, she feels fear. When she's deprived of something she wants, she feels anger. Left alone for too long, she feels the beginnings of sadness. The capacity to experience these emotions is hard-wired into the human nervous system. If someone steps on your toe, you feel pain. If someone steps on your psychological toes—for instance, by being rude—you feel anger. If you don't experience these emotions, it's because you are spending psychic energy to keep them out of awareness. This psychic energy could be better spent on other things.

We can see the expression of similar emotions in higher animals—dogs, cats, horses, monkeys—it's what enables us to feel emotionally connected to them. Darwin pointed out how the infant's ability to express emotion even before the acquisition of language has important survival value for the species—the infant expresses fear, we protect it; it expresses hunger, we feed it; it expresses happiness, we play with it (and thus give it the opportunity to learn through socialization). The function of emotions is to amplify or call attention to the situation that elicits them. If the infant couldn't express these feelings, it would die, because we wouldn't know how to care for it.

Emotions in themselves are absolutely value-free. They are

reflexes, like salivating when hungry or withdrawing your hand from a hot iron. But how we express emotions carries important social and individual values. We have the ability to control how we express emotions, but we get in trouble if we try to control how we experience them. If a man gets angry and beats his wife, that is both condemned socially and destructive psychologically. But if he tells her why he's angry and then tries to work things out, or if he blows off steam by exercise, or throws himself into his work, those activities are both socially approved and psychologically productive. The point is that although we have control over how we express emotions, we've been taught that we shouldn't even feel some feelings—an almost impossible task.

It takes a great deal of practice for the depressed person to learn how not to experience emotions, but we get very good at it. Women get especially good at not feeling anger and men get good at not feeling sadness. All of us stop experiencing much joy or happiness. It seems as if when you lose the ability to feel painful feelings you also lose the ability to feel positive ones. We go through life numbed.

The Function of Defenses

Depressed people overuse certain psychological *defense mechanisms*—denial, isolation, and repression, among others—to help keep feelings out of conscious awareness. The concept of the defense mechanism is one of the lasting products of psychoanalysis. Defenses help protect our conscious minds from awareness that underneath, we are in conflict with ourselves. We are constantly trying to find a balance between our desires, our conscience, the constraints of external reality, and our needs for other people.[1] Sudden change in any area upsets our homeostasis. Defenses distort reality to restore the balance temporarily. When external reality is too much to be accepted—the death of a loved one—we can go into denial. When our desires are in conflict—for instance, sexual desire for someone our conscience tells us we are not supposed to desire—we may transmute the desire into a wish for someone else, turn it into hate, intellectualize it, or any of a number of other possibilities. Defenses are like art, a creative synthesis. The mind unconsciously creates something that was not there before.

Defense mechanisms themselves are necessary for human existence. They are often creative, adaptive strategies for dealing with difficult situations or people. But they can be used by the depressive as ways to try to avoid feeling. They can become habitual and hypertrophied; protecting ourselves from some truly horrible feelings, we run the risk of losing the ability to feel altogether.

All defenses distort reality to some extent, but some do it more than others. So-called "immature" defenses, like denial and projection, can stand reality on its head. In denial, I honestly don't see how my alcoholism hurts others, although it's plain as day to any objective observer. This is why people get so angry at alcoholics. It's very difficult to believe they really don't see things as they are. But the alcoholic lives in a different reality dominated by the bottle. In projection, I attribute my feelings to others. Feeling grouchy and looking for a fight, I interpret my wife's neutral comments as hostile and provocative. Other, so-called "mature" defenses may distort reality only a little. Humor, for example, works by shifting one's perspective: what had seemed all-important and frustrating seems ludicrous, perhaps trivial, with the help of humor. I don't particularly like the characterization of some defenses as immature and others as mature—to me much depends on how they are used—but some defenses let us keep a more accurate perspective on what is going on around us than others. Unfortunately, depressed people use the less accurate defenses too much.

Denial means simply being caught between reality and wish and not accepting reality. It catches us when we learn of a loved one's death—"Oh no, it can't be true." It catches the alcoholic who simply can't see the damage his drinking is doing to himself and to all those around him. The depressed wife of the alcoholic may use denial to protect herself from experiencing the anger and hurt that come from repeated disappointments. Why do wives stay in abusive relationships? There are many reasons, but when a wife says to herself, "He didn't mean it, he won't do it again," that's denial. For the time being, she really believes it.

Isolation is short for "isolation of affect," affect being another word for emotion. Isolation drives a wedge between the experience and the feeling. We are aware of what's happening around us, but we don't experience the emotion that we would expect to accompany the event. Isolation is useful for surgeons, rescue workers, police officers, and others who have to remain calm in very stressful situations. But for the depressed person, isolation can be very destructive. Many depressed people report suicidal thoughts or impulses—like driving down the road and thinking about pulling into oncoming traffic—that seem to come from nowhere, disturbing ideas that have no feeling connected to them. These thoughts are indications that there are painful, agonizing feelings going on under the surface that are not experienced. *Intellectualization* is an elaboration of isolation; we use the cognitive, rational side of our brains to try to understand a difficult situation—nothing wrong with this, in fact it's quite constructive—but we try to use our understanding to avoid experiencing the accompanying emotions.

Repression has two meanings now, both important for depression. One meaning is the opposite of isolation: it's experiencing the feeling without the idea. The depressive gets suddenly sad without knowing why—but the objective observer sees the event that led to the feeling. This may be a criticism, a disappointment, a snub that passes quickly in and out of the depressive's consciousness. The event itself is quickly forgotten, repressed, but the feeling lingers. This leads us to the other, more common, meaning of repression, that of "forgetting" events that are too painful to remember. This is not an uncommon phenomenon with trauma—sexual abuse, combat, disasters. The events are not really forgotten, of course, they come back as nightmares or in other manifestations. The depressive who has been through traumatic experiences will use repression to help keep the feelings associated with the event out of consciousness.

What the depressed person typically experiences instead of emotions are mood changes. One minute we'll be feeling pretty good, then without warning we feel depressed—sad, discouraged, no energy. One of the favorite phrases of depressed people is "out of the blue"—"It just came over me, out of the blue, and I felt so awful again."

The basic principle that the depressed person has to learn is that these mood changes do not come out of the blue—*mood changes are always caused by an unfelt feeling*. The feeling is usually a response to an interpersonal event, although sometimes it is just a response to a memory, something we read about or heard on television. Something happens that makes us angry, makes us feel hurt, sad, or scared—or even happy—but the event doesn't register on our consciousness. The feeling seems disconnected from reality; we don't understand what's going on in ourselves so we feel inadequate, out of control, frustrated—depressed again.

There is nothing like five years of psychoanalysis four times a week to drive home the point that changes in the way we feel are always traceable to some external event. The analytic relationship becomes so close, the analyst and patient are relatively isolated from outside pressures, and there is time to spend on the fine-grain analysis of communication and feeling. The patient will learn that his moment-to-moment fluctuations in mood in the hour are determined by how he experiences the analyst. Does he seem interested, sympathetic, bored, irritated? When the patient thinks of the analyst as an interested audience, the patient feels confident, expansive; when the analyst seems bored, the patient feels empty and frustrated. Of course this is a two-way street; absent depression, mood and feeling are in constant change in response to internal and external stimuli. In my own case, I was lucky to have an analyst who was open to exploring his role in our interaction—too many will take the position that any distortion has to come from the patient's side. That can only reinforce depression.

Short of psychoanalysis, the depressive can monitor his or her own moods to help detect the feelings underneath. Trust that there is always a precipitant to a mood change, and use a Mood Journal to help analyze the connections between events and the change in mood. In this log I'm asking you to describe not only your mood changes and the external and internal events accompanying them, but also how you think a "normal" person might feel under such circumstances. You may know someone you think of as well adjusted, someone who seems to experience a full range of emotion, whom you might want to use as a hypothetical model. Imagine how that person would feel in the external situation you are in, given the thoughts, memories, and fantasies that you are having. Then try to rate the extent to which your mood change is in synch with "normal" feelings.

This is an important and powerful tool. If you use it correctly and regularly, you can begin to get around your own defensive system. *This may not feel good.* You may find yourself worrying more, feeling perhaps a bit more edgy. You are going to become more aware of things that upset you. This awareness is what depressives try to avoid. Just remember that this avoidance sacrifices your true self and makes you depressed. You may see your defenses at work in how you use the Mood Journal. You may forget to use it (repressing a conflict between your wish to get better and your fear of change). You may get mad at it for suggesting things you don't want to hear (projecting your anger at yourself onto an external object). You may think it is boring

Mood Journal

Date, time	Mood change	Externals (who, what, where, other unusual circumstances)	Internals (thoughts, fantasies, memories)	"Normal" feelings	Mood/feeling agreement (1–10)

Instructions: When you detect a shift in mood, write down the change (*e.g.,* from neutral to sad), the external circumstances (what you were doing, where, with whom), and the internal circumstances (what you were thinking about, daydreaming, or remembering). Then, based on those external and internal circumstances, describe how you think a "normal" person might feel (*e.g.,* sad, angry, happy, proud). Then rate how much your mood agrees with "normal" feelings (1 = no agreement, 10 = complete agreement).

and a waste of time (isolating your affect and intellectualizing your feelings). Try very hard to stick with it nonetheless.

Review the Mood Journal every day, ideally at the same time of day, when you have a few minutes and can give it your attention. See what patterns you begin to notice. Follow this intellectual exercise with a relaxation routine (see chapter 7). The time spent in relaxation will give your unconscious mind the opportunity to digest what your review of the Mood Journal has told the thinking part of your brain. We are talking here about changing lifelong habits of thinking and feeling; you need to get all the different parts of yourself working together on this task.

Trying to change yourself in this way is hard work. It helps if you can laugh at yourself. I'm the kind of person who buys self-help books about getting organized, then misplaces them. I've lost the same book on "accounting for nonprofit managers" so often that I finally bought three copies. There *is* a perverse gremlin within us that resists change, especially the kind of change that someone else says is good for us. My strategy has now become to appreciate the gremlin's tricks on me, then try to outwit the little beast. So if you find yourself losing this book, or if you find that life always interferes with completing the Mood Journal, just assume that your gremlin is at work. Laugh ruefully at the games he's playing with you, then see what you can do to be smarter than he is.

After a few weeks' practice with the Mood Journal, you should begin to see the connections between your mood changes, external events, and internal processes. Once you can see that mood changes are caused by what's happening to you, you can stop pretending that they come "out of the blue." What I think you'll also find is that your moods are more closely connected to "normal" feelings than you think they are. The depressed person often feels there is no reason for feeling depressed, and thus feels crazy or out of control. But if we take the trouble to investigate, to get underneath our own defenses, we usually find that there are perfectly good reasons for feeling the way we do. Understanding that is the first step toward doing something about it.

Grief

Most first episodes of depression are the result of loss of a relationship. The incidence of death of a parent in childhood is much higher among depressives than among other people. Freud thought that depression was always the result of a mourning process that couldn't be completed. And the experience of grief is very much like the experience of depression. Yet grief is inevitable, and depression is not. Although painful, normal grieving is not depression. When normal grieving is prevented, depression can be the result. When we suffer a loss, we must allow ourselves the time and opportunity to mourn.

The grieving person is sad and withdrawn, and may feel that his world has come to an end, but he knows that he will probably recover. He doesn't feel the sense of personal inadequacy that the depressed person does, nor does he feel irrationally guilty. His self-esteem is intact.

> Each person must make his way through life encompassing two important facts. If he loves, there will be the great rewards of human intimacy, in its broadest sense; and yet when he does so, he becomes vulnerable to the exquisite agony of loss. And one day—he knows not when or how—he will die.[2]

Grief is the natural process we all go through when we lose someone—or something—we love. The paradigm of grief is the loss of a loved one through death. But we also lose people in other ways; we divorce, we move away, we change jobs, we simply grow apart. And we also lose the meanings of people as they, and we, change. Our parents retire to Florida, and we suddenly realize how much we depended on them. Our spouse has a stroke, and isn't the strong partner we were used to. Our children marry and start their own families, and we wonder if they need us anymore. We can also grieve for things, possessions, opportunities. The victim of a house fire loses the family photographs, and with them a connectedness to the past. The ambitious man advances so far in his career and no farther and must mourn the illusion of success.

All of us now are familiar with the concept of the stages of grief, so familiar indeed that the concept seems patronizing, dehumanizing, "as if some Julia Child of sorrow is trying to provide us with a step-by-step recipe for the perfect grief."[3] What comfort the model can provide is the knowledge that in grief we are caught up in a process. Something foreign has taken over a great deal of ourselves, and we don't have as much control as we used to; but though the experience is bound to be painful, it is predictable, and the pain will diminish.

The initial stage of reaction to grief is one of shock, denial; this may last for some time, and indeed vestiges of denial can linger for years in dreams and reveries that bring the dead back to life. But this phase does end, to be replaced by a period of intense painful emotion; here is where depressives find disaster. The mourner feels unbearably sad; feels that the pain will never end; feels intense anger (including anger at the dead person, for leaving); vacillates from overwhelmed passivity to hyperactivity; feels frightened and wants to regress; and feels guilty as well.

But depressives fear both the experience and the expression of feelings. We try to avoid or control our grief. The loss awakens our "inner bereaved child,"[4] a primitive unconsolable distress, and we marshal all our self-destructive defenses. Fearful of becoming permanently destabilized by the force of emotions we can't control, we reinforce our self-image as powerless. We apply depressed thinking habits (see chapter 8) to the circumstances of our loss, and assume that we are personally at fault, that we will never recover, and that the loss will sap all possibility of joy from every aspect of our lives. We don't display our feelings, and so don't elicit comfort from those around us.

When grief can proceed beyond this middle stage of intense emotion, there is a gradual resolution, an acceptance of the loss. In adapting to and accepting the change in circumstances, we grow as individuals; we take into and make part of ourselves the admired and cherished attributes of the person we have lost. *Identification,* the same defense mechanism that enables children to comfort themselves and grow stronger during temporary separations from the parents, makes us become more like the person we lost. Sometimes this is a completely unconscious and seemingly meaningless activity: a wife who never paid attention to her husband's garden begins to tend it after his death and finds herself as dedicated as he was; a middle-aged man takes up fly fishing shortly after his father's death, not consciously emulating the times they spent fishing when he was a child, but still recapturing the experience. Sometimes it is a deliberate act, a way of showing respect for the dead that also teaches us to value what they valued: a son faithfully maintains his father's stamp collection; a husband starts attending the church his wife attended without him.

Psychologists use the term *introjection* to describe a less mature form of identification resulting from incomplete mourning. Introjection means taking on characteristics of the lost person without integrating them into the self. They become little alien forces that "possess" us at times—they literally don't feel like part of our selves. This explains the fear that most children of suicides have, that they are doomed to repeat the same act someday. But less concrete examples abound in the lives of the depressed. These are the voices of critical parents that speak to us whenever we start to feel good, that reinforce all our self-doubts. We aren't able to achieve a mature, objective perspective on these parents, as perhaps people who had problems and stresses of their own, who sometimes weren't as patient or loving as we needed but who did love and value us. Instead, we still see them from the perspective of the four-year-old; they are all-wise, and they know the real truth about us; and when they say we're not good enough, it's like the voice of God.

People who are truly depressed can rarely achieve acceptance of a loss. In fact, one of the two psychotherapeutic methods proved to be effective with depression, Interpersonal Psycho-therapy, or IPT, assumes that abnormal grief reactions are one of the four primary causes of depression.[5] Interpersonal psycho-therapy work with abnormal grief is deceptively simple: the therapist's goal is to facilitate a normal mourning process by getting the patient to talk about and express emotions about the loss, and to help the patient reestablish interests and activities that can help take the place of what was lost. But the IPT therapists, and others before them, have noted the difficulty of diagnosis: a patient who presents with depression may have absolutely no idea that the depression is connected with a death or loss. In fact, the patient may actively minimize the impact of the loss; that's why it's essential for the therapist to do a thorough history and exploration before treatment is begun.

Anger

Anger is a particular trouble spot for most depressives. We are often aware of a feeling of estrangement from the world, our noses pushed up against the glass watching real life behind the window, and a consequent bitterness, hurt, or resentment is always lurking in the background. At the same time we may feel it is our own fault we feel this way—after all, we could just jump into the midst of life if we chose. So there is a leitmotif of anger in our lives, which we may recognize yet feel we are not entitled to. And this anger and self-blame feeds on itself in a vicious circle, so it is often nearly impossible to be sure that we are justified in feeling the depth of anger we experience in any particular situation. We second-guess ourselves constantly and often end up doing nothing but driving others crazy, Hamlet-like.[6] Some of the defenses we use against awareness of our anger, like passive aggression, just make others angry at us, while we sit in smug superiority looking down on those who can't "control" themselves. In other circumstances, our guilt makes us self-sacrificing: we will absorb ill treatment from others as if it is our due, but eventually we will get pushed too far and explode in a tirade of anger that unloads all the steam we have built up. If we do this often, we get the reputation of a difficult person and we get avoided. If we do this rarely, we get the reputation of a crazy, unstable person who bursts out inappropriately.

It's important to remember that anger, like all other emotions, is neither good nor bad in itself; it's just an innate response we have. Anger can be used for many worthwhile purposes. It's the fuel that feeds our desire for justice, what makes us want to see wrongs put right. What is scary is that it feels as though it can run away with us. But I don't think that is nearly as true as most of us tell ourselves. The wife-beater frequently says words to this effect: "I couldn't help it. She made me see red, and then I didn't know what I was doing. I'm sorry I hurt her, but I lost control." But (usually) he didn't really lose control. He didn't beat his wife until she died; he didn't strangle her or shoot her or stab her; he just beat her until he felt like he'd won the dispute. There was some judgment there, some decision to stop before an invisible line was crossed. Anger usually doesn't take absolute control of us, but its expression can be so heady, tempting, can make us feel so good that we indulge ourselves in carrying the fight forward till our opponent is humiliated. Saying that we were so angry we lost control is an excuse. We had control, but we still did something shameful.

Many depressed parents are deeply ashamed of their anger at their own children, and a great deal of child abuse results from parental depression. Children know when parents are depressed, and it scares them, because they don't know if the parent is going to be capable of caring for them. When children are scared, they often become more demanding and difficult. Mom gets to feel even more depressed because her children won't listen to her. Mom alternates between withdrawal and rage. It's an explosive combination. The same dynamics apply in elder abuse. Caregivers in this position need real help. We've found that a combination of psychotherapy and medication for the depression with concrete, practical, in-home support and guidance in effective skills—in parenting or in caregiving for the elderly—makes the difference.

Anger can't be escaped, but we can tame it, live with it, and make it safe, even use it for productive ends. Practicing assertive communication and behavior, as described in chapter 7, can help make sure that anger is constructively expressed and doesn't hurt people important to us. And as we develop assertive skills, we find that we feel less aggrieved and isolated and thus have less to be angry about.

General William Tecumseh Sherman, remembered now as the wrathful arm of the North who burned Atlanta and took his army into the heart of the South, was a textbook case of a man with a lifelong characterological depression that developed into a full-blown major depressive episode early in the Civil War. Sympathetic superiors sent him home for a rest cure, but not before the newspapers had learned of his erratic behavior, exaggerated fears, and paranoia. He disgraced himself and the Union Army. But within a few months, events cured his depression permanently.

Sherman, like so many depressives, experienced loss early and as a young man always felt like an outsider with something to prove. Sherman's father died when he was nine, leaving his widow impoverished. The family—eleven children—was broken up, the children sent to live with relatives and friends. Sherman was taken in by Thomas Ewing, a powerful politician who treated Sherman fairly—but Sherman always felt in his debt, and resented Ewing for it. Sent to West Point as Ewing's idea, not his own, Sherman found his calling, graduating third in his class and going on to a successful early military career. But he chose as his wife Ewing's daughter Ellen, binding himself further into the Oedipal struggle to prove himself; their letters reveal Sherman's continual need to gain respect for what he felt he lacked inside.

In the 1850s, there were no wars and no advancement for military men. Sherman left the army and went to work for his cousin's banking firm. He showed an aptitude here, too, but a national economic recession caused his bank to fail. Sherman blamed himself, not events. Having persuaded his brother officers to invest in his bank, he repaid them from his meager personal funds when the bank went under. But he didn't give himself credit for doing the honorable thing; instead, his letters from this period reveal a deepening depression, continual self-loathing, and suicidal thoughts. At the outbreak of the Civil War, he was at his lowest ebb.

He rejoined the army, his reputation for skill and integrity winning him a high position, in charge of operations in Tennessee, despite his clearly expressed desire to serve in a lesser role, under someone else. After a few months of service, he was not sleeping, not eating, imagining spies and enemy armies where none existed, demanding reinforcements for no reason that anyone could understand.

He went home to his wife, who not only gave her emotional support to the husband she described as "the soul of honor & full of truest courage & withal so kind and forgiving," but enlisted her powerful family and went directly to President Lincoln, who knew Sherman and perhaps understood a fellow sufferer. She reported back to her husband, "He said he wanted you to know . . . that he had the highest and most generous feelings towards you" and that "your abilities would soon merit promotion."[7]

Brought back into active duty gradually, Sherman developed a relationship with Ulysses S. Grant that lent him some strength and led to a lifelong bond. "He stood by me when I was crazy," said Sherman later, "and I stood by him when he was drunk: and now we stand by each other always."[8] Then, at Shiloh, Sherman's life and character changed permanently. In the first action of the battle, Sherman's party suddenly came under fire; his aide-de-camp was shot from his saddle, and Sherman was wounded. He went on to be wounded again that day, and had three horses killed underneath him. Surprised by the rebels, he spent the remainder of the battle in the front lines, rallying his troops and showing great personal courage. Whether it was because he was emotionally ready for a crisis, or because he was so surprised he didn't have time to become anxious, he proved something to himself and his troops.

It is as if he never looked back from that moment. If in the past he had made his own life hell, he spent the rest of his life giving it to other people. Freud thought of depression as anger turned against the self; Sherman developed the ability to use that same anger against his enemies, much to the dismay of Georgia. He went on to apply the same fire and discipline as postwar General of the Army, earning the respect and admira-

tion of all. At his funeral, in 1891, his most distinguished enemy, Joe Johnston, served as pallbearer, contracting fatal pneumonia by going hatless in February New York weather. "If I were in his place," said Johnston, "and he were standing here in mine, he would not put on his hat."[9]

Joy and Pride

Anhedonia is the technical term for the depressive's inability to experience joy. In the depths of major depression, nothing touches us, not the most intensely pleasurable activities, not the most familiar comforts. We are emotionally frozen. In this state, we either have to get professional help or simply wait for weeks or months until the depression lifts by itself; nothing is going to make us feel better.

Less dramatic than anhedonia but a much more pervasive problem among the depressed is a condition that doesn't even have a clinical name; it's the gradual withdrawal into isolation and indifference that creeps up on us as we live with the disease. Robertson Davies called this condition *acedia*[10]; it's akin to the deadly sin of sloth. But it's not merely laziness, it's a gradual closing down of the world. As depression makes us lose interest or pleasure in ordinary activities, our range of activities constricts. We stop taking chances, we avoid stimulation, we play it safe, and we begin to cut ourselves off from anything that might shake us up—including loved ones. It's the gradual poison that sinks into marriages and makes people vulnerable to affairs. It's the hardening of the attitudes on the job that makes for petty, passive-aggressive bureaucracies. It's the withdrawal from our own children that leaves them questioning why we bother to live.

Pride is what we're supposed to feel when we've accomplished something, but, like joy, it's not something that depressives experience very often. This is partly because of our inherent perfectionism. We rarely feel that anything we've done measures up to our own standards. Remember that depressives consistently evaluate their own performance more objectively than do nondepressives, whereas nondepressed people tend to forget their failures and give themselves more credit than is actually due for their successes.[11] This makes us sadder but wiser, pessimists rather than optimists. Even so, there are times when we do accomplish something that is objectively worthwhile. Do we allow ourselves to feel good about it? Not usually, and not for long. Pride, like joy, is a feeling we don't experience.

One reason why we don't allow ourselves to experience these pleasurable feelings is our wish to remain in control at all times. Intense feelings of any kind are destabilizing; we start to worry that we will keep on inflating with good feeling till we pop like a balloon or float off into the stratosphere never to be seen again. Another is our fear of retribution; we've been conditioned to expect that something bad inevitably follows something good, so we'd better not let ourselves feel too good. Better to feel numb or neutral than to feel the crashing disappointment we fear will follow good feelings. Most important, perhaps, is that for the depressive feelings like joy or pride evoke painful memories of past disappointments. We remember the father who was never satisfied, the mother who didn't seem interested. The bereaved child within us, who has never completed grieving for those incomplete relationships, is awakened at times of celebration, and becomes the ghost at the feast. No wonder we're tempted to stay numb.

Depressives assume that everyone else is happy most of the time, and that there is something wrong with us for not feeling the same way. On the contrary, there is good reason to believe that the normal state of the human mind is one of mild anxiety.[12] Most people, when asked to think of nothing, or when put in situations in which external stimuli are limited, begin to worry.

Thoughts come unbidden into their minds that remind them of things they have to do, old sins, old guilts, current conflicts and problems that have to be resolved. Without something to focus on, the mind experiences chaos. This trait probably has had adaptive value for the species; those who are mildly worried are more likely to survive in the long run than those who are content and satisfied.

But the important implication for depressives is that happiness, instead of being a normal state of being that we don't experience because something is wrong with us, is something that must be cultivated. We need to practice feeling good. When we feel happy, we need to express those feelings to others. When we feel proud, we need to let ourselves sustain the emotion. We will find that we don't explode or float away; on the contrary, we can trust that the mind's normal anxiety will eventually reassert itself without any effort on our part. We will have to face the painful feelings, the old disappointments that get stirred up when good things happen, but every time we do so, we accomplish a little more of our grief work: we grow stronger, and the old hurts have less power over us because they diminish in proportion to new, reparative experiences.

I worry that the symptomatic relief of depression provided by medication or brief therapy only helps the patient regain a previous level of functioning that was depressed to begin with. Acedia, the absence of feeling, makes for empty lives, and it seems to be on the increase. Putting anger, guilt, and shame in their place is not enough for recovery from depression; we also must take responsibility for learning to feel good. We might prefer to play it safe, to avoid or control all emotions, but we simply can't; it doesn't work; our selves and our relationships deteriorate into brittle, bitter, vulnerable shells. While learning to feel may be temporarily upsetting, it is ultimately the only source of richness and meaning in our lives.

Learning to Express

Feeling feelings is not the same as expressing them (although expressing them helps one feel them). Not feeling is an unconscious process—we're not aware of denying or stuffing feelings. Not expressing them can be conscious. It's not healthy, kind, safe, or wise to express all our emotions. We want to feel them and then make deliberate decisions about how to express them. Choosing not to express won't make us depressed, but trying not to feel will.

Expression of feeling serves important social functions. It communicates our meaning to others much better than words alone can say. When we wail and cry in grief, we elicit sympathy. When we get angry, our voice gets louder, our nostrils flare, we fill our lungs with air to make ourselves seem bigger (much like dogs or cats, who can also make their hair stand on end), and the object of our anger may be intimidated. When we yawn, others yawn; when we laugh, others laugh. Emotional expression helps us feel connected to others, a part of society, a part of the group.

Expression also helps us feel our feelings. Ask anyone who has ever acted. When we act sad, we feel sad; when we act happy, we feel happy. For the experienced actor, these artificial mood changes don't last, but in everyday life, "going through the motions" often helps us feel the emotions expressed by the action. This is how role play and reenactment in group and family therapy works. Getting the patient to begin to say the words that have been held back so long opens the floodgates of emotion. Considering the relief achieved through this process, it's remarkable how much people hold back from emotional expression out of habit and fear, not out of rational choice.

If you have a spouse or trusted loved one, you are one step ahead in learning how to express yourself emotionally. You and

your partner can make a deal and take turns engaging in the
following exercise.

1. Sit comfortably in a quiet place where you will be
   uninterrupted for a half hour.
2. Speak freely and uncensoredly about what's on your
   mind. Don't worry about making sense, just let yourself
   ramble. It can just be the events of the day, a problem
   that's absorbing you, a memory, a fantasy. As you speak,
   pay attention to how your body feels. Are you feeling
   sad, downcast, angry, happy? Try to find ways to put
   those feelings into words. Or are you feeling con-
   strained, embarrassed, self-conscious? Try to identify
   what's making you feel that way and move beyond it.
3. Your partner will listen sympathetically with full attention. The only comments your partner may make are
   those that will draw out feelings more. Your partner
   may not intrude his or her own thoughts, ask for
   clarification, voice any criticism, or change the subject.
   Instead, he will say things like "That must have made
   you mad," or "You seem pleased, but I'm not sure I understand why." In other words, the partner's comments
   can be addressed only to the emotions in your communication.

If you don't have a partner, or even if you do but prefer more
privacy for your feelings, you can keep a journal. A journal can
be a very helpful tool for developing self-awareness, for expressing things we normally try to suppress, and for developing an
objective perspective on one's family, history, and future.[13] To be
effective, you should follow these rules for journaling:

1. Write regularly, ideally at the same time every day.
2. Do not censor your thoughts or feelings. Write sponta-
   neously, as thoughts and ideas occur to you.
3. At least once a week, read through your journal. Try to

identify emotional patterns that you may not have been
aware of as you were writing. When you thought you
were so upset about bills, is it possible you were really
thinking more about something else—a loss, a worry?

4. Your journal is yours alone. Do not show it to anyone
else. You may certainly talk about what you learn from
it, but keep your private thoughts private.

After a little practice, you may become aware that you are
feeling more than you thought you did. This is exactly the
desired effect. People with depression tend to be overly controlled in how they express emotions. As you think about how
you are with emotions, is it possible you could begin to be more
expressive now in other situations as well?

I know a woman who, when her depression is coming on, loses
the ability to see colors. Everything turns to shades of gray and
brown. Emotions are the colors of life. Without emotions, life is
just stale, tasteless, dull and gray. Gaining strength in the ability
to experience and express emotions is the first step toward
recovery from depression. The emotional self is a part of the self
that has largely been lost to the depressive; reestablishing contact with it may take time, but it's worth the effort. We have this
unfortunate idea that we should be master of our emotions, that
they are part of our animal nature that must be controlled at all
costs. Instead, we should seek to live in harmony with our animal
nature, to get that side of us and our intellectual and spiritual
selves to live together with affection and respect.

Behavior

PEOPLE WITH DEPRESSION generally are working too hard
but not getting anywhere. There is often a frantic, driven, compulsive flavor to our methods. Sometimes there is an obvious
pattern to how we defeat ourselves; at other times, the pattern,
if any, is very subtle. Regardless, we never seem to make as much
progress as our activity level warrants. We seem to be afraid to
stop, back off, take our bearings, and see if we are still headed
in the right direction. In order to recover, we must change these
habits. This may come as a shock for some people, who experience their depression as something outside themselves, who are
proud of their hard work and stamina and don't want to question
habits that seem part of themselves. I don't ask you to give up
hard work, I just ask you to make sure that it gets you where
you want to go. In this chapter you will be asked to consider
your goals and priorities in life, and see how much of your actual
day-to-day activity contributes to achieving those goals. You will
be learning to evaluate how much procrastination and other
forms of self-destructive behavior interfere with productive activity—and how to relax and have a little fun.

Setting Priorities

A very helpful way of thinking about depression and stress is that they result from our failure to live up to our own standards and goals. Psychotherapists hear over and over again from depressed patients that they are never satisfied with themselves. Often the patient is excessively perfectionistic; sometimes the patient's goals are so far out of reach that he feels too demoralized to even take the first step.

There is a wonderful, sad vignette by Aaron Beck, the originator of cognitive therapy for depression. He had a patient who, despite his deep depression, managed to wallpaper a kitchen. Here's how the dialogue went:

THERAPIST: Why didn't you rate wallpapering the kitchen as a mastery experience?

PATIENT: Because the flowers didn't line up.

THERAPIST: You did in fact complete the job?

PATIENT: Yes.

THERAPIST: Your kitchen?

PATIENT: No, I helped a neighbor do his kitchen.

THERAPIST: Did he do most of the work?

PATIENT: No, I really did almost all of it. He hadn't wall-papered before.

THERAPIST: Did anything else go wrong? Did you spill the paste all over? Ruin a lot of wallpaper? Leave a big mess?

PATIENT: No, no, the only problem was that the flowers didn't line up.

THERAPIST: Just how far off was the alignment of the flowers?

PATIENT: (holding his fingers about an eighth of an inch apart) About that much.

THERAPIST: On each strip of paper?

PATIENT: No . . . on two or three pieces.

THERAPIST: Out of how many?

PATIENT: About twenty or twenty-five.

THERAPIST: Did anyone else notice it?

PATIENT: No. In fact my neighbor thought it was great.

THERAPIST: Could you see the defect when you stood back and looked at the whole wall?

PATIENT: Well, not really.[1]

This is an extreme example of one way to make yourself miserable. The other extreme is to set your goals so low that you can be sure of achieving them, which seems to be what the current self-esteem movement is all about. Our schools nowadays are full of silly-sounding educational, cultural, and recreational programs that reward kids with everything from gold stars on up for what are really minor or insignificant achievements. Calvin, of "Calvin and Hobbes" fame, suggested to his teacher that she stop giving him all those failing grades because failure was bad for his self-esteem. Today's parents are cautioned not to be critical of their children under any circumstances; the message is that unconditional love and acceptance build self-esteem. But the flaw in this logic is obvious. True self-esteem requires an accurate appraisal of one's own abilities in comparison to those of others. With a healthy sense of self, you can accept your weaknesses without feeling like an all-around loser. There are real differences in abilities, which are rewarded differentially by life. Unconditional acceptance seeks to deny those differences and build a phony self-esteem, vulnerable to puncture by life's experience.

Having goals that are either unrealistically high or too easy to attain can contribute to depression. But many of us don't even know what our goals are. Some people think they know exactly what principles are important to them, what their objectives are in life. Others are mystified by this subject, believing that they never think about their values and goals. Both can be very wrong. We do live our lives by certain values and principles, and we do have a sense of what we would like to accomplish for ourselves, but these are largely unconscious. To make these conscious, we have to examine ourselves deliberately. Then we can think about whether our goals are too high or too low.

Most of us have done values clarification exercises. Here's one I like:[2] Imagine I drive up to your house in a big trailer truck and unload a steel I-beam 120 feet long, about a foot wide, in your street. All the neighbors come out to look. I put you at one end, me at the other, and I take out a $100 bill. I ask you to walk across the I-beam without stepping off, in under two minutes; if you do, I'll give you the $100.

Now let's load the I-beam back on the truck and drive to lower Manhattan. I'll hoist the beam up to the top of the World Trade Center. The towers are about 118 feet apart. We anchor one end of the beam on each tower. If you've been up there, you know it's very windy, and it's usually misty. The beam is damp and jiggles a little in the wind. Now will you walk across for $100? How about $10,000? How about a million?

Now let's suppose I'm a different sort of character. I'm on one tower, you're on the other, and I have your two-year-old child. If you're not here in two minutes, I'll drop her. Will you try it? Most people will cross the beam for $100 if their life isn't in danger, but won't do it for a million when it's really dangerous; on the other hand, most are willing to risk it for the sake of their child.

This is an exercise in prioritizing values. If you're making a deliberate effort to get your life in harmony, this is the place to start. What will you cross the I-beam for? If the most important thing in life to you is your family, why don't you spend more time with them? The reasons probably have to do with your difficulty experiencing emotions. One of the most common ways we have of avoiding emotions is that we let ourselves become over-whelmed by busy-ness. "*Things* are in the saddle, and ride mankind," said Emerson. If we want to do what's truly important to us, we have to make a conscious and deliberate effort to prioritize.

The steps in organizing yourself so that you are spending more time doing what is really important to you are to:

1. Identify
2. Synchronize
3. Partialize
4. Review

1. *Identify your goals.* Goals are statements of how we want things to be. I want to have a happy marriage, I want to be financially secure, I want to be healthy, I want to enjoy my work. These are all nice ideas, but they are too broad to have any real impact on how I conduct my life. To be helpful, goals should be specific, concrete, and measurable. What's in the way of my enjoying my work? Mostly, right now, it's the slightly shaky financial condition at our clinic and the impact managed care is having on us. What can I do about this? Well, one practical, achievable goal is to have a balanced budget for this year; another is to raise $20,000 more in contributions next year. If these are the things that I know are really necessary in order for me to enjoy my work this year, this is where I have to put my energy. I'd much rather spend my time seeing patients, but if I do that, our financial situation won't improve and I'll feel guilty, anxious, and depressed.

2. *Synchronize.* Are we in synch with ourselves? Do some of our goals conflict with others? If my most important goal is to run a lean, efficient charitable organization, but I also want to have a big house and vacation in Europe every year, I'm setting myself up for depression. In the long run, we doom ourselves if our goals are in conflict. We are grown-ups and we have to face the fact that we can't have it all, even when it means giving up on some things that are important. And it's necessary to really give up. If you decide that a big house is not a primary goal for

you, make a public commitment to giving up that dream. Talk it over with your spouse and friends. Throw out all the magazines you've been saving with beautiful pictures of mansions. Have a ritual: light a fire in the backyard and burn up something symbolic of the goals you're giving up.

3. *Partialize.* Then go in and start making action plans about the goals you really do want to accomplish. What are your professional goals for this year? Where would you like to be in five years? At retirement? Do your goals for this year take you closer to your long-range goals? If they don't, they should. Maybe you have to focus a lot for the present on simple survival strategies, how to get through the day, week, year. But you will feel better if you can add to your daily activities something that will help you get to your long-term goals. When we feel that our everyday activities are in agreement with our basic values and take us a step further toward who and where we want to be, we can justly feel a little satisfaction. We add to our self-esteem; we have a little more evidence that we can have an impact on our fate; we gain a little more confidence that we can figure out what needs to be done; we may be adding something to our serotonin level; we may be quieting the critical voices of our parents that made us feel like incompetent fools; however it works, it helps us feel better about ourselves.

Make your action plans realistic and concrete. Make them require some effort, but don't make them impossible. Be somewhat flexible, and give yourself leeway for your own state of mind, which may vary from depressed to euphoric. This is important work that is going to shake up your depression. Just as using the Mood Journal challenges your defense mechanisms, thinking about and working toward what's truly meaningful in your life can be upsetting and difficult. Don't expect it to go smoothly. Accept that your emotions will be in some turmoil. At times, you'll feel terrific; at other times, you'll wonder why you started. Just don't give up.

4. Review. Finally, review your goals, and your progress toward them, regularly. Make sure that you have given yourself permission to change your goals. Don't get stuck in feeling bad because circumstances and your priorities have changed. For goals that remain important, look at your action plans. Are there things you should be doing differently? Build some time into your routine when you can review your progress—at New Year's, on your annual vacation, monthly when you pay the bills, on a regular date with your spouse. Give yourself credit for doing what you've done, make new plans for doing what could be done better, and *let the rest go.*[3]

Jerome has been a patient of mine off and on for eight years. He is a real sad sack, the kind who drives therapists to distraction with his self-defeating behavior. Thirty years old, he lives with his mother and stepfather in a very conflictual family. He is only marginally employed, despite his above-average intelligence. For the past three years, he and his parents have been in the process of fighting about moving him into a separate apartment in the basement. It's a battle for control: when Jerome wants to move, his mother finds ways to sabotage his efforts; when his mother wants him to move, Jerome stalls and procrastinates. Jerome's room is full of boxes of things he's accumulated over the years—magazine articles he will read someday, projects he's taken up then put aside, things he doesn't know what to do with but thinks will come in handy. Whenever the idea of moving comes up, the boxes get in the way.

Sometimes therapists can't see the forest for the trees. Jerome never complained about feeling depressed. He has a great sense of humor (often at his own expense), his mood is generally upbeat, he has no physical symptoms of depression like sleeplessness, and he is usually full of energy. Jerome came back to our clinic recently to see if he could get some help with other aspects of his behavior. As he and I discussed how to go about this, we considered the idea of Prozac, which has been success-fully used for these specific problems. With Prozac in his system, Jerome's self-defeating behavior patterns began to change for the first time, and I recognized that all his personality difficulties fit the picture of an obsessive-compulsive personality masking a depression.

Somehow two months of Prozac helped Jerome get to the point where he actually moved into the basement. Not only that, but for the first time he began to make realistic career plans for himself. Instead of waiting for the perfect job that was going to make him perfectly happy, Jerome decided to take the first decent job he could find, recognizing that it would make him a little happier than he is now. He discussed going to the commu-nity college evenings to get some skills that would make him more marketable. "Of course I'll only go if I can be sure I've got the time and energy to put into it," he said. "I've got to get A's." Then he caught himself. He identified this as depressive, self-defeating thinking; the purpose of going to school is to learn, not to get A's. Deciding that you won't go until you can be sure you have plenty of time is just setting up artificial barriers that you don't need.

When you're depressed, it's hard to take action. *But take some action, and give yourself a lot of credit for doing it.* Don't be like Beck's patient.

Working Productively

Most people who are depressed have a hard time being produc-tive. Work—and here I mean everything from paid employment to child-rearing and housekeeping to the kinds of "work" we assign ourselves, like reading a good book or planting a garden—is a chore to the depressed. It drains us, leaves us feeling as bad as before, physically worn out and emotionally depleted. As with so much of depression, there is a real chicken-or-egg question—is work so difficult because we're depressed, or are we depressed in part because we can't accomplish anything? And as with so many chicken-or-egg situations, we face a false dichotomy: the truth is, poor work habits and depression reinforce each other.

Most depressed people are great procrastinators. Procrastination means putting off for a later time what "should" be done now. The "should" may come from without, as with the teenager who dawdles over homework, or from within, as with me planting my garden. When it comes from without, it's easy to see the rebelliousness that procrastination expresses. When it comes from within, it's hard to see immediately what purpose procrastination serves—but it may serve many.[4]

Most procrastinators don't really know how work works. They assume that all really productive people are always in a positive, energetic frame of mind that lets them jump right in to piles of paper and quickly do what needs to be done, only emerging when the task is accomplished. On the contrary, motivation follows action instead of the other way around. When we make ourselves face the task ahead of us, it usually isn't as bad as we think, and we begin to feel good about the progress we start making. *Work comes first, and then comes the positive frame of mind.* Closely allied to this misunderstanding about motivation is the idea that things should be easy. Depressed people assume that people who are good at work skills always feel confident and easily attain their goals; because they themselves don't feel this way, they assume that they will never be successful. But again, most people who are really successful assume that there are going to be hard times, frustrations, and setbacks along the way. Knowing this in advance, they don't get thrown for a loop and assume that they're at fault whenever there's a setback.

Procrastination can also help protect the depressed person's precarious self-esteem. We can always tell ourselves we would have done it better if. . . . The paradigm is the college term paper rushed together in a furious all-nighter. The student protects himself from the risk of exposing his best work by never having the time to do it right. The fantasied sense of the self as special, uniquely gifted, is preserved. This is allied to the depressed person's tendency toward perfectionism, as described elsewhere. Trying so hard to make every single little piece of a project perfect, we doom ourselves to disappointment and frustration—but at the same time, we always have the safety of knowing that we could have done it better if only we'd had more time.

David Burns, in *The Feeling Good Handbook*,[5] has a five-step process for defeating procrastination:

1. Cost-Benefit Analysis. Choose a task you are procrastinating on. Make a list of the advantages of continuing to procrastinate. Now make a list of the advantages of getting started. Be very honest. You may be procrastinating on some tasks because it is not in your best interests to complete them, but you haven't recognized that yet. After listing the advantages and disadvantages, weigh them against each other on a 100-point scale. If the advantages outweigh the disadvantages, now make a similar list of advantages and disadvantages of getting started *today*, and again weigh them against each other on a 100-point scale. If the advantages of starting today outweigh the disadvantages, go on to step 2.

2. Make a Plan. Write down the time today when you will start. Now make a list of any problems or obstacles you can think of that might interfere with getting started. Next, for each of those problems and obstacles, identify what you will do to overcome them. Now you have no excuses.

3. Make the Job Easy. Set realistic goals. Don't expect a perfect product. Don't expect to work for five hours straight. Decide in advance about what you can reasonably

expect to accomplish in the reasonable amount of time you want to allocate to this project. Decide which steps must come first. If you want to paint the house, maybe getting to the store to buy the paint is enough progress for the first day.

4. Think Positively. Identify any negative thoughts and feelings that are associated with the task. For instance, "Painting is boring" or "The house will look okay for another year" or "I should wait till I'm more in the mood." Now for each of those negative thoughts, think of alternative positive and realistic thoughts that will help you feel more productive and motivated. For instance "I can listen to the radio while I paint" or "I'll be proud of the house when it's done" or "I'll feel good about getting started."

5. Give Yourself Credit. Review your progress when you've accomplished the first day's goals. Take time to let yourself feel good about what you've done, which includes taking a step toward dealing with procrastination. Make a reward— an ice-cream cone, time with a book, a relaxing bath—contingent on accomplishing the first day's goals.

There is a simple, useful process psychologists call *chaining,* or making one event depend on another event's being accomplished first. You can make chains that help you get a lot of work done. I want to go play Doom on my computer, but I'm going to let that be my reward for first going through the outdated magazines. As I go through the pile, I find there's one I really must renew my subscription to. Now I have to do that as well before I play Doom. Renewing that subscription reminds me that I have a stack of unpaid bills nagging at me. Maybe I can't get the bills all paid, but I can take twenty minutes to get them organized and make a commitment to myself to pay them tomorrow. Now I can go play my computer game feeling a little less overwhelmed by events and a little more deserving of some time to goof off.

Self-Destructive Behavior

Everyone gives lip service to the idea that depressed people are self-destructive. After all, suicide is the extreme end of depression. Of milder forms, we say, "He keeps shooting himself in the foot," or "She's her own worst enemy." We romanticize the self-destructive tendencies of artists like Dylan Thomas or Kurt Cobain.

What exactly does this mean, to be self-destructive? Freud originally theorized that depression was aggression, the destructive wish, turned against the self, an explanation which still has some poetic or intuitive appeal though it doesn't tell us much about recovery. There are two more concrete meanings. One is to engage in behavior that is clearly dangerous or self-destructive, without appreciating the danger. The other is to engage in behavior that backfires on us. The behavior is not, in and of itself, dangerous or harmful, but it has unintended negative effects. Although this can happen to anyone, for the depressive it often becomes such a pattern that we assume there is an unconscious process at work.

This discussion leads us to two important defense mechanisms, acting out and passive aggression. Remember that defenses are ways of keeping unacceptable feelings, impulses, and wishes out of consciousness. They are as much a part of being human as having fingernails, and they help make life much more pleasurable for all of us. But some defenses are more adaptive than others.

Acting out means the direct expression of a wish or impulse without the feelings or thoughts that accompany it. This is the hallmark defense of adolescence. Juvenile crime is often said to be "acting out"—the child expresses his rage at abusive parents and unreliable authority figures by such things as vandalism, drug abuse, or interpersonal violence. In my relatively tame adolescence one of the favorite activities of my group of boys was "lawning"—driving the parents' car late at night over neighbors' lawns, tearing up grass, shrubs, and small trees. Aside from the obvious attack against the symbols of suburban conformity, what makes me realize it was acting out is that we all thought it was just hilarious and thrilling. We experienced none of the hostility that now, in retrospect, it seems so clear we were expressing.

Therapists often reason that acting out is different from anti-social aggression because the acter-outer wants to get caught. Think of Jason's dropping the marijuana in front of his mother, twice. There is certainly a component of this behavior that is asking for limits, asking for someone to express love by demanding that the behavior cease. People like Kurt Cobain or Dylan Thomas may ultimately die because their fame surrounds them with friends and hangers-on who are unwilling to say no to them. Their aura of genius or tortured artist may get their friends caught up in denial, so that no one sees the danger ahead.

Passive aggression is a difficult concept to explain, though we all experience it. It involves making others feel the destructive energy that we ourselves can't express. In psychotherapy, the patient who threatens suicide when her therapist is about to go on vacation is seen as passive-aggressive—she does not feel her anger at the abandoning therapist, but he gets to be angry with her. In everyday life, anyone in a position of little authority may resort to passive-aggressive behavior as a means of retaining some control—adolescents who refuse to do chores despite repeated warnings, until the parent finally yells, get to feel a certain satisfaction out of being picked on. In the office, the person who insists on doing everything exactly according to the rules doesn't acknowledge his own desire to control everyone else, though they certainly feel it. Passive aggression is also the archetypal guilt inducer—George Vaillant refers to the dramatically self-sacrificing person who "gives away the biggest piece of cake in such a way that the recipient ends up feeling punished."[6]

Viewed in this light, procrastination is a form of passive aggression that the depressive uses very cleverly to make himself feel miserable. The resented authority is not the abandoning therapist or the bossy parent, but the part of the self that says to the depressive, "You really should (get a better job, wash the dishes, paint the living room . . .)." Instead of acknowledging the conflict between this part of the self that sets standards and moralizes and the part that feels entitled to have the biggest piece of cake, the depressive will procrastinate. Instead of washing the dishes, he will go to the store to buy a new sponge and, while there, be tempted by the display of canning supplies and decide now is the time to put up pickles. The next day he'll have more dirty dishes and no pickles, because in the middle of the project he'll get frustrated and sit down and watch *Oprah*. Daytime television was made to give procrastinators something to do. But his depression, his low opinion of himself, his idea that he can't meet his goals, has just been reinforced.

Finding more direct and healthy ways of expressing anger, of developing autonomy, of acknowledging a need for intimacy, are the obvious strategies to disrupt self-destructive behavior patterns. In clinical practice, many depressed patients are completely unaware of their self-destructive behavior, and many patients who come in because their behavior has gotten them into trouble are completely unaware of their depression. Getting these links established is not easy therapeutic work.

Grady may be the worst hard-luck story I have ever run across. A spruce little man in his late forties, Grady was a down-and-out alcoholic for twenty years, like most of the rest of his family. Grady has been sober for ten years now, but that hasn't changed his luck any. Because of his chronic pain, Grady is unable to work. He sits around all day and worries. He appears extremely tense and depressed, his legs and hands twitch and his eyes search the room, his voice is a low monotone.

When Grady was eighteen, there was a fire at his home while his family was in bed. Everyone got out but his twelve-year-old sister, who was burned to death. The investigators traced the source of the fire to Grady's room. Grady had been drinking that night. Most likely, he was smoking in bed, but he can't remember that night at all. Certainly everyone, including himself, blames him for his sister's death.

Grady hit the bottle and stayed submerged for a long time. He did manage to work regularly, and he married and had a child. After several near-death experiences from alcoholic coma, Grady checked himself into a rehab center and sobered up. A few months later, in an accident at his job, Grady fell and broke his back. His employer was able to deny Grady's claim for workers' compensation because of his drinking history, implying that Grady's drinking had caused the accident. No one did a blood test, so Grady wasn't able to prove that he was sober. Since then Grady has lived on public assistance.

Now Grady, still sober, comes to our clinic for help with his depression, which he clearly identifies in the first interview as his primary problem. But in subsequent interviews, the focus shifts. Grady's mother has liver cancer and is dying. Another brother is in another hospital detoxing. Grady's mother wants him to visit his brother and talk him into remaining sober. If Grady won't do this simple little thing for her, she threatens to take herself out of the hospital and stop her chemotherapy. Meanwhile Grady's seventeen-year-old son is in a psychiatric hospital in another state after a drug-induced suicide attempt. He had been living with Grady's ex-wife, but the ex has now washed her hands of the son. The hospital is calling Grady asking him to assume financial responsibility for the boy's care—a man on public assistance, with no assets.

I know enough about Grady's family and about psychiatric hospitals to believe what Grady is telling me, but it's beyond my comprehension to understand how so much bad luck could happen to one person. I truly believe that Grady is a victim, having been blamed all his life for things that were only partially his responsibility. But what good is my sympathy and support to him? I express my convictions to him, and he seems pleased that I'm sympathetic, but it doesn't help with his depression. An old-fashioned AA believer, he is against all medication. What can therapy do for him?

The truth is that Grady is more than a little self-destructive. Look what happens in the therapy. He clearly and specifically asks for help with his depression, but instead of focusing on himself and his feelings, he focuses on others. I don't think that even he believes that if we can clear up these messes in his life, his depression will go away, but he's acting as if he believes that. He puts others first in his own therapy, just as he's done all his life. He puts the therapist in the position of trying to help people who are not in the room—an impossible task. I get angry and frustrated with Grady, but I have trouble acknowledging that. He's been screwed by so many people, I don't want to screw him too.

Grady's boundaries are a mess. He's trying to control things he can't control. All he can do for the people who make so many demands on him is give them his love and attention, but he himself places no value on these gifts. Accustomed from early on to blame himself for everything, he accepts the family role of scapegoat. Nothing he does is ever good enough.

Harry Stack Sullivan said that good therapists must be masters of the obvious. What's obviously missing from Grady is his anger. If he's been screwed all his life, and is still being screwed, isn't he the slightest bit angry about it? How come I'm the one feeling anger? If Grady's therapy is to get anywhere, he's got to learn how to identify and express angry feelings.

Grady is not a therapeutic success story. He dropped out of treatment with me. He still comes to our clinic periodically when he's feeling overstressed, and it helps him to have someone listen with respectful attention, but he's not able to make much progress on the mountain of rage he carries silently around on his back. Blaming himself has become a way of life.

Assertive Behavior

There are now dozens of books, tapes, and classes that you can take to help you learn how to be more assertive. The reason this is such a popular movement right now is that it really has something to teach. Most of us, especially the depressed, suffer in silence when people are rude, threatening, or manipulative, and we end the encounter feeling diminished in self-esteem. Or occasionally we will lose our temper and descend to the level of the other person, which doesn't resolve the dispute and also leaves us feeling bad about ourselves. Acting assertively, on the other hand, strengthens self-esteem. If we treat ourselves as if we are worthy of respect, others are more likely to treat us the same way, and we also get the message: "I'm as good as anyone else."

Being assertive means knowing what your rights are and giving yourself the same respect you'd give the other person. It does not mean being pushy, demanding, controlling, or selfish. In fact, part of assertiveness training is learning to listen carefully, to make sure that you understand clearly the other person's position and that you carefully consider his or her rights as well as your own. Being assertive does mean identifying what you want and asking for it in clear language that maintains respect for others.

There are many good resources for learning assertiveness, some of which are listed in the Notes section.[7] Bourne has a simple outline for developing assertive responses.

1. Objectively evaluate your rights. What's wrong with this situation? Do you have a right to expect different treatment than what you're getting? We all have basic rights we tend to forget about, including the rights to change our minds, to say "I don't know," to be treated with dignity and respect, and to feel our feelings.
2. Choose a time when you want to deal with the situation. For a conflict with a loved one, a coworker, or someone we are in regular contact with, establish a mutually convenient time when you can discuss the problem. But some situations need to be dealt with on the spot, before greater damage is done.
3. State the problem in terms of how it affects you. Make it clear exactly how you are hurt or inconvenienced by the other person's behavior. This may be all you need to do. Sometimes people are unaware of their impact on you. Use calm, objective language that avoids criticism.
4. State your feelings, using congruent verbal and nonverbal language (this takes practice). This is also where "I statements" come in. "When your stereo is loud, I can't get my work done (step 3). I get worried that I can't meet my deadline" (step 4). The other person is not responsible for the way you feel but has a right to know about it. If you don't state your feelings, you're assuming that the other person can read your mind.
5. Tell the other person what you want. Use simple, direct language. Keep it specific: "I want you to help with the dishes," not "I want you to show more consideration for me." Address the other person's behavior, not his personality or character, to avoid putting him on the defensive.
6. Describe the consequences. Clearly spell out what will happen if the other person does or doesn't cooperate. This should not be a threat, but a natural consequence.

"If I can get my work done, we can go out later." When you're dealing with someone you know to be uncooperative, you may point out the natural consequences of his refusal: "If you don't let me get my work done, we won't have enough money to buy the things you want."

People with depression are rarely good at being assertive, and assertive people are rarely depressed. I don't think that assertiveness training alone can cure depression, but learning these skills can certainly have powerful consequences for self-esteem. It can teach us how to express our feelings, remind us of our interpersonal rights, help get our needs met, and resolve confusion and conflict in relationships with others. Most of all, we can't expect to have self-respect if we don't treat ourselves with respect. It's more of the depressive's magical thinking, wishing that self-respect could be given to us like an inheritance. On the contrary, self-respect, like every depression-fighting skill, has to be learned and earned.

Learning to Relax

Joan Rivers being a notable exception, most of us depressed people are not exactly the life of the party. This is not entirely our fault. We would like to be looser, more relaxed, but we literally don't know how. Generally we are either engaged in frenetic activity to keep our demons at bay, or sunk into depressed lethargy, exhausted by our own activities. We have to take ourselves by the hand and teach ourselves to relax.

Herbert Benson published *The Relaxation Response*[8] in 1975 as a study of the effects of Transcendental Meditation on the body. His little book has become one of the most important resources available for people dealing with stress, anxiety, and depression. Benson removed the mysticism from TM and left the discipline—the exercises, breathing, posture—intact. He found that regular meditation, which he called deep relaxation, had a number of effects on the body. In the short run, there was a decrease in heart rate, respiration, blood pressure, and muscle tension and an increase in alpha wave activity in the brain. Over the long run, it was found that regular deep relaxation resulted in a reduction of anxiety and an increase in feeling of well-being, as well as in important cardiovascular improvements.

Benson's approach is easily self-taught. You must find a quiet environment with a comfortable place to sit where you won't be disturbed for a half hour. Spend the first few minutes consciously focusing on points of muscle tension in your body, willing the tension to flow out of those points to be replaced by a feeling of warmth and relaxation. Sit upright, either on a pad in a yoga position or in a comfortable chair with feet on the floor and back supported. Concentrate on your breathing—count your breaths and make them regular—or on a word or phrase that has meaning for you. Adopt a passive attitude—visualize a tranquil pool. When thoughts intrude into your consciousness, visualize them as bubbles in the pool, rising to the surface only to dissipate in gentle ripples. Lose self-consciousness—do not evaluate how you are doing, just concentrate on your rhythmic breathing. Set a timer so that you don't have to worry about the length of your meditation session.

There are a number of other ways of achieving relaxation, including progressive muscle relaxation and guided imagery meditation, which are equally effective.[9] Of course, there are other, more traditional, ways of relaxing. Prayer, in the sense of communing with God, is one. Walking, when it can be performed as a focus of attention in itself, can permit the passive attitude of meditation at the same time as the body is exercised. Sports that demand concentration—swimming, golf, tennis—can have the same result (of course you don't want to be caught up in a competitive spirit, but to pay attention to the movement of your body and its interaction with the forces of nature).

Journal writing, mentioned above, is a form of meditation. Intimate conversation, and indeed the act of sex, can take us out of ourselves and help us relax, as can reading a good book, taking a warm bath, weeding the garden. The important element to add to all these more traditional pursuits is Benson's "passive attitude"—don't worry about the results, trust that the process itself is good for you, concentrate on the experience.

I want to say a special word about music. I never could play an instrument well, but I learned early what music could do to one's soul. In the darkest hours of my adolescence, I would stick my head inside our old-fashioned cabinet record player and get swept away by Borodin's Polovtsian Dances or Strauss waltzes, later by the Beatles and the Rolling Stones, Bob Dylan and Joan Baez. Music short-circuits consciousness and goes directly to the part of our brain that has to do with emotions and mood. It can reliably lift us out of depression—but to do so, it can't be played as background music. You have to stop what you're doing, pay attention to the music, and play it loud. Even sad music can stop a depressed mood. After all, depression isn't sadness, it's the absence of feeling, and sometimes a good cry is healing.

Whatever method of relaxation you choose, practice it regularly. My recommendation is that you perform your relaxation routine directly after reviewing your Mood Journal. The Mood Journal may be mildly upsetting for you; it's meant to help you get around your defenses and see the connections between events in your life and your emotional state, connections that depressives generally try not to see. You may be faced with some unpleasant implications. But rather than think and worry a lot about these implications, I'd prefer that you let your unconscious mind work on them by doing something that disengages you from thought and worry. Once you are good at identifying how events affect your emotions, you can give up the Mood Journal, but don't give up a relaxation routine. Make it a part of your life.

People with depression are good at being responsible. We are good soldiers, honest and industrious. We have high standards and are good at working autonomously. Accompanying these traits are the bad habits of disorganization, procrastination, and perfectionism. Worse still are the self-defeating, self-destructive patterns of behavior that we use to defend against unacceptable emotions. Add to that the difficulty we have relaxing and enjoying ourselves and you get a pretty grim picture.

Recreation means re-creation of the self. What all recreation does is make us stop our driven, frantic behavior to look around and listen. Losing self-consciousness temporarily in meditation or some other form of relaxation, we can come back to our problems with a different perspective. We may have spent all day butting our heads against a wall. When we step back, we may see that there is a door in the wall we didn't notice in our frenzy of activity. We need to give ourselves time to heal from the emotional bruises of the day. As we do, we may be momentarily frightened by feelings, thoughts, and images that we ordinarily try to keep out of consciousness. This is where we have to start learning that our own feelings are nothing to fear.

Thinking

DEPRESSION AFFECTS our ability to remember, think, and work. For instance, people who are depressed have much greater difficulty remembering random information than people who are not depressed. When given new material, they have more difficulty connecting it with what they know already—the information does not get organized in ways that help it get learned or recalled. The cognitive impairment that depression inflicts is most evident on tasks that require complex processing or independent thinking.[1] It's as if it's not bad enough that depression causes us emotional pain, makes our behavior self-defeating, and drives others away from us. On top of all that, if we want to regain self-esteem by accepting a challenge, we're handicapped at the outset because we have more trouble re-membering and absorbing information.

Distorted Perception and Bad Logic

Aaron Beck and his colleagues are the leading researchers on how depression affects thought processes and how the way we think affects our depression. They have identified a "cognitive triad," three patterns of distorted thinking, common to many people with depression. This is not theory, this is fact; depressed people reliably and demonstrably differ from others in the following ways:

1. *The Self.* The depressed person is his own worst critic. He sees himself as defective, inadequate, or deprived. He thinks that he deserves unhappiness because of his flaws, or else that because of his deficits he is unable to achieve happiness. He tends to underestimate and criticize himself, and he lacks hope because he believes he is missing the essential character traits that lead to fulfillment.[2]

2. *Present Reality.* The depressed person interprets interactions with the everyday world—people, events, and inanimate objects—differently from other people. He sees the demands the world makes on him as impossible to attain. He interprets his interactions with the world as representing defeat or deprivation, whereas an outside observer would see some successes in the failures, some gifts among the rejections.

3. *Future Expectations.* The depressed person has a negative expectation for the future. He doesn't anticipate relief from his present suffering, and when he considers trying something new, he expects to fail.

Interacting with the distorted perception of the depressive are a number of ways we consistently make errors in logic and judgment. Beck has observed and categorized a long list.[3] The most important are:

1. *Overgeneralizing,* or the tendency to assume that if it's true once, it's likely to be true all the time. Just because you perform poorly on one test doesn't mean you will continue to do badly, but the depressive is likely to think so.

2. *Selective abstraction* consists of focusing on a detail taken out of context, ignoring other evidence, and drawing conclusions on the basis of the detail. When I give

a speech, I am likely to remember the awkward pauses, the questions I don't feel I answered adequately, rather than the 90 percent of the speech that goes over well. Unless I watch myself, I am likely to judge the whole experience on the basis of a few negative details.

3. *Excessive responsibility.* People who are depressed tend to assume that they are responsible for bad things that happen, while good things are caused by others, by luck, or other factors which can't be controlled. When the car skids on an icy road, the depressive thinks, "I shouldn't have been driving today," rather than, "The road is icy."

4. *Self-reference.* Depression leads to a negative self-consciousness, a tendency to magnify one's own part in things, even to believe that you are the center of attention. The depressed child in the school play thinks that all eyes are on her, that any mistake she makes will be the talk of the town.

5. *Catastrophizing.* Depressed people are well known for expecting the worst. My depressed patient, who is doing quite well in his business, gets a call every weekend from his depressed father: "Everything okay at work?" My patient knows that his father expects things *not* to be okay, that in fact he will be relieved somehow when he's finally told they are not.

6. *Dichotomous thinking* refers to the tendency to see everything as good or bad, black or white. The depressive puts himself in the bad category, people he admires in the good. He doesn't see faults or weaknesses in those he admires, nor does he see strengths in himself. He extends this kind of thinking to include those who seem to like him, deciding that they must be in the bad category, too—uninformed or ignorant if they are stupid enough to like him. Thus Groucho: "I

wouldn't belong to a club that would have me as a member."

It should be evident that these kinds of cognitive errors are self-fulfilling prophecies. If you expect to do badly on tests, your chances of doing well are diminished. The negative expectation may mean that you won't prepare, that you'll be more anxious, and that you'll have difficulty concentrating and remembering. If I selectively remember the negative aspects of my speeches, I'm likely to avoid making speeches, feel under stress when I do make them, and communicate that stress to my audience. The little girl in the school play is more likely to present herself badly because her excessive self-consciousness interferes with her skills. Expecting the worst all the time can lead to never really trying. Dichotomous thinking means never being able to evaluate oneself as highly as others.

Beck has also identified a number of *depressogenic assumptions*—false beliefs that set us up for depression:

1. In order to be happy, I have to be successful in whatever I undertake.
2. To be happy, I must be accepted by all people at all times.
3. If I make a mistake, it means I am inept.
4. I can't live without you.
5. If somebody disagrees with me, it means he doesn't like me.
6. My value as a person depends on what others think of me.

There are many others. They may seem so glaringly illogical that no one could admit feeling this way. But we don't arrive at these beliefs through logic and experience, rather through making assumptions that fit with our own guilt and self-blame. These beliefs are pervasive and insidious in their effects on our lives. We can't possibly be accepted by everyone at all times; some people will want exactly opposite things from us, and we must choose one or the other or run the risk of alienating both. If we feel that we can't live without another person, we're almost guaranteed to scare him or her away from us. If we feel that everyone who disagrees with us doesn't like us, we are likely to distort our own principles and values for the sake of pleasing others, and then we won't think much of ourselves.

We seem to be well able to defend against recognizing these hard truths about ourselves, but everyone makes characteristic errors in logic and builds assumptions that are not accurate perceptions of reality. Beck and his colleagues have found that patients have to discover their erroneous thought processes on their own, through a process of inference and deduction. Patients are first trained to identify their automatic thoughts when negative events occur. Automatic thoughts that a wife might have when her husband is in a bad mood might be, for instance: "It must be my fault," "I'd better do something to make him happy," "He must not love me if he acts this way." When enough automatic thoughts have been observed, common themes begin to emerge—themes like repeated self-blame, a tendency to sacrifice to please others, a tendency to assume rejection instead of other possible explanations for others' behavior. It is then only a small step in abstraction to identify the assumptions behind these thoughts: "I can't do anything right," "If I don't put others first, they won't love me," "If someone I love is ever in a bad mood, they don't really love me."[4]

Cognitive therapy consists of an organized effort guided by the therapist—but requiring the active collaboration of the patient—to change these faulty habits in thinking. Beck generally ducks the chicken-or-egg question—does faulty thinking lead to an experience of the world and the self that we call depression, or is depression something else, one manifestation of which is this kind of faulty thinking? Empirically, the question doesn't need to be answered. If changing thinking patterns leads to relief from depressive symptoms—and it often does—who cares which came first?

Pessimism and Optimism

Martin Seligman is famous in academic psychology for conducting the original studies that led to a *learned helplessness* model of depression. Seligman studied dogs under conditions in which some could escape from electric shocks, others not. Exposed to new situations, those dogs who had escaped in the past continued to escape, but the dogs who had not been able to escape did not even try. Even when it was obvious that safety just required jumping over a small barrier, these dogs just lay down and whimpered—they had learned that they were helpless to control their fate.

These experiments sound cruel, but Seligman was certain of his purpose. He had always been fascinated with the problem of what makes some people bounce back from stresses that make others collapse. As a boy of thirteen, he had seen his father, who seemed so strong and reliable, suffer a stroke that left him paralyzed, despondent, and helpless. As a college student with ambitions to change the world, he saw helplessness in every aspect of society. He was determined to try to explain the problem. His experiments were the beginning of the end for the simple-minded behaviorism of B. F. Skinner and his colleagues, who argued that we learn things simply because behavior that is rewarded is repeated, behavior that is punished becomes less frequent. According to the behaviorists, dogs should have been unable to form cognitions or expectations like helplessness—and man's cognitions were simply artifacts of reward-punishment sequences. The learned helplessness phenomenon was impossible to explain through behaviorism.

Learned helplessness can explain a lot about depression. It

can explain many self-defeating patterns of behavior—the wife who endures an abusive husband, the troubles people have with diets, smoking, drinking, the negative expectations of ghetto youth. Equally important, though, is an aspect of Seligman's work that has received comparatively little attention—some dogs never learn helplessness. In later experiments with humans, in which various noxious stimuli were administered under situations of control and no control, some people never gave up. With both dogs and people, it was impossible to teach about one third of subjects that they were helpless. What makes the difference? What accounts for this determination not to give up in the face of consistent failure?

Although Seligman is a cognitive-behavioral psychologist, he has a different view on the cognitive habits of depressives from that of Beck.[5] Seligman focuses on the concept of explanatory style—the different ways we have of thinking about how the world works. He notes that people who tend to give up easily have certain explanatory styles in common. They tend to see bad events as permanent and good events as temporary, whereas people with an optimistic explanatory style perceive events in just the opposite manner. Thus, when something bad happens to a depressed person, he might think, "I'm all washed up," when a more optimistic person might think, "I can get over this." And when something good happens, the depressive will think, "I got lucky," instead of, "I deserve this."

Besides permanence, another dimension of explanatory style is *pervasiveness*. Pervasiveness refers to how much influence one event will have on the rest of our lives, how much it seems to exemplify a predictable pattern rather than a specific case. Pessimistic people see bad events as more pervasive than specific. "There's no such thing as an honest mechanic" rather than "That mechanic is dishonest." Optimistic people tend to see bad events as unique rather than pervasive: "I don't feel well today" versus "I'm always getting sick." Of course, the reverse is true for good events. Pessimistic people see them as unique, lucky breaks rather than a part of a pattern: "I got lucky on the math test today" rather than "I'm good at math."

The third aspect of explanatory style is *personalization*. When bad things happen, we can blame ourselves, or we can blame others.[6] When good things happen, we can assume that we were just in the right place at the right time, or think that we had something to do with it. People who tend to blame themselves when bad things happen have low self-esteem: "I'm stupid," "I can't do anything right." People with healthy self-esteem are less likely to accept blame: "It's your fault as much as mine," "I refuse to let you make me the bad guy in this argument." Optimistic people tend to think they can cause good things to happen; pessimists think it's just luck.

Seligman, an example himself of optimism and hopefulness, teaches that these explanatory styles, though learned in childhood and shaped by all our experiences to date, can still be changed through a process of evidence collection and logical argument. Following Albert Ellis's rational-emotive psychotherapy, he calls this process *disputation*.

The "ABC" Method of Ellis and Seligman

1. We all encounter Adversity.
2. Our thoughts about our experiences with adversity become systematized as Beliefs.
3. These beliefs have Consequences. They are the direct causes of our decisions about what action to take against adversity. We can believe we are helpless, or powerful.
4. Beliefs can be changed through Disputation. We can learn to question the basis of our beliefs—is there sufficient evidence to prove it? Are there alternative explanations we have not thought of just because we have a negative explanatory style? Even if the belief is true,

are its implications really as bad as we think? Does holding this belief do us any good, or does it just get in the way?[7]

Seligman is the only writer I know to give an operational definition of hope. He says that hope consists of the ability to find temporary and specific (*i.e.*, nonpervasive) explanations for bad events. When faced with a setback, the hopeful person sees it as unique: "I didn't get that job, but the interviewer didn't seem to like me, and I didn't really prepare as well as I should. I'll do better next time." When explanations for bad events are more permanent and pervasive, no one can be hopeful: "I didn't get that job. None of the interviews go well. I always get nervous and make a fool of myself. I'll never get the job I want."

Depression can almost be defined as the abandonment of hope. The depressive feels that hope has abandoned him, but this is a two-way street. Jon Kabat-Zinn[8] and others have suggested that we get in the habit of noticing that we endlessly judge things. Sit in a quiet place for fifteen minutes. Don't try to control your thoughts, but passively notice them as they rise to the surface. Notice how we attach values to them—this is good, that is bad, this is pleasant, that is scary. This judging is a habit. We are not really evaluating things objectively; we are attaching values to them based on old experiences that may no longer be true. The depressive usually judges things as negative, aversive, or frightening. But we don't have to keep on judging; we can learn to take each new experience as unique. In doing so, we may realize that hopelessness comes from our habit of judging.

Identifying and Challenging Beliefs

Cognitive therapists want to arm us with the strengths of empirical science. They want us to conduct research on ourselves— to observe ourselves objectively, to draw conclusions from our observations, and to test the validity of those conclusions against wider experience. They may suggest slightly different methods, but it all comes down to:

- Identifying stressful situations
- Examining our thoughts and behavior under stress
- Determining what beliefs underlie our responses to stress
- Learning to challenge those beliefs
- Identifying alternative responses to stress
- Examining the effects of those responses, incorporating them into our belief system and behavior patterns if successful, modifying them further if not.

A simple form to use for recording these observations is reproduced on page 153. I have to emphasize that there are no shortcuts. We can learn about our beliefs only through careful observation, not through introspection. The depressogenic beliefs we have will get in the way of seeing ourselves clearly, so we have to do the recording. This is part of the work the depressed patient must do to help his recovery, to begin to develop new strengths and skills to replace the old ones that have just reinforced depression.

If this feels to you much like the Mood Journal, don't be surprised. Both are designed to help you recognize characteristic patterns of responding to external events—the Mood Journal to recognize patterns of emotional response, the Daily Record of Dysfunctional Thoughts[9] to recognize patterns in thinking. These dysfunctional feeling and thinking patterns are manifestations of our own psychological defenses at work. They help insulate us from facing some unpleasant truths—you *can't* always have what you want, I *am* mad at my child, I *am* attracted to my friend's wife, I *can't* please everyone. I don't want to tell you that the honest, regular use of either of these tools will be easy. What are defenses for, if not to protect us from harsh reality? But we must keep in mind that reality, though it may be

Daily Record of Dysfunctional Thoughts

Date	Situation	Emotion(s)	Automatic Thought(s)	Rational Response	Outcome
	Describe: 1. Actual event leading to unpleasant emotion, or 2. Stream of thoughts, day-dream, or recollection leading to unpleasant emotion	1. Specify sad, anxious, angry, etc. 2. Rate intensity of emotion, 1–100	1. Write automatic thoughts that preceded emotion(s) 2. Rate belief in automatic thought(s), 1–100	1. Write rational response to automatic thought(s) 2. Rate belief in rational response, 1–100	1. Rerate belief in automatic thought(s), 1–100 2. Specify and rate subsequent emotions, 1–100

Instructions: When you experience an unpleasant emotion, note the situation that seemed to stimulate the emotion. Then note the automatic thought associated with the emotion. Record the degree to which you believe this thought: 1 = not at all, 100 = completely. In rating degree of emotion 1 = a trace, 100 = the most intense possible.

153

harsh, is real, while the depression we create for ourselves in trying to avoid it is not only harsher yet but unnecessary.

Cognitive therapy has become so accepted now as a standard treatment for depression that some are considering depression largely a symptom of dysfunctional thought processes. This runs the risk of encouraging the depressive's thinking that he needs more control, not less. If he continues depressed, he is likely to feel that he has done a poor job of applying cognitive methods, which just reinforces his sense of self-blame and inadequacy. Depressives need to get out of their heads and into their hearts and their bodies. The best therapists recognize that depression is a very complex condition, that changing faulty thought processes is just one of many possible ways of treating it, and that addressing these thought processes is going to have repercussions in other areas of the patient's life—how he processes feelings, how he communicates with those close to him, how he feels about himself.

Relationships

ONE OF THE bitter ironies of depression is that depressed people crave connection with other people, while the nature of the disease makes it impossible for them to connect. David Karp writes, in *Speaking of Sadness:* "Much of depression's pain arises out of the recognition that what might make one feel better—human connection—seems impossible in the midst of a paralyzing episode of depression."[1]

People with depression can be very difficult to live with. We need a great deal from others, but we are embarrassed and confused by our needs, so we don't articulate them well. Some of our difficulty with other people stems from our faulty emotional, behavioral, and cognitive habits, as discussed in the previous three chapters, but a great deal of it comes from our own needs and our unrealistic expectations of others. Instead of focusing on these needs and expectations here, though, I'm going to focus more on how they affect our communication habits and how we can improve our communication skills. Part of the reason why depressed people can have unrealistic expectations for others is that we never state our needs directly, instead keeping secret wishes locked in our hearts. If we can take the risk of being good communicators, we can say what we want of others. They may not be able to give this to us, but they are less likely to abandon us than we think. Instead, we can enter into negotiations and quid pro quos, the stuff of real relationships.

Rejection Sensitivity

People with depression can be very sensitive to the feelings of others. They have great empathic skills—as if they have radar for what others are thinking or feeling. They have permeable boundaries to their selves. Unfortunately their radar is not reliable at all because what they want and need from others distorts their perception. They overuse the defenses of projection (attributing one's own feelings to others) and introjection (taking in the feelings of others and making them part of the self), which means that feelings in a relationship become a confused, contagious mess.

An interesting observation about people with depression is that they seem to react more to rejection, loss, or abandonment than other people do. It is as if they are thin-skinned, very aware of subtle cues of approval or disapproval from those around them, thrown for a loop by little signs of disapproval that might be shrugged off or argued about by another person. A term used to describe this quality is *rejection sensitivity*.[2] People who are excessively rejection-sensitive might seem different from each other superficially, ranging from the self-preoccupied hysteric to the withdrawn introvert; but all would suffer from depressive symptoms when they feel rejected.

The researchers who developed the concept of rejection sensitivity were interested primarily in psychopharmacology, and it seems as if the effects of Prozac and some of the newer antidepressants bear out their ideas. Prozac seems to make people less easily derailed by setbacks and rejection. They are still aware of these events, but it seems as if the medication helps them gain greater objectivity. A patient who was always upset by her husband's teasing now sees it as his way of expressing affection; another patient tries for a promotion she had avoided before because she now sees the world won't fall in if she doesn't get it. Peter Kramer[3] speculates that we will come to see sensitivity, like panic attacks, reified: that we will assume there is a somatic thermostat for sensitivity whose set point is biologically determined and can be changed by medication.

But this is exactly the subject where some of the most exciting changes in psychotherapy have been taking place. In self psychology, the focus has been on the self as "narcissistically damaged"—needing excessive reassurance from other people or from the outside world in order to feel whole, competent, alive. In family therapy, the focus has been on boundary violations—the tendency to be too easily influenced by what others say, think, or feel, the tendency to confuse one's own thoughts and feelings with others'. To use myself as an example: My mother's suicide left me with grave doubts about myself. If she had truly loved me, as a mother is supposed to love a child, how could I account for her abandoning me through suicide? Didn't this mean that I was essentially unworthy of love? Would I not then look to others to help me feel better about myself, but at the same time be afraid of real engagement because of my self-doubts, leaving myself feeling essentially alone and hopeless? In my present relationships, would I not need to take special care that I communicate my wants and needs clearly, not blame others for being unable to make me happy, not seeing it as my responsibility to make everyone else happy? Do I need individual therapy with someone skilled in self psychology or family therapy to help me straighten out the boundaries of my relationships? Or is it just that I have a low threshold of sensitivity and need Prozac to make myself less sensitive?

Maybe the ideal therapeutic regimen would be a little of all three, and maybe any one of the three could be of significant help to me. I think it is no accident at all when new ideas and research converge like this, even though it may make things more confusing for us for a while. We have scientists from different perspectives trying to understand what are the most important psychological issues of our time—a loss of identity, a sense of emptiness or estrangement, and desperate self-defeating attempts to regain a feeling of being centered and whole. These are problems not just for the depressive, though we may feel it more acutely, but for our entire culture. Naturally scientists are trying, albeit from different perspectives, to understand who it is who comes seeking help. We don't have to try to explain Freud's hysterics, with neurologically impossible paralysis or blindness—they have almost disappeared from Western culture because the social conditions that brought on their symptoms have disappeared. We have to try to understand people who are depressed, who put too much stock in the opinions of others, who have the sense of being outside life.

Depression is both caused by and a cause of poorly functioning relationships. We may be born more sensitive to rejection than the next guy, but it's possible to learn how to control this sensitivity and make our relationships work better by learning how to communicate more effectively.

Metacommunication

What's wrong with these conversations?

SHE: What time is the concert?
HE: You have to be ready by seven-thirty.

SHE: How many people are coming to dinner?
HE: Don't worry, there's plenty of food.

HE: Are you just about finished?
SHE: Do you want dinner now?

Regardless of how the questioner identifies the feelings that these responses engender, the questioner now has a choice. He or she can act based on these feelings or can express them verbally. I have the impulse to pick up and throw the nearest object when I'm spoken to this way, because I feel infantilized. But I'm better off to say it verbally: "I feel like you're overprotecting me. You're assuming you know what I want, but you're wrong. Please just answer the question directly." This is a form of *metacommunication,* or talking about how we talk.

The content of a conversation is what we talk about; the process is how we conduct the talking. Content is lyrics, process is music. Which is it that most directly speaks to feelings? From the point of view of feelings, process, like music, goes directly to our soul, while content must be analyzed intellectually. If we feel listened to and respected, we can take a rebuff. If we feel dismissed or patronized, even if we get our way, we're likely to be dissatisfied.

Shifting the focus of the conversation from content to process can be a very effective way of resolving communication problems. When my wife asks what I want for dinner, pasta or chicken, and I say I don't care, what I'm often missing is that she's asking for a little companionship, a little mutual ownership of a decision. If I say, "Chicken sounds good," but say it with a "Don't interrupt me" attitude, I'm still dismissing her, even though I've answered her question. She will feel diminished (and I'll feel guilty, even if I'm not consciously aware of it). What she can do is say, "Don't ignore me like that," or "It wouldn't hurt you to take your nose out of your book for a minute"—shifting from content to process, letting me know that I've been rude, letting me know that she just needs a reasonable amount of attention.

Ambiguous Communication

It seems natural to expect that those close to us understand us perfectly. But it is a wish that grown-ups must abandon. One of the points that marriage counselors have to make is that expecting the spouse to read one's mind is just unfair and silly. If you don't communicate it, you can't blame your partner for not understanding it.

Many of the techniques described earlier as assertiveness skills will help prevent ambiguous communication. A common problem occurs when nonverbal and verbal messages seem to contradict each other, creating confusion. A sulking "Go ahead, leave without me, I'll see you later, I really don't mind" only mystifies the hearer; should she listen to the words (go ahead) or the music (the sulk)? A half-hearted "If it's no bother, can you bring back some ice cream?" doesn't justify a pout if the traveler neglects it. The person who apologetically asks to be treated fairly is shooting himself in the foot. He has a right to be treated fairly, and he doesn't have anything to apologize for at all.

Ambiguity doesn't come only from conflict between verbal and nonverbal communication. Often our words themselves contradict each other. Sometimes we can't put our feelings into words. Sometimes we want contradictory things. Sometimes we just don't know what we want. This doesn't prevent us from getting mad at those close to us when they can't guess what would please us most. Unambiguous communication is more work than we're used to. To be clear, we must know our own mind, and then articulate our desires specifically, paying careful attention to what we say and how we say it. We have the idea that communication should be effortless, that people who are truly close should be able to almost read each other's minds. This is a dangerous belief. But careful, unambiguous communication can become almost second nature as we practice and it becomes rewarded by greater levels of intimacy and satisfaction in relationships.

A depressed patient has gone to a quasi-religious retreat over the weekend. She uses the experience to tell me she's not happy with the way therapy is going.

"I've been disappointed in all my therapists. I respect you, but I wanted something more . . . spiritual. A spiritual guide, a leader. . . . Someone who really understands me, what I want and what I should do. There must be people who are so enlightened that they give guidance and ask for nothing in return. I don't like the money part of therapy, either."

I try to imagine someone who gives guidance and asks for nothing in return. Though there are saints and truly unselfish spiritual leaders, they are rare, and they do ask for discipline. Most people who give guidance expect, at least, obedience.

I tell her that, in a way, the money is a guarantee. She doesn't have to do anything else for me other than pay her bill. She doesn't have to like or respect me. She doesn't have to take my advice or live up to my expectations. When I accept her fee for a professional service, the exchange of services is open and aboveboard.

She reflects on her history of relationships with men. Her husband was an older man who had been her supervisor at work. He seemed so confident and knowledgeable. She felt he could teach her things. But after a short time, she realized he was extremely controlling. If she didn't wash the dishes his way, he would have a fit. He told her she was a child, that she was capable of nothing. Eventually she somehow found the strength to leave him.

But she still wants a guru, someone who she feels can understand her perfectly. She's not ready to give up on the childish belief that someone who loves us enough can understand us without the work of communication. She doesn't see how even a well-meaning guru can do harm because he's not used to the flattery and the power, or that she might find obedience more unpleasant than liberty.

Projection and Projective Identification

Two additional defense mechanisms misused by depressives that contribute to problems in communication are *projection* and *projective identification*. Projection means that I take my feelings, disconnect them from my conscious awareness, and attribute them to you. "You really want to fight, don't you?" People who are very thin-skinned overuse projection. They take their own bad feelings about themselves and project them onto others, seeing themselves as victims of discrimination and collecting grievances everywhere. Projective identification, a confusing process that many therapists define differently, seems magical but really does happen. It occurs when, as a result of your projection, I really do want to fight. I catch the feeling you attribute to me. The projector and the recipient can get bound together in horribly complex webs of feeling from which there seems to be no escape.

Like all defenses, projection and projective identification are attempts to resolve a conflict between our needs, our fears (or our conscience), the expectations of others, and/or the strictures of reality. I need love and intimacy but I can fear it as well. If I let someone get close, I can be hurt. I can take that fear and project it, making anyone who comes close to me seem to be nosy, controlling, officious. Projection and projective identification can distort reality to a destructive, uncomfortable degree. And because they are so much a part of how we communicate in relationships, and because in human interactions things happen so fast that we can all easily get confused, these defenses are less subject to reflective analysis than denial, isolation, or repression. The best way of gaining control over these defenses is by working with a trusted partner in careful communication analysis.

Projection and projective identification are defenses that can be used by anyone, depressed or not. And they are especially likely to be evoked in close relationships, because intimacy, though good for us, is scary—we fear being engulfed, dominated, controlled. People with depression are likely to take their own bad feelings about themselves and project the feelings onto the people who care about them. The depressed husband who has lost his job doesn't believe his wife really means her words of comfort and reassurance; he doubts his own worth but defends against this doubt by attributing it to her. After enough rejection, she stops trying to make him feel better, and he is reinforced in his belief that she doesn't care about him. A couple of weeks more of this, and she really begins to have the kinds of doubts about him that he was attributing to her all along—projective identification at work.

When I assume that I understand you without sufficient basis in reality, the cause can be either projection or projective identification. I think I can read your mind. I become convinced that I know what you really mean, despite all your attempts at clarification.[4] If I keep on accusing you of really being angry at me, eventually you really will get angry at me. That's projective identification.

When I assume that you understand me, it's also a process of projection. When I get hot and bothered because I feel convinced I've made my wishes clear and you just stubbornly refuse to understand, I'm not communicating anything except my stubbornness. These irrational sensations of *knowing with perfect clarity exactly what the other person is thinking* are sure indications of projection. They're fueled by emotion, not logic.

What we have to do, naturally, is check our assumptions. (The old chestnut: "When you ASSUME, you make an ASS out of

U and ME.") Am I understanding you? Am I making myself clear to you? The technique of repeating back what the other person has said ("I hear you saying that you're disappointed I wanted to leave the party early"), while it sounds so simple-minded it's subject to caricature, is the place to start. It's really an exercise in developing empathy.

Aside from our assumptions, we may learn something about our expectations. If I get upset because my wife spends too much time putting the kids to bed, and I tell her about it, she may question me. How much time is too much? What is it exactly that I need her for that her time with the kids interferes with? I may make the unpleasant discovery that I expect my wife to put my needs ahead of the kids. I may have to question whether this is a fair assumption, whether it is congruent with my feelings in other areas. Compromise is possible:

When our children were young I spent all day at work missing them. I couldn't wait to come home and play with them, just sharing in their easy delight. My wife, on the other hand, had spent all day with them. She couldn't wait for me to come home so that she could have an adult conversation—often about how the kids had driven her crazy, which was the last thing I wanted to hear.

After a few months we realized what was going on. I would come in and she would start to complain. I would be impatient and dismissive. She'd get hurt and angry, and I'd feel that the pleasant evening I'd planned was ruined. We developed a compromise: we would play with the kids together for a while, then I'd play with them by myself while she prepared dinner. After dinner, while I helped with the dishes, she'd take the time to vent. It helped that I, having spent a little time with the children, could now remember that all their behavior wasn't totally endearing and that she, having been given a break of sorts, wasn't quite as stressed out as she was at 5:30.

The tempting, easy thing to do when we're feeling misunderstood is to withdraw. This is something depressives are good at. We can be wonderfully resourceful at entertaining ourselves. The feeling of being picked on, misunderstood, and isolated is an old, comfortable feeling. There is something that feels right about it. It confirms our fantasies that we are the ugly duckling, the Cinderella who is just in the wrong place at the wrong time, who can't be happy with all the mean people in the world. Withdrawal can feel self-righteous.

The hard thing to do is to hang in there and try to make the communication work. Don't assume it's all the other guy's fault. Listen carefully and be empathic. Maybe you're missing something important. Maybe at least you can figure out why he's not understanding you.

Successful relationships don't just happen, they take work. Happiness is not a gift someone else can give you, it's not even something you can get for yourself, it just happens as a by-product of living well. Living well usually doesn't mean taking the easy way out.

Relationships under Stress

I've never yet met anyone who has had a stress-free life. Sickness, loss, financial problems, job problems are things that all of us will have to deal with. Yet in reviewing new cases week after week at a mental health center, I'm constantly struck by how often bad luck has played a major part in contributing to people's psychological problems. If I'd had the same string of experiences, I wonder if I'd be coping as well as my patient.

Cognitively, emotionally, physically, stress can affect our ability to function. Under stress, our judgment is impaired; we have more difficulty assimilating information and correctly sizing up a situation. We can feel depressed, anxious, scared, demoralized. We can get physically ill. Any area of low resistance in one's body will react in characteristic ways—back, intestines, respiration, circulatory system. People with depression, under stress, become more depressed. And stress is the precipitant to almost all depressive episodes.

A good trusting relationship can be the best vaccine against stress. The couple has the advantage of their unique relationship, which gives them the chance to express their feelings fully in a manner rare, if possible at all, in other relationships. A crisis can, of course, bring up problems that have previously been dormant, or recognized but put aside. Peaceful times can permit a couple to become lazy like this. But when an outside problem erupts, these spouses will find their resources undermined by unresolved difficulties. A tendency to blame others instead of taking responsibility, for instance, may be tolerable when times are smooth, but it may destroy a relationship under stress.

A crisis can be used for positive ends. A couple can use the experience to learn how to work together, to build up credit in trust and reliance, to develop an appreciation of each other's strengths, to realize sincerely how much they need each other, to have the experience of providing support and helping. One thing that helps is just to acknowledge the existence of the stress and that one is in the midst of a stress response. Stress brings chaos and disorganization. When spouses keep this in mind, they can accept that their strong feelings and dramatic reactions are normal responses. They don't have to be so afraid of losing control. They can say to themselves and each other, "Something terrible is happening to us, and we are having a normal reaction. Under the circumstances, it is the natural way to feel." It's also important to recognize that stress is relative, not objective. What upsets you—for instance, a child's leaving home—may be relatively unloaded for me; but for you to deal with my job problems might be much more demanding.

There are four phases people typically go through when faced with a serious problem:[5]

Phase 1 is anticipation. When something important is not working out, you are usually aware of trouble coming. You are worried, you have emotional ups and downs when you may feel alternately overwhelmed and hopeless or that you are just being silly and making something out of nothing. You may decide there is no point in talking about it because nothing has happened yet. You probably have trouble sleeping, you may have bad dreams, your appetite may change, you may have some of the physical symptoms you usually get under stress. Generally you are confused; you hope the problem will just go away but you prepare yourself for the worst.

In phase 2 the problem becomes reality. It will affect both of you even if only one is directly involved. One or both of you will regress for a while—the symptoms described above will become worse. Confusion, anxiety, strong feelings, and hopelessness will be harder to fight. Even a good relationship will suffer; but now is not the time to decide you have a bad relationship just because feelings are high and normal ways of coping have broken down.

Phase 3 is acceptance of the problem. You may feel more depressed but less anxious, less blaming, less panicky. Some people get stuck here, feeling that there is nothing they can do but have an unhappy life.

Phase 4 is resolution. You start taking action. You need support and encouragement from each other, partly because you can still feel depressed, angry, or scared. You start to realize and accept that you may have to make important adjustments in your life, but you will be working on the problem instead of being obsessed by it.

It may seem self-evident, but it needs to be stated that both spouses are always involved in a stressful situation. If I'm overwhelmed with problems at work, my wife's reactions are very important to me. When my wife is ill, how I am with her—attentive and caring or withdrawn and aloof because I'm scared—is a major factor in her ability to recover. The spouse should have an important role in times of stress, but some, because they believe there is nothing they can do to help, don't offer constructive ideas, don't offer constructive criticism, and don't offer emotional support to confront the problem. What I'm suggesting is that the spouse needs to get deliberately involved. Not involved in offering advice and solutions, unless there is a clear signal that that's what's wanted, but involved in:

1. Listening, drawing out, and accepting feelings
2. Exploring alternatives, brainstorming, playing out different scenarios
3. Offering hope and encouragement, conveying the sense that you are not alone

These kinds of actions have the effect of reducing anxiety, reducing stress, lessening confusion, and providing a feeling that an acceptable solution is attainable. This is exactly what a good psychotherapy relationship can do, and this is why I emphasize that marriage is a mental health factory. Someone who is actively involved in trying to solve his problems is in a very different frame of mind from someone who is overwhelmed, hopeless, and forlorn.

A crisis in our marriage came when my wife developed a thyroid tumor. I was preoccupied with finishing my dissertation just at this time. I heard what the doctors said to her—that these things are almost always benign—and accepted it at face value. I dismissed my wife's anxiety as groundless and got angry that she needed more reassurance.

Worse yet, the fact that she had to have surgery meant she had to stop nursing our son, then a little over a year old. I told myself and her that it was close to time to wean him anyway, not recognizing that for her the nursing experience was very important bonding time with our children and that she didn't want to stop until she was ready. In all, I treated my wife as if she were a needy pest, when she actually did have a lot to be fearful and angry about.

My analyst at the time was kind enough to point out that my behavior was so bad that the pressure of schoolwork wasn't a sufficient explanation. He reminded me of my reactions to my mother's dependency and depression before her death—denying, dismissive, intellectualizing. Of course I was doing the same thing again. I also was scared of the thyroid tumor. I didn't want to lose Robin. But I didn't let myself think about that. Instead of telling her that I cared what happened to her, I told her not to worry and got angry when she worried anyway.

When the spouse doesn't take the bull by the horns and become actively involved, it can poison the relationship. Sometimes spouses not actively affected by a crisis withdraw, sulk, or develop problems of their own. In such a case you can speculate that they have been overly dependent on the spouse who is now preoccupied with the crisis. They feel angry and betrayed because the other isn't emotionally available. They may be aware of these angry feelings but embarrassed about the selfishness that they imply—after all, my wife has the problem, I should feel helpful, not angry, toward her—and thus close down communication. Or they may be unaware and avoid communication, using any of a number of excuses. In any case, the problem is just made worse, because the spouse who is directly affected by the stress will feel resentful and betrayed. In families with traditional roles, this often happens when a child becomes ill. The mother becomes involved with the illness, and the father, feeling helpless, withdraws. Or the father might have work problems that he doesn't share with his spouse, and she, feeling hurt and left out, doesn't pursue him. You set in motion a vicious circle in which withdrawal by one leads to hurt feelings in the other, leading to more withdrawal and more hurt feelings until you have either a blowup or a distant, uninvolved relationship.

So what guidelines are there for dealing with stress in a relationship?

1. When you feel threatened by an important problem, discuss your fears with each other. Take turns listening, exploring, and accepting. Be nonjudgmental. Try to sort out which fears are real and which are just anxiety running away with itself. What's the worst that can happen? If your worst fears come true, would you be completely helpless about coping with the situation? Try to figure out all the questions you need answers to, and separate out those you can answer now from those which you just have to wait for time to answer.

2. When you are actually suffering from the emotional effects of a crisis, don't make it worse by assuming something's wrong with you. Be aware that feeling depressed or scared is a normal reaction to the situation. Share your feelings with your partner. Cry, bitch, whine, moan, whatever it takes, knowing that your partner is committed to you and understands that you are under stress. Do this as often as you feel necessary.

3. In the process of pouring out your feelings, start to accept that there is a problem and that only you can do anything about it. Start thinking about ways in which you can get some relief, perhaps even some enjoyment. Even though it may sound crazy, you don't have to let your whole life be overwhelmed with the crisis. Schedule some time for enjoyable activities. Try to compartmentalize your life so that you have some time set aside for dealing with the problem, other time for doing things that will make you feel good.

4. When you do take the time for the problem, try to use

it constructively. With your partner, explore solutions or adaptations. Maybe all you can do is make the best of a painful situation. If there are different solutions open, don't rush in just to relieve the anxiety. Purposefully delay action until you're sure you have anticipated all the consequences, but don't use this as an excuse to delay action unnecessarily.

5. Give yourself time to heal. We don't bounce back from stress without wounds. We may remain sensitive, hurt, and angry. Try not to take it out on people close to you, but don't deny the feelings. Continue to use your relationship for support.

We can't exist without other people. As depressives, we may be prone to want too much from others, and we may protect ourselves from experiencing and expressing those needs by playing roles that aren't really us. But real relationships—built on trust, honesty, and caring—can give us the opportunity to heal, to build a new self. Children grow out of their childish needs for omnipotent, ever-attentive parents by a process of optimal frustration. The parents disappoint the child by making mistakes, by not always paying attention, but ideally they do it in synch with the child's ability to tolerate disappointment and frustration. The child learns to soothe himself, learns that he can feel safe and loved for a while even without the parents' attention. The child is building a self.

Honest, caring relationships give adults the opportunity to do the same thing. The depressed person can repair a damaged sense of self-esteem through developing intimacy with another person. The other person doesn't enhance self-esteem through artificial compliments or through reflected glory; rather the process of letting the other see oneself, warts and all, and finding that one is still loved and accepted, does the work of repair.

The Self

DEPRESSION IS A LOSS of parts of the self. Instead of experiencing our inner selves as strong, vital, and joyful, we see ourselves as weak, damaged, or blameworthy. We wish that others could make us feel better, but we can't usually express such wishes directly; instead we use various self-defeating defense mechanisms to keep our wishes out of consciousness. And even though we try to keep our deepest needs out of consciousness, we still feel guilty and shameful; we consider ourselves needy, unworthy, repugnant. What can we do to reinvigorate the self, to help us capture or recapture a sense of ourselves as a center of initiative, a participant rather than an observer, a cause rather than a victim of life?

Guilt, Shame, and Depression

Though in common speech we often hear people say, "I'm really feeling depressed today," depression is not an emotion. Sadness, disappointment, and fear are emotions. Depression is an illness. One of the manifestations of depression is a persistent complex of emotions like sadness, fear, and anger. We all experience the emotions associated with depression when we are grieving, hurt, or disappointed.

Guilt and shame, while certainly experienced as powerful feelings, perhaps more powerful than any others, are not primary emotions in the sense that they are there in the infant's repertoire almost from birth. They seem to find expression only after the first year or so of life, when the infant's interactions with caregivers are already complex. Though guilt was the focus of most of Freudian psychoanalytic theory and treatment, shame seems to be more of a factor in today's psychopathology, and is certainly intimately connected with depression.

We feel guilt about things we do or don't do—we take unfair advantage, we break promises, we lie. We feel shame about who we are—we experience ourselves as unworthy, uncouth, repulsive, stupid. The Catholic Church has for centuries known what to do about guilt—all it takes is sincere repentance and a firm intention to change. If we feel genuinely sorry for our actions and resolve to do better in the future, we don't have to feel guilty anymore. Freud then taught us how to address unconscious guilt—drag the guilt-inducing but forbidden impulses into the light of day, and their power over us withers away. But there is no easy resolution for shame. We can't so easily change who we are. It's hard to make ourselves believe that we are good enough.

Part of the reason for the popularity of the recovery movement is that it helps detoxify shame. Alcoholics have always been expected to be ashamed of themselves—they are seen by nondrinkers as weak, irresponsible, lacking backbone, degraded. But when they share their stories with others who are sworn not to judge them, who will praise them for their courage just for admitting the problem, who share the same taint and seem to be able to live with it, the shame of alcoholism is detoxified. John Bradshaw, the author of *Healing the Shame That Binds You*,[1] a

recovery movement bible, taps this theme by constantly reiter-
ating his message of freeing oneself from "toxic shame."

Shame serves an adaptive purpose for the infant.[2] When his
smiles, coos, and gurgles fail to engage a preoccupied parent, he
looks down sadly and seems to experience shame. It keeps him
from making a bad situation worse by continuing to seek a
response when none is forthcoming. Later, he learns to discrimi-
nate better—if mommy looks disgusted at a dirty diaper but
praises the child for BMs on the potty, shame comes to be
associated with messiness, self-esteem with cleanliness. But if
mommy, because of her own depression, anger, or frustration,
seems inconsistently annoyed at some times, responsive at others, the child cannot learn adequate discrimination. Shame
comes to be associated with the self of the child, not the child's
behavior or products.

Shame is also connected to our ability to meet our own
standards. If we have a strict moral code and fail or slip up
occasionally, we may feel guilty. Guilt, in moderation, is good for
us and society. It keeps us on our toes. But if we consistently fail
to meet our own goals—or if we feel that our goals are set too
low so that we are not challenging ourselves—we feel shame.
It's no longer that our behavior is sometimes substandard, but
that we—our selves—are unable to produce meaningful, effective, worthwhile behavior. Reviewing our priorities, then making
a deliberate effort to spend more time and energy in activities
that help us achieve them, as described in chapter 7, can gradually help alleviate this kind of self-blame.

Shame, like guilt, can be forced out of consciousness—denied, repressed, split off. The adult consumed by shame may
only consciously feel some of the symptoms of depression—a
sense of futility, a desperate but self-defeating desire to please,
a focus on aspects of the self (as with anorexia or psychosomatic
illness) as a vehicle for concerns about the whole self.

Depression is an ironic disease, the Catch-22 of mental illness. In a national survey, a significant minority of Americans were found to think of depression as inherently stigmatizing. Guess who these people were? People in this group were more likely than the average person to have experienced depression themselves and more likely to report feeling "really depressed" at least once a month.[3] A pervading sense of shame is a precursor to depression; but accepting the sick role, accepting that one has an illness and needs help, is also too often seen as shameful. But shame can only thrive in darkness and secret; dragging our bad feelings out into the light of day, sharing them with people we trust, can be of enormous benefit.

Another antidote for shame is a more enlightened self-awareness. Use of a log like the Daily Record of Dysfunctional Thoughts in chapter 8 will help the reader become more aware of the kinds of irrational beliefs—often motivated by unconscious shame—that interfere with healthy functioning. Once themes and issues around shame have been identified, joining a group can be the most effective detoxifying experience. Alcoholics Anonymous, Al-Anon, Overeaters Anonymous, self-help groups for depression, psychotherapy groups—exposing our shame to others who are sympathetic can help remove its power over us.

The Importance of Boundaries

I referred earlier to our conflicted feelings about intimacy, about wanting it desperately and at the same time fearing it. One way in which family therapists think about this issue puts it in terms of fusion and autonomy. *Autonomy* implies having a well-developed self, good internal resources of self-esteem, clear boundaries. *Fusion* implies a merging with others, a dissolving of the self, a wish to share responsibility. It may sound as if I mean that autonomy is good, fusion is bad; but a little fusion can be good for us at times, and autonomy can be carried to the extreme of distance and isolation. Fusion makes us bond with others. Everyone who has ever been head over heels in love has experienced fusion. The feelings for the other person have taken over our entire functioning, so that we can't concentrate, our moods have altered, we may feel invulnerable (and in fact anesthetized). It's like a few drops of food coloring in a glass of water; it permeates throughout our selves. Fusion also comes in the midst of fights. Who hasn't had the experience of not being able to remember what started a fight, who said what to whom when? The rage, like love, takes over all our functioning. Autonomy, on the other hand, is the gradual (and constant) struggle to define a self within the context of a relationship. We must learn not to strive to please others or to be different from others, in fact not to define ourselves in terms of others at all, but in terms of an objective evaluation of our strengths and weaknesses, our wants and needs.

We depressives have trouble giving up on the idea that there is a secret to happiness that others know and we don't; that others could make us happy if they loved us enough, but out of perversity choose not to. We often vacillate between fusion—using the other as a self-object, a mirror, an ideal, without an identity of his or her own—and withdrawal, a cold, bitter disappointment when the other has let us down. No wonder we're difficult to live with. If we want to grow up, we will have to give up these ideas and begin to take responsibility for our own happiness, to move toward autonomy.

Having boundaries simply means knowing where I end and you begin, understanding what is my responsibility and what is yours. Boundaries can be too rigid or too loose. We want them to be semipermeable, so that we can let others in when it's appropriate, or keep them out when it's appropriate. The concept has been embraced by the recovery movement, a loose affiliation of writers and practitioners who seem to have organized themselves around the concept of codependency. The paradigm of codependency is the wife of the alcoholic, who is seen as "enabling" his drinking by making excuses for him, by helping him keep out of trouble, by not confronting him with the effect alcohol has on the family. This type of person is seen as having very loose boundaries—she "colludes" with her drinking husband; she puts his needs ahead of her own and the children's; she blames herself for troubles in their relationship, denying the effect of the alcohol; she feels it's her job to make him happy. The payoff for the codependent wife is that she gets to have the illusion of intimacy without taking responsibility for herself.

The recovery movement embraces ideas like boundaries and codependency like a boy with a new chainsaw. Suddenly there are millions of things to apply the chainsaw to, things we had just never noticed before. Now everyone is seen to be codependent, everyone is in recovery, everyone is a victim of trauma (another new idea). But carrying a new idea to extremes doesn't make the original observation wrong. The phenomenon of codependency is real, and boundaries are a helpful concept in explaining what's going wrong, not only in codependency, but in many troubled relationships.

What should be within the boundary of my self? Two things, primarily: awareness and responsibility.[4] I should be aware of my own thoughts, feelings, memories, beliefs, and choices; aware of my wants and needs; and aware of my own unconscious. I should know that others cannot know these things unless I tell them, and that I cannot have this awareness of others unless they tell me (and they have a right to choose not to). I have to take responsibility for my own behavior, including what I communicate, and responsibility for setting direction in my life and making myself happy. I cannot make others happy, I can't make them stop drinking, I can't make my children successful—in fact, I can't make others do anything. If I choose to, I can conduct my behavior so that they have a better chance of achieving the goals I want for them, but their achievement is their responsibility, not mine. Establishing healthy boundaries like these is a first step toward detachment.

But boundaries can be too rigid as well as too loose. Not everyone is codependent; some are cold, isolated, and lonely. Codependent wives are depressed (often without knowing it, because they're so busy taking care of others), but depression is also caused by distance and alienation. We want to have the capacity to let down our guard, to let others in, to share their feelings and let them share ours. We need to remember that close relationships allow us the opportunity to explore our own identity in an atmosphere of safety. We can express our feelings, talk about our hopes, dreams, and disappointments, without fear of judgment or rejection. A truly intimate relationship can tolerate this without leading to fusion, because each partner keeps in mind that he is not responsible for the other's feelings.[5]

Some marriages evolve into a stable pattern that is so familiar every reader probably knows a couple that fit the description: the distancer and the pursuer.[6] Typically they are a hysterical woman and an obsessional man. She is emotional, demonstrative, loud, and highly visible. He is cold, controlled, and fades into the background. She spends much of her energy trying to get a response from him. She may do this by getting angry, by being needy and clingy, by having psychosomatic symptoms, by having crises—any number of ways. It never seems to work. He comes in, fixes the problem with an attitude of resigned impatience—as if she's an incompetent child—and withdraws again. He may withdraw into work, his hobbies, his buddies, alcohol— he has lots of alternatives. She never gets what she thinks she wants—which is for him to love her as much as she loves him—and he never gets what he thinks he wants—which is for her to be worthy of his respect. Neither one of them has to think about their own selves or what really would give their life meaning; they are constantly preoccupied with each other.

Depending on your gender bias, you may take sides with one or the other partner here. But the interesting thing is that they are really both colluding in a complicated dance that always maintains the same distance between them. He can withdraw because he knows she'll run after him; he gets to feel wanted without really risking intimacy. She can pursue him because she knows he'll run away; she gets to feel alive and vital without getting too close to anyone.

Henry and Phyllis showed me how this works. They came in for marriage counseling at her behest. She felt she couldn't get him to take an interest in her or the family. A big, strong woman, she would turn bright red as she yelled directly into his face about how he let the family down. Their children were having difficulty in school, partly because the family was so chaotic. They rarely were told to do their homework, and when they did it, it got lost. Phyllis blamed Henry for much of this; he made her feel unloved and the children so neglected that no one could function any better. Henry was a master of passive resistance and diversion. An overworked health care administrator, he accepted Phyllis's version of reality. He never got upset by her demands, but never changed his behavior, either. He would mollify her and then escape into a work-related emergency.

Then Henry got sick. He had to quit his job. Phyllis went back to her old career and was soon making as much money as Henry had been. I didn't hear from them for six months. Then Phyllis called because the children were in trouble again. When they came in, I was amazed to see the roles exactly reversed. Phyllis was now too busy for the family, and Henry was feeling overwhelmed and neglected. Their personalities hadn't changed. Phyllis was still loud, rude, and overbearing, Henry was quiet and passive-aggressive. But now he needed her, while she was irritated with his weakness and incompetence. They were using their personalities to keep the same safe distance between them that they had always had.

Boundaries are also a helpful concept in thinking about families. For a family to function, there have to be strong but permeable boundaries around relationships. Children need to be isolated from much of what goes on between parents; there needs to be a boundary between the parents and children. Parents' bad feelings about each other are not to be shared with children. Parents' sex lives, financial worries, the secrets they tell each other when they're feeling depressed, are not the children's business. When a parent tells a child or adolescent a secret about the marriage, that's colluding. It may make the child feel special, more grown-up, but it's actually using the child for some selfish purpose—to gain an ally, to gain sympathy, to fight loneliness— which is ultimately damaging to the child's self-esteem. Of course these boundaries change as children get older. Mothers and daughters may have their own secrets, fathers and sons theirs. These grow out of respect for the adolescent's needs for privacy and special support. The children have a boundary around their relationship with each other which can also be quite healthy. Being able to talk to a trusted sibling is a transitional step from depending on the parents to complete autonomy— and often that trust and openness will continue into adulthood, in a special feeling of closeness that is like no other relationship. Note that divorce does not change the need for these boundaries. Divorced parents still need to make many decisions together without involving the children, need to continue to show support for the other's parenting styles, rules, and expectations for the children. Children can live through divorce much better if they still have the sense that there is a parental unit caring for them, that parents may not live together but still make decisions together.

Practicing Detachment

The depressed person makes himself miserable partly by trying to control things he can't control. Indeed, some researchers feel that excessive worrying is the hallmark of depression.[7] Depressives ruminate on their problems, worrying the same issues around endlessly; we find a counterargument for every possible solution to our problems, and so end up taking no action at all.

Grady's case (page 134) is a perfect example. Everyone around him is sick, and tries to make him feel responsible for their recovery. But he can't make his mother cooperate with chemotherapy, he can't make his brother stay sober, he can't manufacture the money to pay his son's hospital bills. What he could do is give these people his time, interest, and love—but he can't because he's been guilt-tripped so badly he doesn't value what he can do. Instead, he exhausts himself in a fruitless quest to please everyone. He keeps pouring oil in the engine without checking to see that the drain is sealed.

In order not to be driven crazy by constantly responding to the demands of the moment, we need to become adept at *detachment*. Detachment implies a certain objectivity, a certain perspective in being able to rise above a situation and consider its meaning within a larger context than the immediate one. Detachment suggests a certain degree of insulation from contagious emotions—not being caught up in others' panic or anger, but making our own decisions about the emotional meaning of a situation. In some ways, detachment is the passive attitude of Benson's relaxation response—it means recognizing that crisis situations eventually get resolved, that even feelings like panic dissipate, and that what we can do about the situation and feelings is limited.

Detachment is not stuffing feelings. It is not repression, denial, projection, or intellectualization. It is recognizing and acknowledging feelings, but maintaining a certain amount of conscious control over how much they affect us. Detachment comes from being able to get in touch with one's most important values, asking ourselves: Does this situation threaten what's most important to me, or is it merely difficult or unpleasant?

Detachment implies an ascetic discipline, an Eastern value system differing greatly from a Western, consumer-oriented society in which the one who dies with the most toys wins. Detachment means giving up—an insulting concept for American males, but one that we should entertain more. We can all see the wisdom of the dying man, retiring from the daily struggles of life to spend more time with his family. But we are all dying, just some of us faster than others. We have to accept reality, to play the cards we are dealt.

It seems as if depressives have an obsessive quality that won't let them detach. They often worry constantly about things over which they have no control, or tell themselves they won't be happy unless something they can't control happens. A woman I know has two gay children. She feels she has accepted their homosexuality, but she is terribly upset about having no grandchildren. She can't be with people her age because they talk about grandchildren so much. This is very sad, but sadder still is that she sees no way out. She feels the rest of her life will be miserable because of this. One of the ways that antidepressant medications, especially Prozac and the other SSRIs, seem to work is that they help people get a better sense of proportion, to stop driving themselves crazy with little things.

Two questions can help gain a realistic detachment: Will this really matter tomorrow (next week, next month)? and What can I realistically do about it? If I'm in a situation that is highly charged emotionally but whose outcome is not really important to me, perhaps I don't have to act just to get some emotional relief. If I'm in a difficult, even an important, situation but my options are limited, I only make myself miserable by wishing I could do more.

At work I have to separate what's urgent and what can be put off, what's important and what's trivial. It's necessary not to get urgency and importance confused. Many things that seem urgent are trivial; many things that are really important can get put off. But urgency carries emotional weight. Emotionally, we feel it's a crisis, we'd better do something about this right now. So we can keep on taking care of urgencies but putting off what's really important. If we could reverse this, if we could take care of the really important things, many urgencies would be resolved or prevented along the way. Having the discipline and wisdom to step back and decide what's really important, then the discipline to follow through on it, comes from detachment.

The Body

Depressives must learn to listen to and take care of their bodies. Divorced from feelings, we tend to see ourselves divorced from our bodies as well. But our "true self" is not up in our head behind our eyes—it is our whole self, body, mind, and spirit. Ignoring body messages like pain, fatigue, and psychophysiological symptoms just sends us off for unnecessary medical care— depressives dramatically overuse physical medicine—and makes us feel more depressed because the medical care is ineffective.

Our clinic recently cosponsored a panel discussion on "Depression and the Body," which drew a crowd of forty, pretty good attendance for a small town. I was amazed to look around and see not a single familiar face in the crowd—these were not people in psychotherapy, but people being treated for physical symptoms, all of whom had wondered if depression were somehow connected to their problems. Somehow the idea of a connection with depression made intellectual sense to them, but none of them (so far as I knew) had ever called a therapist to discuss it—they just kept going to their doctors, being treated for musculoskeletal pain, PMS, Lyme disease, you name it, despite the discomfort and expense involved in the treatment.

Somatization is another psychic defense mechanism, another way of not feeling feelings. It expresses our anger against ourselves (by giving us real pain) and expresses our anger toward others by controlling them (they must take care of us) and making them feel inadequate (they can't really help us). Somatization may be a form of introjection—we make the bad parent, the sadist, the torturer, part of ourselves, twisting our backs, giving us splitting headaches, pain in the heart, crippling menstrual cramps. Remember Jane's headaches (page 28) after her son shot himself.

If you spend a lot of time and money pursuing solutions to physical complaints, my advice is to find one internist, general practitioner, or gynecologist who is enlightened about and interested in mind-body relationships, and make friends with him or her (your therapist or psychiatrist should be able to help you find one). Tell the doctor about your depression, and make it clear you will be needing his or her help in getting symptomatic relief while accepting the limits of physical medicine to help with mind-body problems. Then in the future when you are doubled over with back pain, don't have dangerous surgery, but get some physical therapy and do something about your depression.

Meanwhile, do preventive maintenance. Exercise, regularly. Eat and drink moderately. There are so many exercise, diet, and health resources out there that I don't need to review them for you. Just accept the facts. Abusing or neglecting your body is an attenuated form of a suicidal impulse. Instead of actively cutting your wrists, you passively develop heart disease by not taking care of yourself. Which is better?

Self-destruction is not romantic, but stupid and selfish. The poet Sylvia Plath's father, an educator and scientist himself, instead of taking care of his diabetes, took to his bed and adopted Christian Science, dying when Sylvia was only eight. The child Sylvia correctly perceived his death as suicide, and never forgave him. Her anger and bitterness toward him pervaded her life, and her suicide was certainly an attempt to find release from the intensity of the emotions she felt.

Play

People who know my stodgy current self would hardly guess that I became a complete fool when my children were young. I would come home every night and play silly games—dragging them around the polished floor on sheets or in laundry baskets, playing train; hiding under an old mattress while they crawled on top, playing earthquake; or doing simple gymnastics, playing "funny tricks." As the kids grew up, some of these games evolved into more familiar sports like catch or Frisbee or games of Scattergories.

When my daughter left for college and my son grew into adolescence, I got depressed again. Consciously, I knew I was missing them. I cried when my daughter moved out; I felt lonely as I went for walks without my son. My wife and I became television addicts. As always seems to happen, it took me a while to recognize depression for what it was.

Something reminded me one night of how we had played together. I literally had to sit down on the stairs to catch my breath, the memory was so powerful and painful. This was not recapture of a repressed memory—I had never forgotten these moments—but a sudden appreciation of the impact of the loss. The opportunity to regress, to be a child again, to play with my own children in safety, had been a healing experience for me.

My own childhood had been rather cold and scary; there wasn't enough tickling and hugging. My children had given me the opportunity to make up for some of what I had missed, to parent myself.

Play is essential to nurturing the self. The depressive, trying to hide from his own punitive superego like Adam from a wrathful Jehovah, feels that he better never let his guard down, better always be busy, always be productive. But it's a joyless existence if all we care about is getting the work done. Something as simple as playing catch with the dog for a few minutes after work connects us with a part of ourselves we can lose only too easily—the child who can laugh, who can enjoy silliness, mindless physical activity.

Play changes moods. Play can lift depression. Sad children, coaxed into play, can smile and laugh and forget their sadness. We've all wheedled a grumpy twelve-year-old into playing Monopoly on a summer night. After a while, the grumping is gone. It may come back, but in the meantime parent and child have had a shared enjoyable experience that wouldn't have happened if anyone had tried to analyze or solve the child's problem. We adults are no different from the grumpy twelve-year-old. Our moods are subject to change. Sometimes we resist the invitation to play because if we played we might feel better, and then wouldn't we feel foolish for feeling as grumpy as we did? But we can't depend on others to keep calling us out to play. We have to make our own opportunities.

Play is not work. You can't make play out of an activity whose purpose is to accomplish something, but it's fine if you accomplish something while you're playing.

Play is usually physical. Our bodies are engaged. We move, we use our large muscles, we can sweat.

Play often involves a conscious abandonment of dignity, sometimes by putting us into roles or positions that are outside our usual behavior.

Play usually involves others. Solitary play is okay if there is no one available, but it's more fun with other people.

Play involves being spontaneous, doing what our impulses tell us. This may require planning. Games have rules to keep our spontaneity in safe limits. Spontaneity helps us lose self-consciousness, which seems to be a major point of play.

There are horrible-sounding psychoanalytic concepts like "regression in the service of the ego," "humor as a mature defense," which are the gray analysts' way of trying to acknowledge that joy is essential but hard to analyze. I think the fact that animals play should tell us that play is part of nature, that we need to play to live.

As Carol Tavris writes in *Anger: The Misunderstood Emotion:* "For some of the large indignities of life, the best remedy is direct action. For the small indignities, the best remedy is a Charlie Chaplin movie. The hard part is knowing the difference."[8]

Taking Care of the Self

Depressives must learn to practice self care. We can fix our leaky oil pans ourselves. What this means is a deliberate effort to practice the skills we've been talking about—changing our emotional, behavioral, and thought patterns, changing how we are in relationships, assessing our priorities and trying to live in accordance with our values—and *then letting ourselves feel proud of our accomplishments.* This may be the hardest single thing for most depressives. We have been conditioned never to feel proud. We expect that it's asking for trouble, that the disapproving Jehovah will reach down and smite us like Job. But the point of that part of the Bible was that Job was chosen at random—there were plenty of other self-satisfied men who were never tortured as he was. Our chances of misfortune are exactly the same, whether we feel good or bad about ourselves.

Remember our analogy about the good parent running along beside the bicycle, giving the child a sense of confidence, safety, and security just by her presence? No matter what our childhood experience was like, we all have some parts of that good parent incorporated within us, which we can cultivate and strengthen. Allowing our selves to integrate our strengths and successes builds a sense of a strong, nurturing self which we can rely on in times of stress. We have to do this by allowing some time to reflect and take stock. We can do this in many of the ways described in previous chapters—through intimate conversation, through meditation, journaling—but if we don't take time to do it, any recovery we make from depression will be only temporary.

This applies equally to people who have recovered from depression with the help of Prozac or other antidepressants. There is a superficial belief that the pill has cured you and that when you go off medication you will be subject to depression again. But on a deeper level most people recognize that the medication has just allowed another part of their selves to come out. Peter Kramer's Tess, depressed for twenty years, miraculously recovers on Prozac—she becomes almost a different person, assertive, witty, attractive. When she stops taking the medication, she goes back to her old ways—depressed, passive, lonely—but says, "I'm not myself."[9] She has returned to the self she was for twenty years, but she believes that the Prozac self is the real self. Prozac helps people be who they think they are, helps them act on their abilities, have the courage of their convictions, live up to their own self-image. But its effect is only temporary if we don't allow ourselves to integrate the experience.

I think that depression is best understood as a chronic condition. But we can stay symptom-free if we just take proper care of ourselves. I suggest that part of good care requires that we put some time aside each week to reflect on our experience. Regular use of the Mood Journal can help you understand the recurring issues that are causing you distress, and also help you learn what gives you pleasure and helps you feel good. It is necessary to consider again our priorities and assess the week in terms of how close we came to living in accordance with them, to figure out what we can do differently next time but also to reflect on and integrate what we've done well. It can be done in church, in therapy, in a group, in an intimate conversation, in journaling or meditation, but it needs to be done.

11

Aids to Recovery

As I've said several times, this book is not meant to be a treatment for depression. It is meant to help you recover and to prevent future episodes, but the person who's really depressed needs more help than any book can offer. This usually means psychotherapy and/or antidepressant medication. Though either can help alone, the two together are much more effective. Newer antidepressant medications can be so helpful that they should always be considered. Competent psychotherapy can help you recover more quickly, and help keep you from relapsing. Unfortunately it isn't always easy to get the two together. Psychiatrists, who can both prescribe antidepressants and provide psychotherapy, usually do only one or the other, but not both. Physicians in other specialties can legally prescribe antidepressants but in most cases aren't sufficiently trained and don't have the time to do the necessary follow-up and counseling. Other psychotherapists, like psychologists, social workers, or pastoral counselors, may have special training and experience in working with depression, but can't prescribe medication. You need to find a psychiatrist and a psychotherapist who work together.

Peter Kramer, the author of *Listening to Prozac,* notes that getting Prozac is easy. Patients call him asking not for Prozac, but where they can get the kind of psychotherapy described in his book—respectful psychotherapy, complemented by careful pharmacotherapy that pays close attention to the ups and downs of recovery. The Rand Corporation, with the Robert Wood Johnson Foundation, did an extensive study of the effectiveness of treatment of depression, comparing different means of funding services.[1] Patients in prepaid or capitated plans, like HMOs and other managed-care plans, were compared to patients in fee-for-service arrangements, in which the therapist bills the patient or insurance carrier for each treatment episode. At the end of two years, patients in the prepaid or HMO-type arrangements had gotten worse. They were much more likely to receive medication immediately, then a few visits, then little follow-up. While this argues strongly against "medication alone" treatment, the distressing finding in the research was that patients in the fee-for-service plans improved only slightly; they were much more likely not to have medication but to have many treatment episodes. Kramer rightly asks, How do we plan for the combination of careful pharmacotherapy and respectful psychotherapy that we know to be effective? At this point in the development of the American health care system, the patient is way out on a limb. I have some suggestions for how to cope with this mess and get the help you need.

Psychotherapy

Psychotherapy is the process of talking out one's problems to a trained professional. There are many ways of conducting psychotherapy, but all depend on an open, trusting relationship. For some patients, the opportunity to disclose to the therapist all the guilt and shame accompanying depression without being judged is enough to start recovery. For others, the therapist will need to provide guidance in such areas as assertiveness, communication skills, setting realistic goals, relaxation, and stress management, which are problems that commonly interfere with recovery from depression.

Good psychotherapy can be provided by a psychiatrist (an MD specializing in mental disorders), a psychologist (Ph.D.), a clinical social worker (MSW), a psychiatric nurse, pastoral counselor, or substance abuse counselor. But the fact is that someone with no qualifications at all can hang out a shingle calling himself a "therapist" or "counselor"—these are terms that are not legally defined or regulated. When you call a therapist or see someone for the first time, ask directly about the individual's professional background and training. Ask if he or she is recognized as reimbursable by health insurance—if not, consider finding someone else. Finding someone you trust and can feel comfortable with is most important—you should feel free to shop around. You should ask about the therapist's background, training, and experience with depression. And if after a few sessions you have any doubts or don't feel you're getting anywhere, tell your therapist about it and get a consultation with someone else. New research reemphasizes the old observation that the emotional connection between patient and therapist may be the most important variable in effective treatment.[2] Because medications can be so effective for depression now, their use should be strongly considered along with psychotherapy. Nowadays a good therapist should be associated with a psychiatrist who can prescribe needed medications.

Psychotherapy for depression need not take a long time. Two short-term approaches that have been reliably demonstrated to be effective with depression are cognitive therapy and interpersonal therapy. Cognitive therapy, based on the work of Aaron Beck,[3] identifies a person's distorted thinking habits and recasts them in a more accurate light. For instance, "If my husband gets mad at me, that means he doesn't love me, and I can't live without his love," becomes "If he gets mad at me, that's unpleas-

ant but expected; he can be angry and still care about me."
Interpersonal therapy, developed by Gerald Klerman and Myrna
Weissman,[4] focuses on communication skills: learning to interpret accurately what others are saying to you (instead of assuming you know), and learning to voice your feelings, desires, and
needs effectively. Many experienced therapists will use techniques from cognitive and interpersonal therapies as needed by
the individual.

Patients who request literature on depression from NIMH or
other sources will often find cognitive or interpersonal therapy
cited as the treatment of choice for depression. These approaches have achieved this recognition because they have been
demonstrated, in experiments with all proper scientific controls,
to be effective, at least as effective as medication. But the reason
why they can be proved effective like this is that they have been
elaborated to such a concrete level that one therapist's cognitive
therapy is much like another therapist's cognitive therapy. This
is not the case in most kinds of psychotherapy, where the personality of the therapist is such an important factor. This puts
cognitive and interpersonal therapy at a distinct advantage in the
research, just because there is so little variability; you are evaluating the effectiveness of a set of techniques, not an art. Experienced therapists sometimes denigrate these approaches as
"cookbook" methods because they leave little room for creativity.
But with a cookbook, if you set out to make a cake, you get a
pretty good cake every time.

If I were depressed and seeking a therapist I would consider
the following factors:

1. My gut reactions—Is this someone I feel that I can like
   and trust? Do I feel at ease? Do I have any reserva-
   tions? Psychotherapy is the one chance we get in mod-
   ern life to tell the absolute truth about ourselves. Is this
   person someone I feel can bear that responsibility?
2. References. Talk to friends, your minister, your doctor.

A casual professional relationship isn't a good reference. You want to talk to someone who knows the therapist well—former patients are best.

3. The therapist's experience with depressed patients, including but not limited to familiarity with cognitive and interpersonal techniques.

4. The therapist's openness to medication as part of treatment.

5. The therapist's willingness to be active and directive when it's called for, not to assume that listening is curative in itself, or that the patient's needs for advice or reassurance are infantile and should be ignored.

These last three factors are things you should definitely ask directly of the therapist. We are not gods, though some of us think so, and we will not be offended by direct questions. If you find a therapist who is offended, go find another therapist. As a matter of fact, it's best if you can see two or three people for an initial consultation and choose the one you feel can be most helpful. This is a much more important decision than buying a new car, and we should put at least as much energy and time into selecting a therapist as we do which make and model car we want. Feel free to take a few therapists for a test drive.

None of this is so easy to do in the age of managed care. Many insurance plans will permit you to see only a small number of therapists who are affiliated with the plan. However, if you go to the trouble of checking out those therapists and aren't satisfied, many insurers will then allow you to go to someone who is not in the plan. You should also investigate whether there is a nonprofit clinic or community mental health center in your area, which will probably charge on a sliding scale adjusted to your income, and will probably also let you see different therapists on the staff until you find someone you can connect with. Finally, you should (if you can) consider paying the full cost out of pocket. This not only allows you the greatest freedom of choice, it offers you the most privacy. Managed care plans are accumulating unconscionable amounts of confidential material on their members; therapists have to submit detailed assessments and reports as part of the reimbursement contract. Since effective therapy for depression can be brief, paying your own way may cost you less than a thousand dollars. You can't even get a used car for that kind of money anymore—small price to pay for real help with your distress.

Medical Treatment

When I suggest to new patients that they consider antidepressant medication, I get a picture of all the misconceptions people have about what these medications do. First of all, they are not happy pills; they don't artificially induce a feeling of bliss, euphoria, or unrealistic well-being. No medication can do that, except for alcohol and some illegal drugs, and their effects don't last. Nor do antidepressants insulate you from life, make you not care about important things, or make you insensitive to pain or loss. Tranquilizers can do that, for a while, but antidepressants can't. Also, antidepressants aren't addictive, nor does their effect diminish so that you will have to increase your dosage later on. What antidepressants do is somehow prevent us from sliding down the chute into the blackest depths of depression when something bad happens. We still can feel hurt, pain, worry, but we feel these the way normal people do, without depression. They also can help us sleep better, give us more energy, and increase our ability to concentrate. They seem to help us change our perspective or sense of proportion, so that we can appreciate better the good side of life and not be overwhelmed by the negative.

The way antidepressants work is interesting. There are two chemicals, serotonin and norepinephrine, that have to do with the transmission of impulses between nerve cells in the brain and seem to be associated with depression. It seems as if depressed people use up these chemicals more quickly than other people. Antidepressants help to maintain them at more stable levels in the synapses, apparently leading to feelings of reduced anxiety; more security; and increased self-worth, assertiveness, and resilience.

There is one major drawback to all antidepressants: there is no evidence that their use can prevent future episodes of depression. It is almost as if we use them as we use an antipyretic—something to reduce the symptoms while the fever runs its natural course. When we recover and go off the medication, we remain as susceptible to future episodes of depression as if we were never treated. That is why many people choose never to stop taking medication. But that is also the point of this book—that you can change your emotional, cognitive, and relational habits to make yourself less susceptible to depression in the future.

The older medications include tricyclics, MAOIs, and lithium. Newer medications include heterocyclics and Prozac and related drugs.

Tricyclics

Until recently, tricyclics were the standard treatment for simple depression. These medications include imipramine (Tofranil), amitriptiline (Elavil), Vivactil, Norpramin, Pamelor, and Sinequan. These are all related to antihistamines, and in fact if you take Benadryl with one of these, you may really dry up. They were derived from the serendipitous finding that tubercular patients treated with antihistaminic compounds sometimes became unexplainedly cheerful. In common use today, 40 to 70 percent of depressed patients improve substantially with tricyclics. But although they are really quite effective medications, there are several drawbacks to their use. They usually take several weeks of faithful administration to be effective, which is difficult to tolerate when patients are feeling in real distress. Also it is relatively easy to take a fatal overdose—a few weeks' supply—so psychiatrists are in a difficult position with acutely depressed patients who may benefit from tricyclics long-term but may be given a means to self-destruction in the short term. Because tricyclics require a certain level in the bloodstream to be effective, it doesn't do any good to take one when feeling blue. Some tricyclics are rather sedating, which is a disadvantage for most people, but they can be used at bedtime for patients with difficulty sleeping. In general, tricyclics should only be used on a short-term basis (up to a year), unless the patient has a long history of severe mood disorder. They are not addictive and there is no perceived high with their use. They must be used with care with patients who have cardiovascular disease.

MAOIs

Monoamine oxidase inhibitors—Marplan, Parnate, and Nardil— are a different class of drugs and have a different action in the brain. These drugs are useful for some patients who do not respond to tricyclics. In Europe, these are generally considered the first line of treatment, preferred over tricyclics, while in the U.S., they are often resorted to only when others have failed. They have some unpleasant side effects, but the main disadvantage of MAOIs is that they may cause a stroke if certain foods containing the compound tyramine (cheese, red wine, pickles, among others) are consumed while they are being used. However, they are so effective with some people that the disadvantages are far outweighed by the relief they provide.

Lithium

Lithium is as close as psychiatry comes to a magic bullet, a specific cure for a specific disease. It is generally the treatment of choice for bipolar disorder, the cycle of manic highs with depressed lows. Lithium in the correct dose reduces by about 50 percent the chances of another manic episode within a year.

Mood swings become fewer, shorter, and less severe. The success rate for lithium treatment is 70 percent, and 20 percent of patients become symptom-free. It is generally seen as a maintenance drug—once on, the patient is on for life. Compliance is an issue for many patients, partly because they miss the manic highs that come with the disease. Side effects, including weight gain and skin rashes, also make it difficult for some patients to follow their prescription. Lithium can be toxic and must be used carefully. It should be dispensed only by a psychiatrist who is familiar with its use, not by a general practitioner. Because it can gradually build up to toxic levels, patients must have the amount of lithium in their blood checked monthly. These factors make it difficult to use lithium effectively with patients who are disorganized or impulsive, a frequent problem with bipolar disorder.

Prozac and Its Cousins

Prozac, of course, is the glamour drug of the day. It has been followed into the marketplace by many other new antidepressant medications like some close relations, Zoloft and Paxil, two near cousins, Effexor and Serzone, and some more distant cousins, notably Wellbutrin, Desyrel, and BuSpar. As opposed to tricyclics, which affect the levels of both serotonin and norepinephrine in the brain, Prozac, Zoloft, and Paxil affect only serotonin. Hence they are known as "selective serotonin reuptake inhibitors," or SSRIs, meaning that they prevent or slow down the reabsorption of serotonin. Effexor and Serzone affect both serotonin and norepinephrine, and the others have more complicated effects. All have been shown to be effective in the treatment of depression. The choice of which of these medications to use for a particular individual has much to do with their dosage and side-effect profile. Paxil, for instance, seems to have a soothing effect on anxiety that Prozac lacks. Effexor has the reputation of being more energizing than Prozac.

Prozac has acquired a mystique, making the cover of

Newsweek, currently being prescribed a million times a month. It has developed a reputation as a drug that you can take for cosmetic purposes—to make yourself feel better than usual about yourself, even if you're not depressed. "Better than well," in Peter Kramer's phrase.[5] Like Powdermilk biscuits, Prozac is reputed to give you the courage to do what needs to be done. And there have been anecdotal stories of dramatic changes in patients who were chronically depressed, people finding that after a couple of weeks on Prozac they were "the person they always thought they should be." At my clinic we haven't run across any patients yet who feel that taking Prozac makes them "better than well," but we have had a few very dramatic successes, people who have suffered severe depression for years who describe living in a new world now.

As Kramer has described so well, there are complex symptom/character questions engendered by the cosmetic use of these drugs. But since depression is so underdiagnosed, I suspect that people who think they are taking antidepressants cosmetically and feel better were, in fact, depressed to begin with. What usually happens to people is some slight positive change— an increase in energy level, a better ability to concentrate—but more definitely a reduction in negative symptoms. People still feel themselves, they feel happy or sad appropriately, but they stop sinking into the depths of depression. It's not usually a dramatic change, but more that people usually realize it's been several days since they felt as horribly depressed as they used to every day. It's as if the bottom trough of the sine wave of mood has been raised.

Another reason why Prozac and its cousins are popular is that the side effects are usually slight, compared with those of the tricyclics. Tricyclics can give you dry mouth, make you constipated, and actually slow you down, whereas Prozac has none of these problems and gives you a little more energy. However, there are some side effects with the newer antidepressants that have been somewhat underplayed. Most notable among these is a reduction of interest in sex and difficulty maintaining an erection, which many of my male patients have obstinately affirmed—after having been cautioned to go slow—on the first night after taking medication. Although the male performance problems usually go away after a few weeks, many people on SSRIs report a continued diminished interest in sex, which can certainly contribute to marital problems. In addition, for the first few days SSRIs can make you feel an increase in tension, ringing in the ears, and difficulty concentrating. And although there seems to be little risk associated with continued use of newer antidepressants, in truth they are so new that there are no reliable data on long-term use.

If these medications are so effective, can they be used to treat depression without psychotherapy? Sometimes, but there are risks associated with their use. First of all, Prozac and the other new drugs are really no more effective than the older tricyclics; their popularity is due to the lack of side effects and ease of administration. Although research has shown that some patients improve with medication alone, the same percentage usually improve with psychotherapy alone; a higher percentage improve with medication and psychotherapy in combination. And medication alone will not reduce the likelihood of future episodes, whereas the lessons learned through good psychotherapy may very well help the depressive avoid falling back into depressogenic behavior. Eli Lilly, the manufacturer of Prozac, has placed ads in the psychiatric journals decrying the overuse of Prozac as "trivializing a serious illness," suggesting that psychotherapy and close clinical monitoring are necessary parts of the treatment regime. It seems likely that Lilly is crying all the way to the bank (it made $1.2 billion from Prozac alone in 1994), staking out a sanctimonious public position at the same time as its detail men suggest Prozac to general practitioners for all kinds of ills.[6]

Why is Prozac such big news? Partly because we're in an

epidemic of depression, partly because of marketing. *Time* and other magazines now regularly have a twenty-page news magazine–style section called "Health On Track," or some other deceptive title, which has little articles about health-related topics like prostate cancer, migraine, allergies, how having pets may keep you healthy, and so on. In small type on some pages you see the words "Special Advertising Section." And you see advertisements for prescription medications for prostatitis, migraine, hay fever, and (nonprescription) dog food. I don't remember seeing advertisements for prescription medications geared to the general public until a few years ago. I don't know if such advertising was held to be illegal under FDA policy or if the manufacturers just hadn't felt this was a rewarding way to open up markets. But now advertising is clearly saying to people, if you have a symptom that bothers you, go to your doctor and ask for this medication by name. This is an expansion of the idea of illness, and the message is, if there is something that causes you discomfort or you don't like about yourself—like hair loss— don't just accept that as part of life, part of growing older. It's an illness, and it can and should be treated.

Newsweek[7] reports that most of the million prescriptions a month for Prozac are written by nonpsychiatrists. They quote a family practitioner who's giving it to her patients for PMS, and an osteopath who's giving it to his patients for back pain (both may be disguises for depression), and report many business executives taking it to make themselves less anxious, to give themselves an edge.

There is tremendous pressure on doctors to give patients a prescription. Face it, we leave disappointed if we leave the office without a scrip. Doctors can do one of three things when we present with a nonspecific symptom like headaches or depression—they can determine it may be something serious and order tests to run it down; they can determine it's not serious and treat it symptomatically; they can determine it's not serious and not treat it. When is the last time that happened to you? Bed rest, a change in diet, a change in exercise, or the counsel to adjust to the limitations of aging are not acceptable anymore. We want a pill. Most doctors will give a pill without even seriously investigating the patient's alcohol consumption, which is an underlying cause of many complaints.

Although there are some general practitioners who have informed themselves about Prozac and other antidepressants and are interested in their potential uses for things like back pain, I think most MDs who prescribe them are really insulting their patients. They've come to the conclusion that the patient's complaints have no discernible cause, and are therefore probably just "in his head," and so they're dismissing the patient. They are prescribing the current equivalent of Lydia Pinkham's tonic—it can't hurt you, and it may help you, so what's the harm? One harm is that you may have a real illness, perhaps depression but perhaps something else, that is not receiving adequate treatment. Another is that if you are depressed, and medication doesn't help on the first go-round because it's not being used correctly, your depression—and the idea that there is no help for you—is reinforced.

Regarding patients who go to their physician requesting Prozac because they want an edge, they want to feel better about themselves, it's hard for me to blame either the patient or the doctor who complies with the patient's wish. But it is very scary how much of a drug culture we live in. I do think such patients should be referred to a mental health professional who knows something about both psychotherapy and pharmacology, but I know that MDs hold back from making such referrals. We have such awful stereotypes about emotional problems and the mental health field that the patient is likely to feel insulted. I wish mental health had one percent of the advertising budget of the drug companies to dispel some of the stereotypes about psychotherapy that scare people away.

Electroconvulsive Therapy

Electroconvulsive therapy (ECT, or "shock therapy") is still used. It went out of fashion in the 1970s because it was overprescribed (also because of its image in the media, as in *One Flew Over the Cuckoo's Nest*), but it does seem to be safe and effective with some patients who are seriously or dangerously depressed, especially those who are agitated and confused. It can dramatically stop an episode of intense, suicidal depression, and there's no doubt that it saves lives this way.

I have some concerns about some of the recent literature on depression that comes out of NIMH and the medical establishment, in which ECT is discussed sometimes as a third alternative to psychotherapy and medication. I know one purpose is to remove the stigma and fear, to make ECT more acceptable to patients who really need it. But I also can't help thinking that this is an effort to market what should be a procedure of last resort as something that the public should accept without question. I'm afraid that the effort will backfire, that people will avoid treatment for depression if they think that ECT is a common alternative. No one should be considering ECT for you until other treatments have failed or unless you're suicidally out of control.

Self-Help

At this point there is no organized effort to provide self-help for people with depression. There is no AA and no group like CancerVive (for victims of cancer) or Red Hot Mamas (menopause). There are some very good books available, both in the inspirational/codependency line and in the disease/cognitive framework (Recommended Reading, page 344). Many mental health centers and hospitals either have professionally led depression groups or lend space to self-help groups. Organizations like the National Alliance for the Mentally Ill, which has a chapter in every state, maintain lists of groups. Their address, along with those of other national organizations that provide information and advocacy about depression, is given in Appendix A. For those who have access to the Internet, the newsgroup alt.support.depression provides the opportunity to talk and exchange information with fellow sufferers on-line. Web pages like Wing of Madness (http://members.aol.com/depress), Alt.Support.DepressionFAQ (http://stripe.colorado.edu/~judy/depression/asdfaq.html), and Dr. Ivan's Depression Central (http:/www.psycom.net/depression.central.html) provide useful and interesting information, but like everything on the Web, all are uncensored and contain bad advice as well as good.

Without a specific self-help program for depression, many depressed people find tremendous help in groups that are not specifically about depression, such as AA, Al-Anon, those for sexual abuse victims, and gender issues groups.

The fact that there is no organized self-help movement for depression is really quite remarkable in these days when you can find self-help groups for everyone from victims of Satanic ritual abuse to the death of a pet. The fact that more and more people are getting only minimal psychotherapy, or medication prescribed by their general practitioner, certainly makes it seem as if the need is there. Perhaps the nature of the illness makes it difficult to believe that much help can come from other sufferers. But I've been using the principles described in this book in a group in my clinic in which I am both a member and the convenor. I take responsibility for presenting some helpful material in every meeting but it's not group therapy. The same responsibility could be shared by other group members. The same type of group could be run in other settings, without professional help or with only a professional adviser for backup.

We've found that the experience of dealing with depression in a self-help context is very positive. We've also found that the model and structure of AA are very useful for depression. Depression is a disease the way alcoholism is a disease—recovery comes only from a change in behavior. But alcoholics know that mere abstinence is not the cure; the cure comes from "living the program"—applying the principles of the AA philosophy consciously and deliberately. Alcoholics know that drinking—and the habits of denial, rationalization, and manipulation that accompany drinking—changes their personality. But they also know that they can change themselves again by living the program.

Depression also changes us. The skills that we develop with depression in a vain effort to save ourselves pain—skills like emotional control, isolation, putting others first, being over-responsible—prevent our recovery. Our group meetings start with sharing; each of us having been depressed, we know the power of words to heal and to hurt, and we practice acceptance and support. At the same time, we know that we have to integrate the principles of recovery from depression; so we encourage each other to experience feelings, to practice assertive behavior, to pursue self-expression and creativity, and to challenge depressogenic assumptions.

A dry drunk is someone who has stopped drinking but still thinks and acts like an alcoholic. They live in constant fear because their sobriety is shaky and they're just going through the motions of life. There are a lot of people with depression who have been helped a little bit by medication or psychotherapy, but they still think, act, and feel like a depressive. They too are always in danger of relapse and always anxious because they know they don't know how to live. This book doesn't teach people how to live any more than AA does, but it presents a program that will help them discover it for themselves.

Starting a self-help group for depression is really not as intimidating as it sounds. Churches will donate space, mental health centers will help spread the word. All you really have to do is distribute some flyers and make up the agenda for the first meeting. After the first meeting, group members should come up with their own agenda, which might include some time for sharing problems and experiences, educational programs on topics of interest, sharing of activities, and advocacy. Basic rules should include respect for members' confidentiality, a prohibition against criticism, an encouragement but not a requirement to share. Other useful resources are *The Depression Workbook*, by Mary Ellen Copeland,[8] and *The Feeling Good Handbook*, by David Burns.[9] Both have many exercises helpful in recovery that can easily be adapted to serve as exercises for a group.

Family Support

Living with someone who's depressed can be one of the most frustrating experiences there is. We want to help the sufferer, but we don't know how; often it seems that whatever we do makes it worse. Sometimes we get angry at the depressed person, but feel guilty afterward. So many of the interpersonal habits of depression are self-defeating: socially, depressed people have an intense need for love and acceptance, but are unable to reciprocate in a way that reinforces others. Their tone of desperation or self-sacrifice may turn people off. They may be acutely uncomfortable in social situations because of the intensity of their need for acceptance but their persistent expectation of rejection.

The depressed person often has little energy left over to think about others, so may appear overly self-absorbed, often with a host of minor physical complaints. Their problems don't respond to good advice or common sense. Then they may change, feel guilty about their self-absorption, and try too hard to undo, or relentlessly seek reassurance or forgiveness. Sometimes the sufferer ruminates about his past and is filled with remorse and guilt over what may be trivial incidents, and he hopes for some sort of magical solution to his current plight.

Anger seems to accompany depressed people like a dark cloud overhead. Sometimes they feel it themselves; they may feel that life isn't fair, they may feel bitterly that they've been deprived of something they deserve. Or they make others around them angry with their self-pity and pouting. Typically others may experience anger but refrain from expressing it out of fear of hurting the victim.

Clearly, people like this can be very difficult to live with. Something that can be of immense help to a friend or loved one is *to get an accurate diagnosis.* It's much easier to put up with difficult behavior from someone we love if we understand that he or she is in the grip of a major illness and not provoking us deliberately. Depression is an illness; it can develop very gradually or very quickly; it can come in response to life events or as a result of changes in body chemistry; it can strike anyone regardless of age or sex, wealth or poverty; but it is an illness and it can be cured.

It's important to remember that depression is not an emotion, but a defense against emotions. The depressed person is keeping a lot of feeling bottled up inside. He generally expects that no one will understand him. It helps lift the depression to express the feelings. For loved ones and family members, those feelings may be unpleasant to hear. He may be angry at us for no good reason that we can see or he may be consumed by guilt over seemingly trivial incidents. He may be very fearful or very self-centered. If this is someone we love and respect, we don't want to hear these things, but it is important that the depressed person learn that honest emotions don't drive people away.

The depressed person needs understanding, patience, and acceptance from those close to him. As friends or relatives, we may feel uncomfortable around the sufferer; we want to tell them to snap out of it, we want to give them good advice, we want to tell them how we handled similar situations. This just makes the depressive feel worse by reinforcing his feeling of inadequacy. We need to listen to our friend with care and concern. My group put together a fine list of how their loved ones can help:

1. Try to be considerate, thoughtful, and empathic. If your spouse had a broken leg, you would expect that their abilities and energy would be restricted, that they would be in pain at times, and that they can't heal themselves more quickly just because you want them to. Think about depression the same way.

2. Don't be provocative. Every relationship has the little hot buttons that can start a fight at any time. Dirty socks on the floor, the remote control misplaced, the car low on gas. You know what your partner's buttons are. Don't push them while he/she is in a depressed state.

3. Small acts of kindness are appreciated, and do help, even if the recipient doesn't reciprocate. When I retreat to bed, my wife makes a point of breaking in to kiss me good night. Even though I often don't act very glad to see her, I would feel worse, lonely and unloved, without her attention.

4. Easing your partner's burden in small ways can help a great deal. Offer to do the shopping, empty the garbage, do the laundry, take the kids out for pizza. It communicates more than words the feeling that you understand how difficult these mundane chores can seem at times.

5. "Advance directives" can be a contract loved ones arrange while the sufferer is not depressed, describing what to do when depression sets in. It can be in stages:

stage 1, leave me alone; stage 2, be kind, patient, and attentive; stage 3, insist I call my therapist; stage 4, take me to the hospital. One patient loses her ability to see color when depression sets in. From experience, she has learned to let her husband know when this happens, because she won't let him know when it gets worse.

6. Take the trouble to educate yourself. Learn all you can about depression. Be willing to talk to your friend's therapist. It's amazing how seeing it in print or hearing it from an authority can change your perspective. Even if you believe you understand that depression is a disease, that the patient doesn't choose to be depressed, and so forth, you need all the education you can get. These are facts we don't want to believe. Learning the facts helps you help your friend, and also shows that you care enough to take some trouble.

I have to say that I don't believe members of my own profession have been very helpful to family members. Though occasionally there are family meetings when a patient is hospitalized, there is a long tradition against involving family members in outpatient treatment. Typically, this is seen as a protection for the patient's privacy: the patient is a competent adult who chose to consult me on his own; if I were to talk directly to family members about his condition or treatment that would be infantilizing him, undermining his competence. But of course the patient can voluntarily give up his right to privacy; therapists rarely ask, "It seems like your parent/spouse/child is having a lot of trouble understanding what you are going through. Do you think it would help if he/she came to one of your sessions? Perhaps I could explain something about depression as a disease, and we could work together on communication between you." Nothing goes on behind the patient's back, no one is undermined. By assuming that the family member is willing to help but just doesn't understand, we model for our client the principles of effective treatment and recovery we espouse: that we are responsible for making ourselves understood, that there are communication skills that can increase understanding, that we shouldn't assume we know how others feel.

Part 3

Putting the Skills to Work

1 2

Self and Society

I HAVE BEEN suggesting that depression is a disease that affects the whole self, body, mind, and spirit, and that people need to recover by a deliberate process of acquiring new skills. These skills—abilities or habits would be equally effective terms—of feeling, thinking, doing, interacting with others, and reflecting on our selves—must be consciously practiced. Though we have the fantasy that depression is something that has been laid on us from outside, to be removed by the magic of psychotherapy or a pill, that is a fantasy we must abandon. One effect of that fantasy is that it makes us feel that deliberate attempts to change ourselves are artificial or unnatural. Though we may feel awkward and self-conscious when we first behave differently than we are used to behaving, in fact that is how we are when we attempt anything new. Ask anyone who's been learning golf, ballroom dancing, contract bridge, or computers. After a certain amount of practice, what felt awkward becomes natural, part of the self, not to be forgotten—like riding a bicycle. In just the same way, practicing new methods of dealing with feelings, new ways of thinking, acting, relating, becomes easier and seems more natural as time goes on. Eventually we build a new, stronger, and more resilient self structure that can make us less vulnerable to depression.

In the next several chapters I want to explore the implications of these ideas about recovery from depression in the important areas in which we live our lives—work, marriage and the family, and the community. It leads us into considering some questions about the nature of happiness, accomplishment, and mental health. Now I can confess that it is only after years of running a mental health center that I've finally found a definition of "mental health" that I like. It's really not easy to define at all. In technical terms it is the opportunity to engage in responsive self-object experiences that are in tune with the changing needs of the individual through the life cycle.[1] In nontechnical terms I'd say mental health is composed of healthy self-esteem, a basic liking for one's self, which has its roots in a successful experience of being loved as an infant and owes something to the child's innate endowment and fit with parents' abilities. This affection for the self grows in two directions:

1. A wish for mastery—to have an impact on the world— coupled with a realistic sense of one's own abilities and limitations
2. The desire to gain intimacy through relationships based on caring and trust

Mental health is dependent on society; the culture must give parents the opportunity to love their children; must honor justice and fair play; must provide hope through opportunities available to all. Thus the world of work, the family, and the larger community all affect not only the current state of mind of the individual but the ability of the individual ever to achieve a state of emotional health. This idea suggests some reasons why depression is so epidemic in the U.S. today.

Depression, when considered in these terms, can be a result of failure in any area: a failure to internalize a positive self-image as a child, a frustration in the wish to have an impact in the world, an unrealistic sense of one's abilities and limitations, an inability to achieve intimacy. Understanding how marriages and families work can help us prevent depressive episodes in ourselves and our spouses and recover more quickly when they do occur. This understanding may also help us immunize our children. Understanding what we need in employment, or in the meaningful activities that take up our time instead of paid employment, can help us spend our time in ways that reinforce a positive feeling about the self. The vaccine against depression won't be found in a laboratory; it already exists in our society with its opportunities for expression and fulfillment, and in the family and human relationships with their opportunities for intimacy and generativity.

1 3

Work

NO ONE SEEMS safe from "burnout" these days. Certainly we live in stressful times. But in reality "burnout" seems to be just another term for depression. Perhaps it is a more palatable term to some because it implies that the sufferer has sacrificed himself to do a good job. But that is precisely what every depressed person I've ever known has done. Perhaps they haven't had the energy or resources to resolve the problem, but they've done their best.

Burnout can be defined as what happens when we rebel against ourselves; we can't keep on doing what we've been doing to ourselves, so we quit, usually in some dramatic, self-destructive way. I recently learned of a child protection worker who defines burnout for me. She can't keep on top of all her cases, so she puts in longer and longer hours; she doesn't talk to anyone about anything but her concerns about her clients, and then she won't listen to good advice; her coworkers and her boss tell her to go home at the end of the day, and she says "I can't, I can't, I can't." They fear she's headed for a break of some sort but feel there's nothing they can do. She's caught in a very high-stress job, feels completely overwhelmed, and is unable to accept help; she's a walking time bomb.

People can stand high-stress jobs like this only when they are selected carefully for the job and when their employers give them a lot of support. Vietnam taught the American military the importance of employee support. Unlike World War II, in which units trained, fought, and were eventually furloughed and discharged together, in Vietnam each soldier served a tour of duty as an individual, being sent as a replacement to a unit already in the field. Denied the sense of belonging to a group that had a future together, the individual soldier was much more vulnerable to the trauma of combat. Some jobs are just as obviously stressful as the soldier's—those of the police officer, the emergency room nurse, the child protection worker—while others are stressful in more subtle ways.

As we move into a more service-oriented society, more occupations exact emotional stress instead of the physical stress that comes with labor. All positions that require managing people— from salesman to bill collector to waiter to day care worker—require us to manage ourselves, to play a role. No one cares if the factory worker has a cranky day, but the day care worker can't afford to be cranky. We have to put on a front and control the expression of our true feelings. As we will see, such control must come from a conscious, thoughtful desire to do a good job, not from the assumption that our feelings themselves are unacceptable.

Learning to manage stress really means managing the anger and anxiety we feel in stressful situations. Only when these emotional by-products of stress are under control is it possible to think about facing the situation creatively.

I once had a client pull a knife on himself. He was trying to get me to call his girlfriend to ask her to come back to him, to say in effect that it was my professional opinion that he couldn't get along without her. When I refused, he calmly opened a huge knife, counted down his ribs to his heart, and pressed the point

against his chest. "I don't think you realize how serious I am,"
he said.

This was a moment of pure anxiety for me. I hadn't the vaguest
idea what to do in this situation. I knew I would be just an agent
of his manipulation if I called the girlfriend, but how could I
let him stab himself? I remembered some advice one of my
casework instructors had given our class—"When you are com-
pletely stuck, get up and go to the bathroom." I got up and left
the room, saying I had to get some consultation. I went down
the hall and told a colleague what was going on. Then our boss
walked by, and I repeated the story. My anxiety was catching,
and it took ten minutes or so of discussion before the three of
us finally decided I would have to call the girlfriend. But when
I went back to tell my client, he was gone. Deprived of an
audience, he must have begun to feel foolish holding a knife to
himself. He called me later in the day, furious at me for walking
out on him, but that was okay with me.

I got lucky. In pure panic, I remembered a mentor's advice,
and it turned out to work better than I had a right to expect.
But by disengaging myself from the anger and anxiety of the
situation, I had created the opportunity for something to happen. When we're caught up in our emotions, when we feel on
the spot, pressured to come up with the vital solution that seems
out of reach, our ability to think is just about absent. Our bodies
are full of fight-or-flight hormones, which give us extra strength
and energy. Our heart rate and blood pressure increase. Our
senses become highly attuned to the danger of the situation. All
these responses had an adaptive value when we were trying to
flee from saber-toothed tigers. But they don't help, in fact they
absolutely hinder, creative problem solving. We can't come up
with new solutions; we can only think of what is instinctual or
what we've done before in similar situations. Whatever we do,
it is just *more of the same* stuff that hasn't worked before.

A crisis is our emotional response to a very difficult situation. Burnout is what happens when we can't get out of the crisis mode.

How do we break this cycle? There are a number of ways. In general, when we're stuck in the crisis mode, we want to step back, disengage. Counting to ten is the simplest example. Taking a deep breath. Going for a walk, a drive. Talking it out with someone who is a good listener. Playing with the dog, the cat. Listening to music—music speaks to a part of our brain that is emotional in nature—if you immerse yourself in music, you forget your problems for a while. Putting it aside and sleeping on it. There really is an unconscious, and buying ourselves time to let our unconscious work on a problem can be of genuine help. From out of nowhere, during the morning's shower, comes a creative approach to solving a nagging problem.

When you find yourself stuck just doing more of the same with a problem that you can't resolve, do something instantly to break the pattern. Do anything. Smell a flower, say a prayer, take a deep breath, go to the bathroom. Think of someone you really respect. Look out the window. Sing a song. Now, in future, make a list of five of these pattern breakers you can use anywhere, and memorize the list. When you're in a crisis, you'll be so caught up in the fight-or-flight syndrome that you won't be able to remember to do any of these positive alternatives unless you really make an effort to memorize them. If you do that, when you are in crisis you can quickly turn on one of these positive interruptions.

Stuck in a stressful situation, you have only three choices: you can alter it, you can avoid it, or you can accept it. Each of these may be the best solution for a particular situation; none of them is inherently any better than the other. Western culture values action—we admire people who take action to alter their predicaments—and so we are conditioned to assume that altering the situation is best. Avoidance sounds shameful, and acceptance sounds passive. But there are many things in life we can't alter and others that are not worth the trouble; wisdom has to do with knowing what's worth fighting about. Caught in the road with an eighteen-wheeler bearing down on you, don't fight about the right of way: *avoid* getting run over. We practice avoidance like this all the time but don't acknowledge it. And acceptance means just facing reality. With the stress of an illness, for example, there is no avoiding it and there's no one to fight about it with, though many people fire their doctors for giving them bad news. The point is to review your options and make a conscious decision; don't beat yourself up if you can't change an unalterable situation. Don't vacillate between making half-hearted attempts to change it and trying to accept it. Think about it: alter, avoid, accept.

If we're in a job with a temperamental, unpredictable boss, and there is no altering the situation, we may still use the other strategies. We may avoid him by learning his habits. We may confine ourselves to written communications, work with our door closed, keep a low profile at meetings. One of the best strategies for acceptance I've heard of is the "brain tumor" strategy. When we're forced to be with someone who is just insufferable, it may help to imagine that their obnoxious behavior is the result of a brain tumor. They can't help being so awful; in fact, they deserve our patience and pity, because the brain tumor is controlling them. Try looking at the person who bothers you the most at work tomorrow and telling yourself that he's yelling at you because of his brain tumor.

Making Work Rewarding

Mihaly Csikszentmihalyi, a psychologist at the University of Chicago, has spent a lifetime studying what gives us pleasure.

Using a method in which subjects carrying beepers are paged at random times during the day and asked to rate their enjoyment level and describe their activities, Csikszentmihalyi has had some surprising findings.[1]

When people were paged during times when they felt challenged and felt that they were using their skills, they were described as being in *flow*. Not surprisingly, the more time a person spent in flow, the better he felt about his experience. People in flow described themselves as feeling strong, active, creative, concentrated, and motivated.

The biggest surprise to come from this research was that flow experiences were much more frequently reported at work than at leisure. When people were paged when they were actually working at their jobs (which was only three-quarters of the time they were at their place of employment), they reported themselves in flow 54 percent of the time. At leisure, only 18 percent of responses were in flow. Most leisure responses fell into the range the researchers call apathy. People in an apathetic state were more likely to describe themselves as passive, weak, dull, and dissatisfied. Some jobs were clearly more stimulating than others, with people who have more autonomy more likely to be in flow than clerical or assembly-line workers; but clerical and assembly-line workers still reported feeling in flow more than twice as often at work as at leisure.

People in the state of flow, either at work or at leisure, reported it as a much more positive experience than not being in flow. They felt happier, more cheerful, stronger, more active, more creative, and more satisfied. These differences were very significant statistically and did not change very much across different kinds of work.

However, when people were at work, they were much more likely to report wishing they were somewhere else, even if they were in a state of flow, than if they were at leisure. "Thus we have the paradoxical situation: On the job people feel skillful and challenged, and therefore feel more happy, strong, creative, and satisfied. In their free time people feel that there is generally not much to do and their skills are not being used, and therefore they tend to feel more sad, weak, dull, and dissatisfied. Yet they would like to work less and spend more time in leisure."[2]

The reason for this paradox, however, is not hard to understand. Most of us have been conditioned to think of work as an imposition. Even if we are feeling challenged and stimulated, it is for someone else's benefit, not our own, and we tend to see the time spent at work as subtracted somehow from the time we have available to enjoy our lives. How much better off we would be if we could change our working conditions or our perceptions of work so that we felt that our time spent at work was an opportunity for happiness, for attainment of goals that were meaningful to ourselves, not merely time subtracted from our life span.

Csikszentmihalyi describes the state of flow as lying between anxiety and boredom. When we feel that we do not have the ability to meet the tasks that need to be done, we feel anxious; when we feel that what we have to do is not challenging, not stimulating, we feel bored. When we feel that the task is a mild stretch for us—that it makes use of our skills, makes us concentrate, makes us grow—we feel in flow. As our skills grow and become habitual, we need different challenges to make us feel in flow.

Csikszentmihalyi and his researchers have also attempted to determine what it is that makes some activities enjoyable, others aversive. They have found that enjoyable activities have the following factors in common:

1. Enjoyable activities—work, leisure, physical or intellectual effort—are goal-directed and have rules. They challenge us to use our skills. If we don't have the skills, they are boring or anxiety-provoking. Reading requires

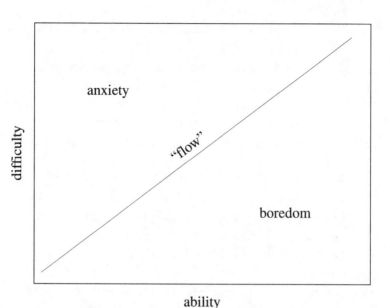

The state of "flow" as a balance between the difficulty of a task
and the ability of the individual.

a set of skills focusing on the author's technique, allowing ourselves to be swept up in the characters or plot
development, reading to learn. Watching television is a
low-involvement activity, requiring little concentration
or skill.

2. Our attention is focused on the activity, with little left
   over for other stimuli.

3. The goals are clear and well defined. Nothing is more
   demoralizing than vague or changeable rules.

4. The activity provides prompt feedback, which enables
   us to correct our behavior. Working with a patient, I
   often know immediately when I've made an error—I
   can see it on his face or hear it in his associations.
   Working with a budget or a long-range plan, I get no

feedback until we are already fully committed to its implementation.

5. There is a deep involvement that helps one forget all the unpleasant aspects of life. All the troubling thoughts that pass through our minds unbidden when we are left to ourselves are prevented from bothering us.

6. These activities give us the sense of being in control in difficult situations. This is why so many enjoyable activities involve a risk, whether it is rock climbing or performing; although there is a risk, there is the opportunity to learn very specific skills that minimize risk.

7. We lose self-consciousness; we forget about ourselves temporarily, but we finish the task feeling better about ourselves.

8. Our sense of time changes. Time may pass very quickly, as in an enthralling film or play, or very slowly, as some performers report who are focused on the minute details of their skills. The sense of freedom from ordinary clock time seems to help us feel empowered and renewed.

Whether our work involves running a drill press, managing people, or caring for children, we all have some control over how enjoyable the activity is. For instance, in many jobs—raising children comes to mind—there is little immediate positive feedback. Children and spouse don't tell you often enough what a good job you're doing, but you can expect to be told whenever anything goes wrong, even if it's completely outside your control. We have to increase positive feedback by structuring in opportunities for it and by raising our own sensitivity to it.

For example, the routine cup of coffee with a neighbor or telephone call with a grandparent that so many mothers build into their day is an opportunity to be reminded, perhaps in indirect but important ways, that the job of child-rearing is significant and meaningful and that you're doing a pretty good job at it. Spouses may need reminding directly that parents stuck at home with small children all day need confirmation and validation. Though in marriage counseling we often hear, "If I have to ask for his attention, it doesn't mean anything when he gives it," in fact it is still meaningful and it's possible to structure reminders—like a fixed time together after dinner to discuss the day—that reduce the necessity of having to ask.

Raising our own awareness of positive feedback, examining our definition of what is an accomplishment, is another strategy. A few minutes of quiet reading time with a fractious child is a major accomplishment, not only because it's difficult to achieve, but because it may be the one good thing that's happened in the child's life that day, and it may add significantly to his ability to control his own moods in the future. The assembly-line or clerical worker who monitors her own performance and can feel good about herself for a productive day is likely to be happier than her coworker who works grudgingly. Of course it helps if management is enlightened enough to actually reward employees for helping to make a good product.

Another way of enhancing enjoyment on the job is by seeking out opportunities to learn and use new skills. The parent at home with children may find time to practice cooking or recreational skills that both occupy the children and are intrinsically rewarding. There is always a better way to do the job at hand, or ways to train oneself to do a more challenging job.

At this point, I can hear my depressed patients: "This is all easy for you to say. But when you're down, it's impossible to look at life as a series of opportunities for growth and challenge. When you're down, life just seems like a whole series of tests that you're doomed to fail. It's just about impossible to get up the energy to even try."

This is true, and I hope that by emphasizing the positive I don't add to anyone's depression. This section is meant for those who are coming out of depression, who are looking for ways to make sure that they don't return to old bad habits in the future. People who are really depressed can't use this kind of advice yet. They need time to recover, they need understanding, medication, support, psychotherapy, whatever it takes to get themselves out of the pits.

It's also true that, much to our collective shame, there are far too many people who will never have the opportunity to engage in meaningful work—because of discrimination, because of the failure of our educational system, because we have changed from a producer society to a consumer society, because of individual bad luck. Those of us who have the chance to do anything with ourselves that is at all meaningful and stimulating should thank our lucky stars.

The hard truth is, we either grow or die, challenge ourselves or stagnate. Growth and change are hard work. Depressed people—all of us—want an amulet, Prince Charming in a pill, some charm or trick or secret that means we will never be unhappy again. This wish is a holdover from our childhood, when we had the illusion that the magic of parental love could protect us from all harm. It *is* an illusion.

One of the great truths is that life is difficult, says Scott Peck.[3] Accepting that it *is* difficult, that this is the normal state of affairs, and that it never will be otherwise allows us to transcend its difficulty. Giving up the wish for the magic charm means giving up the resentment, anger, and bitterness that go with wishing for what we will never have.

14

Love

AS THE MENTAL health professions work more with families, parents, and children, we learn fascinating things about what leads one family to divorce, another to a successful and stable marriage. Considering what leads to "falling in love" may be unromantic but quite useful in understanding how to make marriages work better.

There are unconscious factors in falling in love, in why two particular people decide to marry each other out of all the people in the world, which can have repercussions later on in various stages in the family life cycle in terms of marital conflict, children with emotional problems, or adolescents in rebellion. People who are in Alcoholics Anonymous, Al-Anon, and the recovery movement have faced this unpleasant truth, and out of it comes the whole concept of codependency. I choose to marry you so that I can take care of you, so that I can rescue you, so that you can rescue me, and so on ad infinitum. But the issue is much larger than substance abuse and codependency. Falling in love, by definition, is a crazy process; it's completely out of conscious control. Who I fall in love with, no matter how normal or well functioning I am, is determined by my particular psychological needs at the time I'm ready to enter a relationship.

Those needs have to get addressed somehow in the relationship, or it will never work.

What we see in practice is that families in trouble often present themselves to clinics with an "identified patient"—the depressed mom, the alcoholic dad, the symptomatic child, or the acting-out adolescent—whom the rest of them want fixed. But the assigning of that role to someone in the family has its roots in the unconscious needs of the couple at the time they got together, the reasons why they chose each other out of all the other people in the world. Divorce is often the result of a power struggle between the parents to define who is sick, bad, or to blame. These are all scenarios in which the marital pair has either been unable to come to terms with the needs that attracted them to each other in the first place, or else those needs have changed over time, perhaps in one partner more than another, and the relationship hasn't kept up.

There is a useful point of view that postulates—with good clinical reason—that one attraction between future spouses is that each sees the other as a way of solving his or her own self-esteem issues. The idea is that unconsciously we think, "I have this problem about myself—I feel unworthy of love, and this person loves everyone; I can't stand to make decisions, and this person will do it for me; I've been ignored and neglected, and this person will supervise me." But the catch is that too often the spouse shares the same problem, just has a different, *only apparently better,* way of dealing with it. As in a distorting mirror, we see our spouse's defensive system as the ideal solution to our problem; but the spouse, inside that suit of armor, is only too aware of its chinks and weaknesses and is looking at our armor as what he or she needs.

Sharon was an attractive woman in her thirties stuck in her third unhappy marriage. Her second husband had shot her, then killed himself, in the presence of their children, because she wanted to leave him. She recovered from her wounds but seemed remarkably uncurious about why she would have had this effect on a man.

Sharon was enormously conflicted about sexuality and needed continual reassurance that she was desirable, but in no way was she a flirt or a tease. She seemed like a wholesome, mature woman whose primary concern was her children. Her third husband was about ten years older, very attractive in a hypermasculine way (given to leather jackets, cowboy boots, and big belt buckles), apparently very self-confident about the issues that she was so conflicted about.

I worked with Sharon for about a year, and we couldn't seem to get anywhere. She wanted to leave her husband—he didn't like her children or treat them well, he continually tried to force her to choose him over them, making her feel like a prize in a contest. But she didn't leave; he kept charming her, seducing her, and she would come in for our session feeling guilty and ashamed. Then one day she appeared after having had a couple of drinks, and she said, "This couldn't possibly have anything to do with anything, but you ought to know . . ." and revealed incest by her brother when she was thirteen. We went from there into deeper memories of her childhood—her feelings about her mother being blind to her, her attention to minor defects in her physical appearance, her wish for plastic surgery—as expressions of the feeling of being damaged, shameful, and unlovable from childhood.

Finally, after she'd worked through some of the guilt about the incest and the anger at her mother, and started to feel better about herself, she started to see her husband objectively. She began to wonder: If he's so confident, why does he get jealous when I give my children attention? If he's so self-assured, why does he need to flirt with every woman in sight? Why does he need this kind of reassurance? This man, who had been some kind of magical, mystical Svengali, became suddenly in her eyes

pathetic, vain, needy. She realized, "Every man I've ever mar-
ried, I thought was strong. It's always turned out that I've been
the stronger one."

Every marriage faces a crisis of disappointment, when one or
both partners realize that the spouse is not able to help solve
one's own neurotic problems. Sharon's second husband tried to
kill her when she attempted to disengage from him. In her third
marriage, she finally realized that her search for a strong yet
seductive man represented a problem she had to solve for
herself. In stable marriages, these crises reoccur throughout the
life cycle of the family, as people deal with different developmental issues, but let's focus on the initial crisis.

Say I'm mildly depressed. I'm ill at ease in social situations, I
have poor self-esteem, I'm socially restricted because I worry
constantly about whether people approve of me. I marry someone who looks as if she has all the self-confidence in the world.
A few years later I realize that she looks this way because she's
really rigid, compulsive, and afraid of people—or perhaps I don't
see this, but she gets sick, becomes weak and needy, and I can't
stand it. What attracted us to each other was a defense—a
different defense, but against the same conflict. Likewise she
realizes that, though she saw me as the strong silent type, my
silence comes from anxiety rather than strength. What once
were virtues now are defects. It's as if we have a new set of eyes,
and the things that once attracted us to our mate, we now see
as weak, needy, controlling, interfering. Instead of loving those
qualities, we hate them. We de-idealize each other; that initial
stage of being "in love" is gone.

This is when relationships become work. But let there be
no mistake: no good relationship survives without conscious
effort from both parties concerned; and it is the "work" of relationships that leads to our most meaningful opportunities for

self-exploration and self-expression. In doing this work, we strengthen our selves so that we become less vulnerable to depression.

At the same time, there is no doubt in my mind that the most stable relationships still have a foundation in the "head over heels in love" state of idealization that began the relationship. Even after fifty years, relationships are based on affection and caring, basically irrational processes that make us tend to see our partner's best qualities and tactfully gloss over the worst. There is more than a vestige of the unconditional acceptance of parental love. Knowing that we are loved in spite of everything we hate about ourselves can be powerful medicine.

Male-Female Communication

An important way of understanding the difficulties men and women have in expressing their love comes from the study of how the sexes communicate. In Deborah Tannen's book *You Just Don't Understand*[1] she explores the thesis that men and women speak different languages, or at least use language in entirely different ways for different purposes. This confusion in language, she asserts, accounts for a great deal of the conflict that goes on in male-female relationships, not only in marriage, but in the business world, the professions, the playground, in all areas where males and females interact. You know that you're getting your message across when you become the object of satire. Tannen's point of view was skewered in the movie *White Men Can't Jump*, in which a female character gets angry at her boyfriend for bringing her a glass of water when she says she's thirsty. She says, in essence, that's the trouble with men; they always want to fix things and gloss over feelings. What she was asking for, she says, was understanding and support: "I understand; I know what it is like to feel thirst." Despite the ridicule, and despite the fact that this line of thinking can quickly be carried to extremes, Tannen has a perspective that is useful in understanding how men and women deal with depression.

Tannen says, in essence, that men and women in the United States today grow up in different cultures, which reinforce their use of words for different purposes. Women use talk for inter-action, men for information. Men see the world in terms of hierarchies, and hear all communication in terms of "Who's in charge here?" Women, on the other hand, see the world as a vast network of connections, and all communication as the pur-pose of establishing connections. For men, then, communication is work; it always has something to say about status and one is constantly on guard against being put into a lower status posi-tion. But for women, communication is like breathing; it's nec-essary to keep oneself connected, to be part of the world.

Consider, for instance, the stereotyped play of children: Boys tend to play highly organized games in large groups, in which there are elaborate rules. There is always at least one leader, whose function is to make and enforce the rules, and a whole hierarchy of status positions under the leader. One of the func-tions of play, for boys, is to compete for higher status. Girls, on the other hand, tend to play games that emphasize cooperation, not competition; there are no winners and losers and all must take turns fairly. If a girl tries to push herself forward, she will get criticized for being bossy. Tannen makes some broad gener-alizations, and I'm greatly oversimplifying, but there is some truth in what she says. *Lord of the Flies* could not have been written about a group of girls isolated on an island with no adults.

Tannen gives the example of a friend of hers who is recovering from a lumpectomy. In talking with her sister and with a friend, she says how upsetting it was to have been cut into and how distressing it is now to see the stitches and see how the contour of her breast has changed. The women say words to the effect of, I know, I have felt the same way. Tannen's friend feels supported and comforted. But when she tells her husband about the same feelings, he says, "You can have plastic surgery." Whereas her friends' comments were heard as supportive, she hears her husband's comment as just the opposite. He's telling her to have more surgery just when she's telling him how miserable she feels about *this* surgery. Like the Senate Judiciary Committee, he just "doesn't get it."

So she protests, and she also assumes that he is speaking for himself; that he wants her to undergo further surgery because he doesn't like the way she looks now. But now it's she who "doesn't get it." He protests: "It doesn't bother me at all." "Then why are you telling me to have the surgery?" she asks. "Because you were saying *you* were upset about the way it looks," he says. "I was just trying to help." And she knows, based on their history together, that this is the truth. So why does she feel so bad? Tannen says that she wanted the gift of understanding, but he gave her the gift of advice.

Now I've heard this same scene played out many times over in my office between husbands and wives (also between parents and adolescents). The poor schmuck is "only trying to help," but it's not the kind of help she needs. When a man's wife or child is in pain or in trouble, he wants to fix it and make it go away. He sees this as his responsibility; he feels guilty or inadequate if he can't protect his loved ones. But often it's best for the wife or child to work things out on their own, and very often they know this. They're not asking him to fix it, they're asking for empathy, understanding, commiseration.

It gets us all into a great many difficulties. Men tend to resent commiseration. They hear it as taking away from the uniqueness of their own experience, whereas women tend to hear it as caring. Women tend to resent men's offering solutions; men don't understand why women complain and don't take action. For women, "troubles talk" is intended to strengthen relationships: "We're the same; you're not alone." What they hear from men is "We're not the same; you have the troubles, I have the solutions." Women show concern by probing, asking for more information. Men change the subject. Women see this as a failure of intimacy on the man's part. Men may see it as respecting independence. Men often refrain from giving sympathy because to them, in their hierarchical worldview, it sounds condescending. This is why, in the early stages of training, women make better therapists than men. The motto among therapists is "Follow the affect"—if a subject is obviously upsetting or disturbing to the client, ask more about it. This comes more naturally to women than to men.

Why do men hide behind the newspaper when their wives are asking for contact, recognition? This is much more than a cartoon or TV comedy situation. Even Freud was moved to ask, "What do women want?" Men are scared of women's emotional needs, and they hide. Women feel hurt and rejected. It's what leads to trouble in many marriages. According to Tannen, for many men the comfort of home means freedom from having to compete and impress through verbal display (remember, communication is work for men). They see the marital relationship as one where talk is not required. "I bring home a good paycheck, I don't cheat, I play with the kids, I work around the house. Doesn't all that prove that I love her? What more does she want?" But for women, home is the place where they feel the greatest need for talk with those whom they are closest to. The comfort of home means freedom to talk without worrying about how their talk will be judged.

If spouses are unable to talk about these differences, depression may be the result. If I continually feel that my attempts to comfort and support my wife are rejected, I feel diminished. If she feels that I'm unsympathetic and just want her to shape up, she feels diminished. We are the most important people in the world to each other. If we feel that we can't help or understand each other, that's depressing.

Marriage

A GOOD MARRIAGE is a system for ensuring the emotional well-being of the partners and the children. People who are not married don't live as long as those who are. A good marriage helps us deal with and absorb and respond to the stresses of everyday life in a much healthier way than isolated individuals can.

It's reasonable to understand one's life as a whole series of complicated maneuvers around the issue of intimacy.[1] The feeling of trusting, opening up, being close to someone, being understood, is something that we all very much want. If we are isolated, we go to great lengths to avoid feeling alone—we go to bars, we go to meetings, we go on blind dates, we go to work. At the same time, we fear intimacy as well, and when we are close to someone, we find ourselves putting barriers in the way. We drink, we watch TV, we read the paper, most of all we just don't listen or we listen in particular ways that lead to misunderstandings. This ambivalence—to be afraid of intimacy as well as to need it—seems to be a normal part of being human. What a marriage supplies is the opportunity for intimacy and, through a whole series of shared developmental tasks that the partners are forced to take on together, the opportunity to grow in the ability to trust, to be honest, to care and share. Those things are all good for us emotionally; they lead to positive mental health.

Besides the opportunity for intimacy, marriage can also supply us with someone to blame for our own unhappiness. Though each spouse brings his or her own characteristic defenses to the relationship, marriage seems to offer a special opportunity for projection to operate. Defenses are unconscious habits by which we protect ourselves against uncomfortable or unacceptable self-awareness. In projection, we take unacceptable parts of ourselves and attribute them to others. "*You're* awfully grouchy this morning." Projection can get institutionalized in the marriage so that the couple play roles that they've assigned to each other that are more or less mutually acceptable: the weak one, the strong one, the one who can't make decisions, the detail person. It can also be the fuel for divorce: "It's not my fault, it's your fault, that I'm unhappy, unsuccessful . . . " (fill in the blank).

How to Fight Fair

You never want to say to a marriage counselor that you have a marriage in which there are no arguments. We will lift both eyebrows at how naive you are—with good reason. We have all heard from abandoned wives or husbands who can't understand why their spouse left them without warning—"We had a *perfect* marriage; we *never* fought." What they are saying is that they had a relationship in which disagreement was not permitted and there was no way to resolve conflict—and that contravenes human nature. We all have different wants and needs that are going to come into conflict. It's an inevitable part of being human. In these marriages, disagreement was so taboo that one spouse had to leave rather than express it.

A good fight is healthy for a relationship. It solves problems, clears the air, reinforces communication skills, provides objectivity and insight into one's own behavior (sometimes more than one wishes for), enhances self-esteem, and reinforces the value of the spouse. Good fights, paradoxically, are expressions of caring. We don't argue with people whose feelings and opinions are unimportant to us. Unfortunately, most fights are bad ones, destructive fights that only damage the relationship, hurt each partner, and cement uncomfortable positions.

There are several rules for good fighting, which I've learned painfully over the years:

1. No "kitchen sink" arguments, in which one grievance leads to another and you find yourselves dredging up all the dreck from years of unresolved arguments. Stick to the subject at hand. If you find yourself thinking about old grievances, bring them up when you have set aside some time to work on your relationship.

2. Use "I statements." "I think" or "I feel" rather than "You should" or "You shouldn't." Don't try to control your partner's behavior; rather, make your reactions part of the shared agenda the two of you must address.

3. Never say "never" (or "always"). As in "You never think about me," or "You always put yourself first." Avoid generalizations. They are inherently unfair and can't be answered; they only put your partner on the defensive. If something is bothering you, be specific and concrete.

4. Listen, no matter how painful it is. Try repeating what your partner said, just to make sure you heard it right. Try never to lose sight of the fact that this is someone who might tell you an important truth about yourself.

5. Be assertive, not aggressive. Be very specific about what you want, what's bothering you, how you'd like things to change. Be prepared to say what you'll do if things don't change (but don't go out on a limb in the heat of the moment). Do not threaten, nag, or intimidate. Do not call names or make judgmental statements. Cruelty is never acceptable and almost unforgivable.

237

6. Never get physical. If you don't think you can control yourself, or if you think your partner might lose control, get out. Go for a walk, not a drive.

7. Don't fight when drunk. Better yet, don't get drunk. But even one glass of wine can impair your judgment enough that you might say something you'll regret.

8. Before you open your mouth, be sure that what's bothering you is really something your spouse is responsible for. Most fights have to do with feeling diminished in self-esteem, wounded somehow, and sorry for oneself. Sometimes we don't even realize this until we find ourselves angry at our partner over some little thing. But think about whether this little thing is really responsible for the way you're feeling.

9. For the children's sake—don't fight in front of them. Save it for when you're alone together. If you feel that it can't wait, you're too angry and need to cool down some anyway.

10. Always have a way out. One couple I know found they could not stop fighting before things got ugly. They developed a "surrender hat." They found an old hat and kept it handy. When they started fighting, either one of them could put the hat on anytime. The hat meant, "We have to stop now. I'm getting too upset to feel safe with myself or with you—or I'm just frustrated because we're going around in circles."

Depressed people have trouble with these rules. They tend not to be assertive, and they tend to store up grievances until they burst forth in an explosion of accusations and generalizations. It's important for the depressive to understand that what feels natural (like stuffing feelings) is in fact a bad emotional habit that has to be unlearned. We don't blame ourselves if we don't know how to fix a car or a computer when we've never learned the skills; likewise we have to face the simple fact that there are skills to life and relationships that make things go a lot better. These are skills that are not taught in school and probably weren't taught at home. Our ignorance of these skills is nothing to be ashamed of, but if we know they are there and refuse to learn, we have only ourselves to blame for what happens to us.

Responses to the End of the Honeymoon

When we wake up in the morning and realize that our bed mate snores, and has bad breath, and gets on our nerves, and we're committed to him or her for life—when we realize that we've fallen out of "love"—we can do three things: we can let the relationship stagnate; we can seek a divorce; or we can get to work.

1. The first alternative is that we can come to a number of more or less stable adaptations to the situation, which outsiders see as unhappy marriages or troubled families. Couples can be

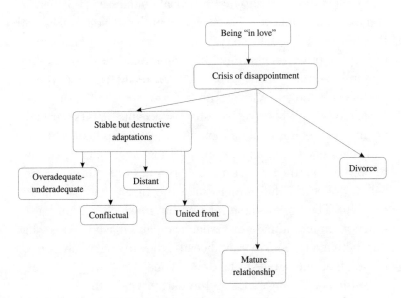

Responses to falling out of love

miserable together for a lifetime, and these marriages can be remarkably resistant to change. Each partner gets a lot out of maintaining the status quo, though each alone will complain endlessly about the other. Some of these scenarios are so familiar that family therapists have developed typologies of stable but destructive marriages we are familiar with.

One is the *overadequate-underadequate* marriage, in which one partner looks disturbed or sick while the other one takes care of him or her. The sickness may be a physical illness or an addiction or a psychophysiological condition. The caretaker, the overadequate one, gets exasperated with the spouse's disturbance but is not willing to do anything to remedy the situation. Codependency is a subtype of this kind of relationship. Frequently when the "sick" one gets better, it's very upsetting to the whole relationship. Many alcoholics attain sobriety only to have their spouses leave them; the hypothesis being that the spouse was getting something out of taking care of an alcoholic. But many phobic or sexually dysfunctional couples are this way. If you talk to a couple who have a sexual problem, you usually find that they've defined it in a way that assigns the responsibility to one or the other—she's frigid, he's impotent. But if you explore in depth, you find that maybe she's not really frigid, maybe he just doesn't know how to arouse her; and she is either afraid to explain or so self-blaming that she just accepts that it's her fault. Or maybe he's not really impotent, he's just impotent with her, and that's got something to do with how angry she is, or how remote or unattractive she makes herself; but in this case, he's willing to be the fall guy, to take the blame and say it's his problem. They get a stable relationship in which neither has to function on an intimate or sexual level, and maybe this is what they both really seem to want, because they're both really scared; it's just that one agrees to take the blame.

In the *conflictual* marriage the partners take turns trying to make the spouse take the underadequate role, to blame the other for the self's unhappiness. The same projection processes are going on, but the spouse refuses to accept the projection. They spend most of their time blaming each other for their own misery. This can be quite a stable system because the payoff for each is that they don't have to take responsibility for themselves. When I worked with one couple like this I ended up with a severe headache after every session. I couldn't imagine saying the kinds of things they said to each other. I had to get up and leave the room or blow my police whistle to get them to listen to me, when ostensibly they were consulting me for help. The agenda for couples like this in marital treatment is to get the therapist to agree with them that it's all the other guy's fault, that it's the other guy who has to change; and of course we won't do this. You have to separate them, get them each working on themselves in individual treatment, in order for anything to happen. But often nothing will, because they are really very comfortable with things just as they are.

A third type of marriage is called the *distant* relationship, sometimes called emotional divorce. Here the spouses have withdrawn from real interaction with each other because they've refused to accept either blame or responsibility. They may medicate or sedate themselves somehow, they may watch a lot of TV, they may even get along well enough superficially so that everyone thinks everything is okay. In *Ordinary People,* it takes the death of the older son and the breakdown of the younger for the family to realize that the mother has been cold, withdrawn, and angry for years. The father doesn't realize this; he thinks things are normal until he realizes she hates their son and doesn't really care much for him. When people are in a stable relationship like this, they don't deal with the reality of each other, they just go on forever silently blaming the other for their own unhappiness.

A fourth scenario is the *united front* family, in which the spouses have stopped blaming each other and focused their energies on someone outside the marital system, frequently a child. A common script is that both parents are conflicted about sexuality. They have a distant, unsatisfactory sexual relationship but neither will discuss it with the other because each is afraid. As the female child in the family approaches adolescence, mother begins to worry too much about how her daughter is going to express herself sexually. Daughter picks up that something anxiety provoking but really fascinating is going on here. She may not understand a lot, but she does get the idea that boys are forbidden fruit. What may begin as normal adolescent sexuality gets escalated because mother, and father too, get invested in trying to control the girl. They ground her, they listen to her phone calls, they read her diary, they try to limit whom she can associate with. The family soon spends all its time worrying about the daughter's sexuality, and the parents never have to worry about their own. This sometimes results in the game Eric Berne[2] called Uproar, in which fourteen-year-old Susie announces that she's going to run off with twenty-three-year-old Johnny, who rides a big Harley and has served time in prison. It's called a game because the purpose of Susie's announcement is to get a response from her parents; otherwise she'd just do it.

You can take the same scenario we've been talking about with girls, moms, and sex, and apply it to boys, dads, and aggression. The harder the family tries to control the kid, the more his antisocial behavior escalates; but we speculate that the kid is accurately reading the double messages he's getting; his aggressive behavior serves a purpose for the family.

2. The second response to this crisis of disappointment, when spouses realize that their partners do not really possess the idealized curative powers we thought at first, is, of course, divorce. Divorce is so intertwined with depression and so much a factor in society's problems today that I've given the subject its

own chapter. Here, let's focus on divorce briefly as a response to the failure of spouses to be perfect self-objects for each other.

Sometimes divorces are justified. Sometimes couples can honestly and realistically come to the conclusion that their differences are too great to resolve and that separation is the only answer. But what makes divorce really tragic is that usually it is a continuation of the blaming process and a continuation of the false hope that someone else will be able to solve my problems for me. Divorce becomes a battle over fixing the blame, not only over the failed marriage, but also over all the years wasted not getting on with one's own life. It's an out-of-control emotional process, the dark side of falling in love. It's a life-and-death struggle, because the one who loses is usually doomed to a life of depression.

Though occasionally mature people can agree that they've grown apart and need to go in separate directions, and occasionally there are couples who bring out the worst in each other and really need to separate, for the most part divorcing couples are fueled by anger, projection, and blame. Divorce brings out our strongest feelings of anger and rage. What's interesting is that the rage feels good. It's righteous indignation. It comes out of very basic needs to protect our own self-esteem, as a way of saying it's not my fault, it's her/his fault.

But of course it is, to some degree, our own fault. This crisis of disappointment in the spouse, which is inevitable in every marriage, and will be repeated with variations throughout the marriage, is closely related to depression. It has us feeling let down, deflated, perhaps hopeless. If we don't want to go for the quick but inadequate fix of divorce, and we don't want to get stuck in a stable but destructive marriage, what do we do?

3. The last potential response to falling out of love is the most difficult but most rewarding. If we have good communication, real affection, and are willing to own our own problems, we can

talk about our mutual disappointment, acknowledge that there is a common problem, acknowledge that some of our disappointment in the other is based on unfair expectations, and form a stronger alliance and a mutual support system out of it.

In general, in a mature, strong marriage, the spouses function as reliable self-objects for each other and minimize projection. This requires affection, attraction, patience, understanding, humor, and commitment. What defines a marriage, more than anything else, is commitment. People say "till death do us part" and mean it, hopefully. It takes that commitment to carry us over some of the disappointments that are an inevitable part of marriage. We realize that being married doesn't mean eternal bliss; it doesn't mean being free of worry, stress, sickness, or financial strain. It does mean having a partner to share these things, and the good times, with. We want to take responsibility for our own lives, for making ourselves and our partner feel as good as we can, and we want to avoid blaming. There's a great deal to be said for consciously striving to make another person happy; we never feel so good about ourselves as when we behave altruistically. We want to recognize that we can't *make* our partner happy, but we are responsible for creating the conditions in which happiness can grow.

By definition, depression means a withdrawal from intimacy into the self. Life experience, heredity, trauma, can always precipitate a depressive episode in someone who is otherwise fully engaged in a committed, intimate relationship. But true intimacy can come very close to preventing depression. If we accept that life is often difficult and that our spouse can't make us happy, but that we can help each other be happier and reduce stress in our lives by working together, we're giving ourselves and each other the opportunity to be as emotionally healthy as possible.

16

Families

AN ARTICLE in the *Family Therapy Networker*[1] describes recent changes in the field of family therapy, which has long prided itself as being avant-garde. Reviewing a groundbreaking article from thirty years ago, which focused on the father's obligation to exert authority over a mildly delinquent son by prohibiting him from smoking cigarettes, the author notes that the focus seems "sweetly antique today, when, by some estimates, 25 percent of all fourth graders have tried marijuana and 50 percent of all high school students get drunk at least once every two weeks."[2] The implication is that what used to be avant-garde has been left in the dust by social change—and the change seems to have happened while our backs were turned.

In those days family therapists used to move heaven and earth to get the whole family in to deal with what was assumed to be a family problem that was manifested only by the child. The child was assumed to be "triangulated," "the symptom-bearer," "acting out a family problem." Part of the resistance so many family therapists faced was the trouble getting father in to the office, away from work, or the bottle, or wherever he was hiding. We assumed that mother was colluding in father's avoidance, but that if we could get them together, we might be able to deal with the underlying marital problem that was usually assumed to be the hidden cause of the child's behavior.

Although there's a lot to be said for the theory, we just don't see many families like that anymore. First, the marriage has probably already ended in divorce. We have a father who is really inaccessible, or divorced parents who continue their conflict at a higher pitch of anger because the divorce has just added fuel to the fire, or step-parents who are taking a much more active role with the children. If the family is still together, chances are that both parents are working, and since the therapist and his or her own spouse are probably trying to juggle two careers and a family too, it's less fashionable to assume that the parents are merely resistant or avoidant if they can't get to the office for family therapy. And if we do get both parents in, we often find that they are truly concerned about their child's behavior, willing to look at their own part in it, willing to try to address the problems in their marriage—but they're too stressed out to do it.

In our heads we may still assume that the "normal" family is father as primary breadwinner with mother perhaps working but still available for the kids after school. After all, many of our social institutions—schools, day care, recreation programs—are still built around those assumptions. But that family is an endangered species. As we approach the end of the century, the family as we used to define it has come apart.

Parents ask therapists tougher and tougher questions, and there are no simple answers. What is good for my child? What is acceptable behavior? What is normal? We no longer have the luxury of thinking of the family as the moral center of the universe. Children and adolescents are left on their own with mass culture and the schools to guide them, and parents are playing catch-up. Therapists find themselves helping families find whatever works to get their kids grown up, rather than prescribing from ideals or standards.

Jimmy was sixteen, very bright, a misfit at the local school. He had never been popular but used his intellect and creativity to define a role for himself as a boy artist/computer nerd. At school he drew attention by arguing a strong nihilistic line, feeling that there was no point to living, and in fact let some of his acquaintances at school know that he was planning to end his life in accordance with some astronomical event. Word got back to the school counselor, who told Jimmy to drive over and see us. Mother met him at our office. Jimmy was open about his suicide plans, and in fact it didn't take much for the therapist to penetrate his intellectual facade. He was quite depressed, and no one in his family had ever noticed. We insisted on medication, and Jimmy improved a little. His suicide deadline passed without incident. Just when we were breathing a sigh of relief, Jimmy's older brother attempted suicide.

John was a nineteen-year-old young man who had just barely finished high school, despite being bright and talented. He lived in a separate suite in his parents' large house, worked around town, and did a fair amount of drugs. He got involved with a young woman who was extremely jealous of his attention to other friends. With his parents' reluctant permission, the girlfriend moved in to his room. One night, after another evening of screaming at each other, fueled by alcohol, they decided on a suicide pact. They took everything they could find in the medicine cabinet, and more alcohol, and went to sleep. Luckily John woke up a couple of hours later, very sick, and called 911. His mother found out what happened when the ambulance showed up. Jimmy, asleep upstairs, didn't know until the next morning. Father was out of town on business.

While John was in the hospital, we met with the parents. Father said: "I never thought John would crack. I always thought it would be either me or Jimmy." It was the first we knew of father's troubles. For the past four years he had been working at a job that kept him in another state during the week, only home on weekends. Despite his talents and job experience, this was the only job he could get after his previous employer folded. They had moved to their community and bought a very impressive house on the strength of that previous job, at the height of the real estate boom. When he lost that job, they immediately put the house on the market, but they could not begin to recoup their investment. Now his current position was due to end in two months, and despite his efforts, he had no other employment on the horizon. He was bitter, pessimistic, and angry. When we said he was depressed, he agreed. We soon had three family members on Prozac.

Mother also worked, in an office job that demanded her presence from nine to five every day. She seemed to be the quiet, phlegmatic one in the family who was holding everyone else together, but she was unable to be firm with the boys when dad was away. Lonely herself, she got sucked in to being their buddy; this made it more difficult for her to see objectively when some of their behavior was really inappropriate or dangerous. The parents' financial plan was that they would go bankrupt when father's employment ended. They could not possibly pay the mortgage.

However one explains what was going on in this family, depression was clearly the family disease. What sort of solutions does the therapist have for their very real problems, and how do we help this family make the decisions they have to make? Dad's depression seems perfectly understandable under the circumstances. John has his depressed girlfriend sleeping with him in his parents' home. Is this evidence of the parents' lack of vigilance, or just the way things are these days? Then, discharged from the hospital, John moves into an apartment with his girlfriend, both of them still suicide risks as far as we're concerned. We want the parents to prohibit this, but is this fair to expect of them? Jimmy moves into John's room, where John had just made his suicide attempt, where one can come and go without other family members knowing, and paints it black. How should we, and the parents, deal with this? John is admittedly using alcohol, Jimmy is probably using marijuana. Father, home on weekends, agrees he drinks too much, is not a good example, and gets crabby with his wife and sons, but he doesn't want to quit drinking; it's the only time he feels good. Living in a motel five nights a week with nothing to do, stuck in a job that's due to end, shouldn't we give him credit for hanging in there with his family? In a traditional world, both boys should be going to college, and we would see the parents' failure to encourage this as symptomatic of abdication of their responsibility. But given the parents' circumstances, could we do better? Besides, both boys say college is a waste of time. Why should they spend four years in school just to wait tables? They can do that now. We can't argue with this as forcefully as we'd like; kids today can't assume that education leads to career leads to happiness. Jimmy still talks of suicide. What about having a potentially suicidal teenager, possibly high, driving himself to and from school, to and from his work, to and from friends? We don't like it, but given where they live, what is the alternative?

Children today grow up in a world of fear. In kindergarten they are taught about stranger danger; in fourth grade they are taught about the dangers of drugs; in junior high, the subject is AIDS. On television, politicians disgrace themselves, sports heroes become murderers, but no one takes responsibility. No one is to be trusted. Parents don't have neighbors or grandparents to help them with parenting. While it used to be that the whole community was involved in child-rearing, now there is no community. The task falls solely on parents and professionals, who seem to be more and more at odds. If a neighbor takes it on herself to reprimand a child for misbehavior on the street, she's opening herself up for a lawsuit. Parents and children alike are overwhelmed by mass culture, without a support system to reinforce any alternatives.

In order to ward off depression, children must develop the capacity for intimacy—to engage in committed relationships in which the partners share their true selves—and the capacity for mastery—to engage in activities in which they can achieve goals that are personally meaningful. Given the culture we live in, how can we help our children develop these strengths?

Depressed Parents, Depressed Children

Good child therapists know that often when a child is in trouble, parents are depressed. Though the parents often feel that the child's behavior is the source of their distress, it usually makes more sense to hypothesize that the child is reacting to the parent's depression. I know of extreme cases where the family has somehow "expelled" the troublesome child from the home (through private school or placement with relatives; or the child has run away) only to have the next child in age step into the troublemaking role. We often explain to parents that the child is really trying to get a rise out of them, to get them to be parents, to put their foot down, enforce rules, and pay attention. The parent may never have realized that, in reality, he or she is quite depressed. When we can treat the depression successfully, the parent has the energy to pay attention, to set limits, to be firm and consistent, and the child's behavior improves. I work in an agency where, besides treating the adult's depression, we have parent aides who can go into the home and teach, step-by-step, effective child care and discipline; the psychotherapy and the teaching of parenting skills reinforce each other, and our success rate is very high.

There is a great deal of research documenting that children of depressed parents are at high risk for depression themselves, as well as for substance abuse and antisocial activities.[3] A series of studies[4] has suggested that depressed mothers have difficulty bonding with their babies; they are less sensitive to the baby's needs and less consistent in their responses to the baby's behavior. The babies appear more unhappy and isolated than other children. They may be difficult to comfort, appear listless, and be difficult to feed and put to sleep. When they reach the toddler stage, they are often very hard to handle, defiant, negative, and refusing to accept parental authority. This, of course, reinforces mother's sense of being inadequate and a failure. Her parenting is likely to remain inconsistent, because nothing she does has any visible effect. At our clinic, we have become so used to hearing from single mothers of four-year-old boys (a particularly difficult combination) that we have a standard treatment plan: get mom some immediate relief (day care, relatives, camp, baby-sitters), then treat her depression, teach her to defuse power struggles, and start slowly to rebuild an affectionate bond between mother and child.

When the depressed parent isn't able to get help like this, the outlook isn't good for the child. He or she grows up with dangerous and destructive ideas about the self—that he's unlovable, uncontrollable, and a general nuisance. He doesn't know how to get attention from adults in positive ways, so gets labeled a troublemaker. He doesn't know how to soothe himself, so is at risk for substance abuse. He doesn't know he's a worthwhile human being, so is at risk for depression.

Counteracting Mass Culture

Television is so powerful that we're all scared of it. When my son was small, I didn't want him to watch "He-Man" cartoons. I thought they taught violence as a means of solving problems, were sexist, and were more than a little scary—much the way parents today think about "Power Rangers." For a while I held out, but all Michael's friends at school watched "He-Man" every day. It was the major theme of their play. Michael begged, and I relented. Now that they are adolescents, I wish my children wouldn't watch MTV, or listen to much of the music they seem to like. The values are so unhealthy: *Buy this, and be cool. Adolescent sex is perfectly fine. Intimidation and violence are how people get what they want. Sex is raunchy. The world is divided between winners and losers. Parents know nothing. School is boring. Work is boring. Life is boring.* Alcohol and drugs are a constant subtext.

Fifty percent of children age six to sixteen now have a TV in their rooms, watching programs specifically marketed for them—and designed to turn parents off.[5] Now, instead of watching one program together, we have "his" show, "her" show, the teens' show, the preteens' show, ad infinitum. If we want to have any relationship with our children today, we must take on the television monster. One suggestion is to watch television with our kids—watch "Beavis and Butt-Head," or "Yo! MTV Raps!" You may not even have to say very much. Children will be embarrassed at what's on the screen merely because you're present—you are their chief arbiter of values, their external conscience. Because you're there with them, they see the screen partly through your eyes, and they can't get sucked so far into the tube. If you do say something, don't make it an obvious put-down. They will feel obligated to defend their culture, and you won't win the argument. Instead, ask questions: What does it mean that that rapper has five girls in his bed? Or go back to the subject later, when the television is off—tell your kid what you found disturbing, and why, and ask him how he feels about it.

The painful truth is that MTV is just an extension of the values of adult culture. Our society defines us as consumers; we are marketed and manipulated twenty-four hours a day; our leaders don't lead but instead follow the ratings. Older ideas of the dignity of labor seem quaint. Anyone who works hard today is a fool; the smartest person makes the most money with the least effort. Since parenting and making a marriage are also hard work, those who keep at it are also fools. It's easy to walk away from a marriage. When was the last time you heard anyone criticized for divorce?

This is indeed a depressing picture. The popular culture of our time is shallow and narcissistic; those who are immersed in it will become depressed when their sources of narcissistic supplies dry up—when they grow old, when their money or drugs run out, when they wake up alone. Those families who stick together, who make time for each other, who teach communicating and caring, will be in much better shape for the future.

Pursuing Your Child into Adolescence

In our culture, adolescence comes earlier and earlier. When children are only four, they're likely to be in preschool or day care programs where they spend a great deal of time with peers. By third or fourth grade, children may spend every afternoon in lessons or sports and every evening with the TV or homework. By sixth or seventh grade, parent and child may be speaking directly to each other only about chores: Is your homework done? Did you feed the dog? What time is practice tomorrow? In actuality, the child is much more strongly influenced by the 95 percent of time he or she spends with peers. And the peer culture, in turn, is influenced by the media, by the desire to fit in, and the fear of being different. Parents may see their children going about their business and be vaguely aware that they don't really know what's going on in the child's head, but decide "If it ain't broke, don't fix it."

This is a fatal assumption. Parents need to be nuisances. It's part of the job description to be intrusive. It's how our children know we love them.

After age five or six, children don't make it easy for us to cuddle them, to display affection directly; they squirm away when we reach out. They get absorbed in the business of growing up and don't like to be treated like "babies" anymore. Some parents feel rejected by this normal developmental stage and withdraw from their children. Parents who are better prepared psychologically just shift their tactics—they pursue the child into this new stage. The questions sound inane, and the child will roll his eyes and act as if you're *so stupid* for asking: "What did you do in school today? What do you think of your new teacher? How are you getting along with your friends? What did you think of that show on television? Did you read the story in the paper about the fossil they dug up in South America? What kind of music do you like now? What's the difference between rap and hip-hop (punk, alternative, techno)? Do you think girls should play Little League? Do you want to go to a movie tonight?"

Remember the distinction between content and process, words and music, in a conversation. Emotionally, content doesn't matter very much; the child hears the music. And the constant refrain is "I care about you. You are an interesting person. What you think and how you feel matters to me." Although the child in latency needs to push away and not respond directly to these parental overtures, he gains in confidence and self-esteem with every encounter. Then you may also find those rare occasions when the child will make himself available for some conversation that goes beyond the superficial—because he knows you're interested.

Teach Responsibility by Example

As children grow out of the toddler stage, they leave behind that phase of development in which they unabashedly worshipped mommy and daddy as powerful, beautiful, and wise. Sometimes the rapid shift from idealization to treating you like an embarrassment, an incredibly dense and insensitive failure who can't understand the simplest thing, is a little hard for parents to take.

Often, the child will treat you affectionately one minute and contemptuously a half hour later, and you don't have any idea what caused the change. This stage can last from about age six through sixteen. It can eat away like acid on parents' self-esteem.

Although children at this time seem to have as their goal driving parents crazy, what they actually need is for parents to demonstrate resilience and dependability. Therapists' offices across the country are full of depressed adults who are grieving over their disappointment in their parents, never realizing that their parents were doing what they thought their children wanted. A son who perceives his father as having inexplicably withdrawn from him as he entered adolescence never thinks that father may have been hurt by the son's own withdrawal and gone on with other aspects of his life. A woman whose self-esteem is damaged by promiscuity and drug abuse in adolescence feels that her mother deserted her in her hour of need—not understanding that mother responded to the daughter's insistence on pushing her away. Although children treat their parents with evident contempt, there is still a piece inside that needs to feel that mom and dad are safe, reliable, and competent. If parents can't project that image despite the child's testing, the child will fail to internalize a sense of himself as safe, reliable, and competent.

Parents need to remember that they are the patterns on which the child builds his personality. To self-consciously try to do the right thing in a difficult situation because we want our children to think well of us is not hypocrisy, it's good parenting. How we deal with anger and frustration, how we cope with anxiety and stress, how we communicate intimacy and affection—these are habits our children will learn from us. We don't have to be perfect. They can change their habits as they grow up. But we can change, too. Sometimes wanting to set an example for the children brings out the best in us.

Who wasn't moved by Atticus Finch in *To Kill a Mockingbird?*

I've heard Gregory Peck reflecting on the hundreds of attorneys who have told him they chose their profession after seeing that film as children. The image of a strong, kind parent who faces evil and teaches tolerance inspires us to try to be better than we are.

Keep Perspective

The depressed reader who is a parent may now feel more depressed than at the beginning of this chapter. I've been saying that parental depression is responsible for all kinds of problems in the later life of the children, and I've been holding out very high standards for good parenting to prevent children from developing depression as adults. If the reader who wants help with his or her own depression now feels that it must be a real challenge to be a good-enough parent, I can't blame you for feeling that way at this point. But there's no point avoiding the truth. For those of us who have the opportunity, parenting is the most important thing we do with our lives. It's not easy, and how we are and who we are with our children will affect them until the day they die.

But there are two things I can say that can help. One is that in parenting, effort and desire count more than actual success. Above all, our children need to sense our continual caring and concern. We don't have to be perfect. We can be angry or irritable, even depressed and defeated, and our children can accept that if only we can still show that we love them.

The other point is to restate the message of this entire book: Depression is treatable! People get better all the time. More than 80 percent of people who get just a few months of psychotherapy and medication show great improvement. But if you're a depressed parent, you can't be one of the two-thirds of depressed people who don't seek help. You owe it to yourself and your children to get better. It's not as hard as you think.

1 7

Divorce

THE "FATHER KNOWS BEST" family, in which it's the first and only marriage for both parents, dad is the sole breadwinner, and mom stays home to care for the children, is now down to about 5 percent of the total population. The divorce rate is currently about 49 percent. It seems to have leveled off at that point after rising for the last twenty years but shows no sign of declining. Of children today, about 45 percent will go through a parental divorce. More than twice as many children of divorce compared to those from intact families will see a mental health professional during their lifetimes. In a national sample, men and women who were sixteen or younger when their parents divorced reported significantly higher divorce rates, more work-related problems, and higher levels of emotional distress than those who grew up in intact families.[1]

While I'm sympathetic to people who feel that they are stuck in a loveless marriage, I do think our society has blundered by making divorce seem like too easy and attractive a solution for very difficult problems. We have the idea that marriage should be based on romantic love and that once married, we should live happily ever after. This is somewhat of a social and cultural anomaly. Through most of history and in most cultures, it's been understood that the purpose of marriage is to raise a family, not to be happy. Now too many spouses think that the first sign of trouble means that the marriage isn't working and that divorce is the answer. Often cut off from older family members who could put problems in perspective, the bride gets her idea of what is normal from watching Montel Williams or Jenny Jones, the groom from Bud Light commercials.

By emphasizing external solutions to problems rather than helping people develop their own internal resources, we contribute further to our epidemic of depression. We should never expect that our spouse will make us happy, any more than we should expect that going to a bar means intimacy and love, that the right kind of car brings us fulfillment, or that a credit card brings us inner peace. Relationships take work.

Effects on Children

One of the chief risks of divorce, of course, is that the child will blame himself. The child imagines that his angry feelings or his bad behavior are the real reason daddy left. Children hear parents argue about the kids, and think that they have caused the problem. It's the healthy child who can talk about these fears and get reassurance. The child who is more vulnerable will keep it inside, may keep it from consciousness, may internalize it into a feeling of badness that doesn't go away—thus you get some adolescents whose whole identity is tied up with being bad. More mildly, this may get played out in the relationship with father. Believing that father is justifiably angry, the child may be tense, silent, withdrawn. The father may interpret this to mean that the child doesn't care about him, and feel rejected. Father's visits may become less and less frequent, and the child may feel, "I was right all along, Dad doesn't love me"—a classic example of a self-fulfilling prophecy.

Perhaps the most common problem children have with divorce is that of divided allegiances. When the child still loves and idealizes mother but father no longer shares those feelings, the child is confused; what had seemed like the bedrock of his experience—that of having his perceptions confirmed by the most important people in his life—is now seen to be unstable. When parents actively try to get children to take sides, of course, that makes matters worse, because they are being asked to discount the evidence of their own senses—to believe that their own feelings and experience are wrong. Children in this position often grow up with a severely damaged sense of self, a lack of confidence and trust in their view of reality—the ideal-hungry depressive referred to in chapter 4. These children may become good at manipulating, having learned that they can be rewarded for telling people what they want to hear.

Another danger in divorce concerns abandonment fears. Children, especially preschoolers, haven't developed a cohesive sense of themselves as separate from others. They are in a state of absolute dependence on their parents. It's likely that a child will fear that if one parent left, the other one will too—so children's typical reaction to divorce is a lot of generalized anxiety, a reawakening of separation anxiety, at a time when the parents' resources are strained. Parents, especially mom, who is likely to feel the brunt of this burden and is likely to be feeling vulnerable herself during the divorce period, may resent or ignore the child's increasing dependence—or get angry at the child.

A last possibility is that the child will resort to various maneuvers in order to get the parents back together—getting in conduct trouble, grade trouble, developing psychosomatic symptoms. This is especially true when during the marriage the child has played a role in keeping the parents together. Besides the obvious self-destructive aspects of this behavior, it also gives children too great a feeling of control. It destroys boundaries between children and adults—if the children really have this much power, who takes care of whom?

One strain that is common to these plots, in addition to the problems that are going to accrue to the child because of the confusion, deception, the lack of parenting at crucial times in development, is that in all the child is being used as a self-object by the parents; the child is used by the parent as a container for parental problems. Without a sense of being valued as a unique individual, with only a sense that he is useful for what function he can perform for others, the child loses the ability to feel genuine emotions, genuine pride, uniqueness, and vitality. You get the adults whom we see so often now: full of rage, but unaware of it, expressing it only through self-destructive behavior; empty depressions, feeling a pervasive sense of despair; blaming themselves for their own unhappiness; continually trying to please others, with no sense of inner direction.

Adam, fifteen, was referred after he failed ninth grade. He didn't do any schoolwork, and was known as the class clown. Adam's father had had no contact with him since Adam was four. He had two older siblings, both of whom had been through a stormy adolescence, full of conflict with mother. Mother was a slight, soft-spoken, intelligent woman with a great deal of charm, but one got the odd feeling that there was something wrong with her. Bad things always happened to her; she would get terrific headaches and go to bed for two days; she would not return phone calls for a week. She brought Adam in not because he was failing school or friendless or depressed, but because he started talking back to her. She projected a kind of distant amusement about her son's behavior, but he dropped hints about her rage that seemed entirely out of character.

Adam was about five feet three, 105 pounds, with Coke-bottle glasses. Looking back, I now wonder if he was a fetal-alcohol-

syndrome child—he had the large head, small frame, and vision difficulties that go with this condition. Secret drinking would also have explained mother's erratic behavior. Adam was into the greaser look—now he'd be called a punk or homeboy. He knew his mother expected me to fix him, and he had no interest in being fixed, but he was too compliant to refuse to come in.

As we talked and I didn't challenge or correct him, he opened up somewhat. He started telling me about the world as he saw it. There were always fights—in school, after school, in the mall, in the bowling alley. It was usually several bigger, older guys who were ambushing Adam for no reason he was aware of. Fortunately, Adam was an expert in martial arts and always managed to fight his way out of these situations. As time went on, the numbers and sizes of kids Adam was beating up kept increasing, their wounds got more and more serious, till I finally caught on that what I was hearing wasn't really happening at all. But Adam was telling me these stories with a perfectly straight face. He had nothing to gain by conning me. Was he psychotic? I went to see my consultant.

The consultant said I was being given the privilege of participating in Adam's reparative fantasies—his daydreams, if you will. These fantasies helped prop up Adam's very shaky self-esteem, and they were about the only thing he had going for himself. Clearly, Adam did see the world as a very dangerous place in which he was essentially alone, where he could trust no one, and there were powerful forces lying in wait for him. This was not a paranoid vision, but an accurate portrayal of the world as he knew it. So what should I do? How could I take this understanding and help Adam get along better in school?

The consultant said that Adam had plenty of people to help him with school, and that if I could keep my mouth shut and enter into Adam's world, he would eventually trust me enough to let me help him a little in a different way. I was shocked—why shouldn't he trust me? Wasn't I on his side? But I did as

I was told, and as the summer went on, Adam stopped complaining about keeping his appointments and even started bringing me fish he'd caught.

That fall Adam was in trouble in school again. He was now a year behind, taking all the same classes for the second time, with many of the same teachers, who were not thrilled to see him back. As he started to tell me little bits about how his teachers treated him, I could imagine what kind of provocative behavior on his part had elicited those furious responses. I went to school and sat in on a staff conference on Adam, and I'll never forget the gym teacher: "This kid just needs taking down a few pegs." I felt I understood the problem between Adam and the school: what Adam needed was taking up many pegs—but he was so scared, so mistrustful, that he wouldn't let anyone see that. Instead he acted cocky, uncaring, obnoxious, clowning, all those things that drive teachers crazy. He was already caught in a situation in which he wouldn't let anyone reach him. For him to accept a directive from an authority figure would literally tear apart the fragile false self he had built, the karate expert who cut a swath through hordes of enemies every night.

A child who yearns for a missing father feels unworthy of love; a child who is used by his mother as a confidante, a weapon, or a punching bag, depending on her mood, will not trust anyone. He's going to feel absolutely alone, frightened, and defenseless.

Adam found an interesting solution; he dropped out of school and got a job as a plumber's helper. He had to start work at five every morning, carry heavy equipment in all kinds of weather, and do most of the dirty work involved in plumbing. From all reports, he did this cheerfully and energetically. I was surprised at his attitude change, but Adam patiently explained it to me: because the plumber was paying him (treating him like an adult), the plumber earned the right to tell Adam what to do.

Taking orders for money was okay; taking orders just because adults are bigger and in authority wasn't.

Though he never returned to school, I felt that Adam had turned a corner. He never was able to articulate his rage at his mother, but he began to be less influenced by her. He was able to find a way to take pride in actual accomplishment, not live in his fantasy world all the time. Through the medium of money, he was beginning to find a way to interact with adults that enabled both parties to treat each other with consistency and respect. He was able to drop his cocky facade and relate to his boss like one adult to another. I hoped that these new skills would form the basis for an adaptation to adult life.

Research on Divorce

In 1989, Judith Wallerstein published the results of an important study of the long-term effects of divorce on children and families. The study began in 1971 and followed sixty families with 131 children.[2] Participants were selected purposely to represent "normal" families. People with severe emotional disturbance or children with severe learning disabilities were screened out. The families seemed to embody traditional values—in almost all, it was the first divorce on either side of the family.

The study was to last one year, following the then-prevalent expectation that after a year families would be back on track again. But at one year, the researchers found most families still in crisis, their emotional distress not having subsided. Many adults still felt angry, humiliated, and rejected, and most had not put their lives back together. There was an unexpectedly large number of children who seemed on a downward course. They had worrisome emotional symptoms and school-performance problems, and their peer relations had gotten worse.

Wallerstein and her researchers went back to the same group

after five years. At this point, one-third of the children were doing well; they had good relationships with both parents, and the parents were no longer fighting. The divorce seemed better than a failing marriage, and the children seemed back on track. But more than a third of the children were significantly worse off than before. Many were clinically depressed and not doing well in school or with friends. Some early disturbances—sleep problems, school performance, conduct problems—had become chronic. Amazingly, after five years a majority of children in the study still hoped their parents would reconcile. At the same time they were intensely angry at their parents for giving priority to their own needs. Few really seemed to understand the reasons for the divorce, even when parents thought it was self-evident. Many of the children were still exposed to intense bitterness between parents, either in direct confrontations or in complaining to the child about the other parent.

At this five-year point, the majority of adults felt better off, but a large minority didn't. Half of the men and two-thirds of the women felt more content with the quality of their lives, but the rest were stalled or felt worse. Not surprisingly, the men were doing better financially than the women. In this study, they were usually paying child support; but in many cases it didn't even cover the cost of child care for the working mother.

After these surprisingly negative results from five years after the divorce, the researchers went back and did ten- and fifteen-year follow-ups. *Second Chances* was based on the results of these follow-up studies.

Wallerstein concluded that children's experience of divorce is very different from that of adults. It is simply not true to rationalize that because an unhappy adult is probably not an effective parent, whatever makes the adult happy is necessarily good for the children—the "trickle down" theory of family functioning. An exciting love affair or a stimulating job change may make an adult very happy and at the same time make him or her less available as a parent. Parents are often forced to choose between their own happiness and that of the children, and that is simply a fact of life. And the love and affection between spouses in a second marriage does not necessarily extend to the children. Before the divorce, children can be quite content even when their parents are miserable. Only one in ten children in the study experienced relief when their parents divorced. Children need the functions of a parent and the structure of the family, aside from their love for the parents as individuals. They feel that their childhood is lost forever, that divorce is a price they pay for their parents' failures. They feel angry at parents for violating an unwritten rule—parents are supposed to sacrifice for children, not the other way around.

Perhaps the most disturbing news in this study was what Wallerstein called "the sleeper effect." At the ten-year follow-up, children who had appeared to be relatively unruffled by the divorce, whose parents did everything the right way, began in their early twenties to show rather serious problems that they themselves linked to the divorce. These problems included depression, anorexia, self-destructive behavior, risk taking, difficulty getting close to others, and difficulty trusting. These young adults talked of doubts about the permanence of relationships, doubts about one's judgment of others, and anxiety about and expectation of betrayal. The sleeper effect was generally a phenomenon of young women, because boys are more predictable; if they're going to have trouble, they show it early on. But issues from the childhood experience of divorce get reawakened in each child as he or she enters adulthood—some merely think about it, others act it out.

Wallerstein's study didn't have the rigorous controls necessary to demonstrate a new phenomenon like the sleeper effect with real scientific validity. We don't know the number of young people from intact families who have the same kinds of difficulties. But those of us in clinical practice would support the observation wholeheartedly with our own experiences. There seem to be a large number of young people who are profoundly and permanently troubled by their parents' divorce. Many of them are outwardly well-functioning, successful, attractive, intelligent, popular—but they feel an inner core of depression, anxiety, mistrust, self-doubt, rage, and guilt.

Over a third of the young adults sound remarkably depressed ten years after the divorce. They drift through life, have no goals, have limited their education, and have a feeling of hopelessness. Some are staying home well into their twenties, others are drifting. Many have dropped out after a year or two of college and are in unskilled jobs. They are clearly underachieving. The authors make a clear link between this pattern and a feeling of abandonment by the father. They feel that girls in early adolescence, boys in later adolescence, go through a period when father's love and good opinion become needed much more intensely. If the father does not respond, they internalize his lack of caring—if I were a better person, he would pay more attention to me.

Many of the young people had made an attempt to reestablish a relationship with father, after having lost contact with him for years. Fathers remain a significant psychological presence in the lives of their children, whether they visit regularly or are never seen. In the study, only one child, an infant at the time of the divorce, fully substituted his stepfather for his biological father. Most children do not give up on their biological fathers, even if the fathers have abandoned them. Most mothers in the study did not deliberately subvert visitation, but many previously loving and involved fathers did not regularly visit, partly because visitation is so painful and uncomfortable.

Visiting requires frequent separations that can lead to depression and sorrow in men who love their children. Society needs to define a role for the visiting father. Visits were consistently interpreted differently by fathers and children. Most fathers felt they had done pretty well by the kids, but three out of four children felt rejected; they felt that their fathers were present in body but not in spirit. What matters is not the quantity of time, but the extent to which the father and child have been able to maintain a relationship in which the child feels valued.

Another surprising finding was the lack of paternal support for college. Child-support payments legally stop at eighteen. Most of the fathers in this study rationalized that their responsibility for the children's education ended at that point—including some very successful men who could easily have afforded to help. Most of the children in this study had dropped out of school earlier than their peers, partly because of financial pressure. Few were willing to even consider confronting father directly with the need for help, although they felt that father should have done more. Colleges base financial aid on the income of both parents and refuse to deal with the dilemmas involved if one parent refuses to pay his share. College-age children feel cheated, mothers feel angry, and fathers feel guilty—the direct effects of divorce continue long after the decree is obtained.

At the follow-up interviews, disturbingly high proportions of children were involved in delinquency and substance abuse. Of the boys in the study, after ten years close to half were unhappy, lonely, and had difficulty in relations with women. Many of the children used promiscuous sex to deal with loneliness. Twenty-five percent of the girls became sexually active in junior high and continued a high rate of sexual activity.

Generally, parenting was not found to improve after divorce, despite our assumption that an unhappy marriage interferes with parenting. At ten years, over a third of the good mother-child relationships had deteriorated, and over half of the good father-child relationships. There were many examples of children getting manipulated by parents into taking sides, though this was difficult to report on statistically because both parents and children were reluctant to discuss the issue. The adults would deny their role, insisting that the children were acting on their own. The children would speak like little adults, strongly identified with the aggrieved parent.

What Helps Children Accept Divorce?

Given all this depressing news, but assuming that divorce is the best response to a bad situation, what can parents do to help their children? Many states are now requiring divorcing parents to participate in divorce-education programs designed to help minimize the impact on the child. Wallerstein found these factors to be associated with children's positive adjustment to divorce:

1. Protection from open conflict. When parents were able to cooperate with one another for the sake of the children, the children benefited from the protection. Even though cooperative parents were sometimes some of the angriest, they kept the children protected from their feelings.

2. A continued good relationship with each parent after the divorce. When father continues to be a parent, to enforce standards and values, to be on call in emergencies, to contribute financially, children do better.

3. A close mother-child relationship. Mother is usually the custodial parent. She usually has to work and is set back financially, but if she can take an active role in the child's life, this is the single most important factor in the child's future adaptation. When mother is stable and can continue to be a parent to her children despite her desire or the pressure to wipe out the past and start over again, children fare best.

4. A high degree of structure. Meals are on time, the family eats together, bedtimes are consistent, rules about

everything from when you do your homework to experi-
mentation with sex and drugs are clear and consistent.
Visitation is regular. The rules can be different in each
parent's household if the child feels loved and valued.

5. A good relationship with step-parents. Step-parents
   should not expect to replace the biological parent for
   the child, but if they are concerned, loving, and consistent they can be very important figures to the child.

6. A stable relationship with grandparents (including step-
   grandparents). Grandparents provide an opportunity for
   children to get love and caring that may be temporarily
   in short supply at home. If they can refrain from taking
   sides in the divorce battle and remain empathic to the
   emotional needs of the grandchildren, they can help
   the child significantly.

What Divorce Does to Adults

At ten years after the divorce, a quarter of the mothers and a
fifth of the fathers had not gotten their lives back on track. They
were found to be chronically disorganized, unable to meet the
challenges of being a parent, leaning heavily on the children for
emotional support. The children were being used to ward off
the serious depression that always seemed to threaten the parent. These are "overburdened children." One child was left
alone for months while mother was visiting her lover out of
town—putting herself to bed, feeding herself, getting to school
by herself. One six-year-old taped a note to the foot of his bed:
"Go to sleep, Jimmy. Don't be afraid."

Women who divorced while in their twenties or early thirties
were found to be significantly happier and better off financially
ten years later than those who divorced later. There was no
depression after divorce for these younger women; the depression had already occurred during the marriage. The divorce is

seen as a second chance, invigorating and energizing. Not all were successful at getting their life back together; some repeated the same mistakes, but many had successfully juggled career, children, and a second marriage. In working hard, they developed a new sense of confidence and self-esteem and were proud of their achievements and independence.

But of the men who divorced while in their twenties, most were seriously derailed ten years later. Forty percent were struggling financially; nearly half had lost ground economically. Every one of them had remarried, but ten years later, almost all of these second marriages had failed. Half were unable to establish stable careers. Only 30 percent could meet child-support obligations.

When a couple in their twenties divorce, it is usually at the wife's initiative, and she usually gains from the process. Divorce does not give the young men a second chance; rather they interpret it as a failure. Ten years later, they still blame themselves and have more respect and affection for the former spouse than any group in the study.

The situation was almost exactly reversed when divorces occurred later in the woman's life. Usually under these circumstances it was the husband who left. Often he was able to establish a new relationship, often with a younger woman, while the wife and children were more or less abandoned. These wives were likely to feel permanently damaged by the divorce, were much worse off economically, and felt that they had little control over their futures. The husbands, on the other hand, felt much better about themselves and their futures.

Divorce and Depression

In most divorces, there is a clear winner and a clear loser (aside from the children). Jockeying for these positions becomes an important part of the identity of the divorcing parents. It is an effort to prove competence, certainly, and can be part of a creative challenge; but often it is just a continuation of the same battle that fueled the divorce, the crisis of disappointment. It is a way to prove to the world and the self: "Look how well I can do without him/her." It is as if one partner is destined to end up depressed by the divorce, while the other apparently is strengthened and unburdened.

Usually, the one who leaves is the winner, the one left is the loser. Usually, the one who ends up better off financially is the winner. In their twenties, women leave men and usually end up winners; in their thirties, men leave their wives and end up winners.

But in reality if there is a contest, both lose. If men "win," they usually establish financial success but at the expense of their relationship with their children. If women "win," it is usually in emotional terms; financially they are still worse off, and their children don't have a father. Both end up more prone to depression.

By making divorce a contest, we deny ourselves the opportunity to do the grief work of divorce. Grieving means going through the familiar stages of denial, bargaining, anger, and ending up accepting the loss. Acceptance means achieving a balance in feelings about the lost person; no longer colored by rage or hurt, but tolerant and objective. If we're unable to do this, we go on projecting our misery on our spouse, who is no longer even there to respond. We keep ourselves in a depressed position, unable to digest our grief. If we're going to divorce, we have to commit to going all the way through it—to giving up on the fantasy that our partner is to blame for all our unhappiness, to accepting the sadness of our lost hopes, to taking responsibility for our own lives and our own decisions.

1 8

Community

I GREW UP in the sixties, a time of optimism for our country. To some of us, there was a rebirth of caring, of empathy and egalitarianism. A popular song referred to the prisoner, the drunkard, the hobo, with the refrain "There but for fortune go you or I."[1]

We assumed that, if things were bad, they could be changed, and we might even trust our government to direct the change. When President Kennedy signed the original community mental health bill in 1963, the idea was to set up a nationwide network of centers where people could go to get affordable psychological help when they needed it, for all kinds of problems, big and little, chronic and temporary. There were supposed to be crisis services, partial hospitalization services, community education programs—there was supposed to be an emphasis on preventing emotional disturbance. There was even supposed to be an effort to promote "mental health" as a positive concept, as if it was something more than the absence of mental illness. Thirty years later, if you feel that your community has a mental health center that provides these things and that you feel comfortable going to, write to me—I'm maintaining a very short list.

That our culture today fosters depression is borne out by the increasing prevalence of depression among young people. A series of studies[2] has shown that people born between 1940 and 1959 suffer depression more frequently and earlier in life than those born before 1940, not only in the United States, but in most of the Western world. Rates for mania, schizophrenia, and panic disorder have stayed about the same, suggesting that something cultural is at work. Our society is depressing. We don't feel optimistic about the future, we don't trust our leaders, we don't see opportunities to engage in rewarding careers. Is there anything we can do as a society that might slow down or reverse the epidemic of depression?

The Failure of Community Mental Health

What happened to the optimism that fueled movements like community mental health and inspired young people to work for social justice? I don't have all the answers, but I can give a brief review of community mental health that suggests some of the forces at work. The short version of why community mental health failed is that federal responsibility was axed by the Reagan administration in 1981, but the truth is that the movement was in trouble and there was no solution in sight. The reasons have to do with overoptimism among the mental health professions, the national economic retreat, and the crisis in the health care industry.

The small number of community mental health centers that were built were caught in the bind of dealing with sicker and more dangerous patients, with increasing federal mandates but without additional dollars. They began to go after the patients who could pay for services, and got on the merry-go-round of Medicaid, Medicare, and private health insurance that holds out the promise of enough money to operate an agency but at the cost of paralyzing bureaucracy. With a few exceptions, they did not provide innovative, aggressive treatment for the sickest patients, instead beginning what became known as "revolving door" treatment. The patient would be discharged from a state hospital and given an appointment at an outpatient center. The center would make no special effort to make sure that the disturbed and vulnerable patient got the help he needed to follow through with medication, housing, job training, and other necessities for a stable life. When, inevitably, the patient would decompensate, he would be readmitted to the state hospital, often several times a year—the revolving door. Meanwhile, the centers tried to make themselves more attractive to patients who could pay higher fees.

Now the picture has somewhat reversed itself. The large community mental health centers have taken on responsibility for caring for the most disturbed patients, seeing that funding for those patients is fairly secure. The more entrepreneurial staff who always wanted to be treating neurotic patients have left the centers for private practice. Both institutions and individuals seem to have forgotten about community education and prevention programs and other things that were to go into positive mental health.

And you don't have to be an expert to see that the mental health of our society hasn't improved. The number of homeless people out on the streets is a disgrace, and it's hard not to despair for our country. During the Great Depression, Steinbeck wrote *The Grapes of Wrath* and John Ford made a powerful, touching motion picture of it. Such conditions were just not acceptable in America; they were cause for outrage. Today it seems as if we've given up. People seem to be desensitizing themselves to the plight of the poor, the homeless, the mentally ill, the AIDS baby, the crack user; the problems seem so overwhelming that it's hard to blame people if they just want to go home and turn on the VCR. New York's Project Help, which provides rudimentary mental health care to the most impaired homeless with a mobile outreach van, says, "These days, people are telling us not to even bother asking them for money. They seem disappointed that so much money goes into a service that doesn't 'cure' people."[3]

Drug abuse, crime, the gap between rich and poor, child abuse, divorce—the rates keep going up in all our most distressing social problems. It's hard not to wish the problems would go away. It's very hard to feel, "There but for fortune go you or I." That kind of empathy, letting down the walls we put up to keep ourselves snug and secure, can be very painful. In the case of the young man who wrote the song with that refrain, it may have cost him his life.

The Risk of Caring

Phil Ochs sang "There but for Fortune" at Newport in 1964, and Joan Baez made something of a hit of it a year later. Ochs was one of the leading lights of the folk-protest movement of the late sixties. He showed up at the Chicago convention in 1968 and led the crowd in "I Ain't Marchin' Anymore" and "The War Is Over," two anthems of the peace movement that he had written. His guitar was entered into evidence as a defense exhibit at the trial of the Chicago Seven. Pete Seeger said, "Phil was so likable, so earnest. And good golly, he was prolific. He'd have a new song every two or three days. And they were good, too."[4]

But after 1968 Phil's candle started to flicker. His marriage ended in divorce; his recordings, though respected, were never the breakthrough hits he wanted; he started drinking more and composing less. He developed a mysterious stomach ailment that had him believing he was dying for almost a year. When it was diagnosed and cured, he went on a manic drinking spree. He took on another personality, calling himself John Train. John Train was loud, obnoxious, and violent.[5] He became paranoid and started carrying weapons. He got thrown out of the clubs he used to headline. Once he was arrested after running up a limousine bill he couldn't pay. The police allowed him to call his lawyer to come down to the station to bail him out. Ramsey Clark, the former Attorney General, showed up at the precinct station.

By December 1975, Phil was past the manic episode, worn out, depressed, and broke. He went to live with his sister on Long Island and spent his days watching television and playing cards with her children. In April 1976 he hanged himself with his belt from the back of her bathroom door. He didn't leave a note.[6]

This was a gifted and beloved young man who threw his life away. I can't help thinking that part of the reason was the pain his vision cost him—the pain of putting yourself in the place of the "other guy," of not allowing yourself to feel safe and superior to a faceless, anonymous other, but knowing that except for a few lucky breaks you might be in that position yourself. The best, the most compassionate, of psychotherapists live with that every day. We have to temper it with our professional skills, but it's what enables us to engage people, it's what enables those in trouble to trust us in the first place.

It's possible that today we might do more for Phil Ochs. His friends tried to get help for him, but nothing worked. Today we have some different medications and, I think, a better understanding of the psychological treatment of depression. But the truth is, with our still limited abilities we can't force treatment on people who don't want it, and that's for the best. We can't hold people against their will or medicate them unless they are a clear and present danger, and anyone who is smart and determined can get around those standards very easily.

I'm very glad I live and work in a small community. Being small helps. People need to feel cared about. When people know each other, they tend to care about each other. Jesse Jackson is onto something when he reminds urban youth, "I *am* somebody!" Those kids don't think anyone cares about them, and so they don't care about themselves. They may believe that they matter only when someone they look up to tells them. Many children where I live know without being told that they are somebody. They know that there are people who love them, who will tell them the truth; they know that they live in a community where there are basic standards of opportunity and justice. But when kids have experiences that suggest the contrary, they don't feel as if they are someone. And there are also many kids even in my small town who have those kinds of experiences all the time.

What's the community's responsibility in preventing depression and other mental illness? It's very great indeed. Every time the school system breaks a promise—when a teacher talks big but is obviously just a time-server. Every time the wealthy and powerful get preferential treatment. Every time adults are not able to respect each other's differences, we lose a little of our community mental health. Children learn that their self-esteem is vulnerable because truth and fairness don't always work. On the other hand, when we're able to organize something like a community food bank, when a neighbor takes in a foster child, when the ambulance squad drops everything to respond to an emergency, we gain a little bit in terms of caring, giving opportunities and hope, showing a belief in social justice.

Consider mental health through the life cycle of the individual. The child is born with a unique combination of innate strengths and deficits, most of which will be manifested later only as he or she grows and faces developmental hurdles. The child is born into a family that may operate out of love, respect, and fairness, or out of abuse, abandonment, and blame—more likely a combination of some of the positive qualities, some of the negative. The family's ability to nurture and support the child is not fixed or innate. It changes in response to stress, to success, to bad luck. Most of our clients wouldn't need us if not for bad luck. The community decides how families in trouble are to be treated. Are they to be helped, by whom, to what extent?

The child grows up in a community and enters society through institutions like the school, the church, the day care center. These institutions offer the child the opportunity to develop, to strengthen assets, to overcome weaknesses. The extent to which these opportunities are seen as fairly distributed affects the child's sense of himself as able to affect the course of his own life. As our children grow, some of the more vulnerable break. Does the community deny them, or own them? Do they get sent out of state, or into special classrooms, or into long-term-care facilities? As those who grow up more or less success-fully enter the life of the community as adults, what's the community's responsibility in terms of offering opportunities to earn a living, marry, raise a family? And if they choose an alternative lifestyle, how tolerant will the community be? And as these people move through the stages of adulthood into old age, their sense of how caring, how fair, their community is, directly affects their thinking about whether life is good and worthwhile.

I feel very lucky to live in a community that's small enough so that people know each other and are not just faceless strangers, and small enough so that many people, if not most, at least have the impression that their presence and participation makes a difference. Perhaps it can't work on a big scale, or perhaps our cities and our country must take active steps to get people to care about each other. We can't ignore society's failures, but neither is it enough to send them away, to pity them, and to throw money at them as long as they stay at a distance. Nor can we blame them and turn away. We are all *interdependent* with each other; it costs us to recognize this—but it costs us more to ignore it.

I said before that there are only three things we can do with a difficult situation: we can seek to alter it, we can try to avoid it, or we can accept it. I also said that Westerners tend to overvalue action and to assume that avoidance or acceptance are second-class solutions. But when it comes to our social problems today, we seem to be too ready to give up. More and more people want to avoid facing reality by tuning into a mass culture that presents a false image, by trying to amass personal wealth that may insulate them. They can drive in their air-conditioned cars from their burglar-proof houses to the mall and back again and try to avoid awareness of the world in between. We have lost faith in political leaders and have bought the idea that government hurts more than it helps—we accept the idea that there are no real solutions for social problems. We have given up on the idea that a health care system should be accessible to all, turning a blind eye to the truly offensive profits that are being sucked out of the system.

Taken to the extremes we do today, avoidance of social problems and belief in our powerlessness to do anything about them doesn't really get us off the hook. These are excuses, rationalizations, defenses against facing unpleasant choices. Remember unconscious guilt. Having been told from childhood on that we are our brother's keeper, we can't abandon that burden without feeling that we have failed. We can anesthetize ourselves with alcohol or television, we can amass the trappings of success, but we live a meaningless life.

Depression is a disease that hits us both as individuals and as a society. Let's expand our vision: the paranoid, self-centered "I've got mine" outlook leads to depression; the expansive, inclusive "Let's work together" attitude, though uncomfortable and challenging, is life-affirming and joyful.

I don't have any easy solutions for what we can do about our epidemic of depression. However, I believe that if we set out to undo our own depression, by definition we will be adding meaning, engagement, and vitality to our own lives and to those close to us. Perhaps we could take it one step further. Perhaps each of us could do something regularly to make a contribution to the larger good. Based on what I know about depression, of course that means more than writing a check. It means taking the trouble to get involved, on a personal level, in a way that challenges our comfort.

19

Special Risks

PEOPLE AT CERTAIN stages of life, people who undergo certain kinds of experiences, seem to be more vulnerable to depression than the average person. Children, once thought to be invulnerable to depression, are now recognized to suffer frequently, though their symptoms may be difficult to detect. Young people in adolescence, always recognized to be a difficult time, have increased their incidence of suicide alarmingly over recent years. Older people, often facing longer life spans through better health care but without a meaningful way to spend their extra years, develop clinical depressions that are very different from loneliness or the effects of aging. People who abuse alcohol and other drugs, and people who undergo psychological trauma, are at especially high risk. And grief, the normal reaction to the loss of someone important in our lives through death or separation, crosses over and is indeed related to depression in a very special way.

In all of these risk categories, we must apply what we know about recovery from depression to the circumstances of the victim. The wish to not feel, the cognitive errors and self-destructive behavior patterns that we see in the general development of depression, also apply in these particular cases. The same sorts of strategies, adapted to the circumstances of the individual, can be used to facilitate recovery.

Men, Women, and Depression

I've alluded elsewhere to the higher incidence of depression among women than men. This is a complex and difficult subject, complex partly because of the possibility of sex-role bias on the part of theorists and researchers, difficult partly because of the complexities of reliably diagnosing and counting an amorphous disease like depression.

The most widely accepted research comes from Dr. Myrna M. Weissman, who with her colleagues has been studying the epidemiology of depression in the U.S. and around the world for twenty years. Her most recent publications conclude without ambiguity: "Epidemiologic studies conducted in the United States [and in other countries] all show convincingly that rates of depression are higher in women than in men, with about a twofold difference on average. . . . These studies also show that the gender disparity in the rates of the first onset of depression begins early, around 13 to 15 years of age, and is maintained throughout life. There is a peak in first onsets during the child-bearing years and a decrease in onsets after age 45. There is no evidence for an increase during the menopausal years."[1] Based on her research, Weissman sounds a definite warning: since depression seems to be largely a disease of women of childbearing age, and since pregnant women and new mothers tend to get excluded from research (because of the possible effects of treatment on the fetus or the child), we need to do systematic research to remedy this important gap in our knowledge.

But what about the perception that men seek treatment less, not only psychological help but all medical help, and thus are less likely to be identified as depressed than are women? This is apparently not a factor, since Weissman's studies are essentially door-to-door samples, not samples of only those who seek help.

And what about the idea that depression is a biased diagnosis: that the male-dominated mental health professions mistakenly define behavior (like showing emotion, listening instead of arguing, accepting rather than attacking) that is essentially feminine as pathological? Or that women who are unhappy with their traditional, male-defined, lot in life are sick merely because of their deviance, as Stalin's enemies were assumed to be crazy? This thesis was originally put forward by Phyllis Chesler in 1972.[2] Despite great argument to the contrary (Maggie Scarf, reviewing Chesler's work in 1980, wrote: "Women simply *are* more depressed, in the aggregate, than are men, in the aggregate. Beyond the shadow of a doubt."[3]), this is an idea that will not go away. Like it or not, psychiatry represents conventional values; it is an important means of social control and subject to abuse. If women are made to feel that there is something inherently inferior about being women, they are more likely to feel depressed. If women are made to feel that there is something pathological about being feminine, they are more subject to conventional social control. Carol Gilligan[4] argues that from Freud to Erikson to Vaillant, all our standards of normality have been inherently male-centered, focusing on career and self-assertion, rather than family and connection, as defining the ends of life.

Colette Dowling[5] makes the issue vivid for depression. She describes a 1990 report of the American Psychological Association's Special Task Force on Women and Depression, which raised the specter of whether or not use of antidepressants could encourage passivity, dependency, and a victim psychology in women. Dowling points out that antidepressants aren't addictive and that women who seek treatment to remedy their unhappy life situations are likely to feel stronger and more capable, whereas women who don't get treatment are likely to stay depressed and disempowered. The psychological profession, she implies, was using feminism to disguise an anti-medication bias.

It's very hard to read the epidemiologic studies and conclude anything else than that women are twice as likely as men to feel what we define as depression. There are a number of possible reasons why this might be the case. One is that women may have more to be depressed about than men do. Anyone who defines himself in terms of other people is at risk for depression. The more sources of gratification one has in one's life, and the more predictable and controllable those resources, the less risk for depression. If a woman is taught to define her worth in terms of keeping her husband happy, she is too dependent on an arbitrary and capricious source of gratification. If she is taught that her worth is measured by raising happy and successful children, her self-esteem depends on forces over which she really has very little control. If a man, on the other hand, believes that his self-worth is measured by success on the job and in the family, he has at least two sources of support. And a strong case can be made that the rewards in the world of work are distributed more fairly and predictably than at home. We have personnel policies, job descriptions, union contracts that define in some detail how to do a good job at work; not so at home. That this theory might have some validity is supported by recent studies showing that, with a blurring of sex-role boundaries, men's risk of depression is rising, while women's risk for substance abuse is also on the rise.

Another factor in sex-role differences, at least in American society, has to do with the tremendous social pressure women, especially young adolescents, experience to try to make their bodies something other than what nature intended. The thin, emaciated look glamorized by popular culture is simply impossible for most women to achieve. Incidence of anorexia and bulimia is rising at an alarming rate among young women; but these symptoms are really a response to an underlying depression. As boys grow into puberty, their bodies become more like that of the idealized man—broader shoulders, better muscle definition—but girls' bodies go in the opposite direction, becoming rounder and more fatty. Fashion dictates an ideal of a pre-pubescent girl; so when girls find their bodies taking them away from the ideal, no wonder they become dissatisfied with their bodies and themselves.

Another possible reason why women are more likely to be depressed is that their moods are, to a greater extent than men's, influenced by hormonal changes. Many women with depression report an expectable waxing and waning of symptoms that coincides with their menstrual cycle. Attuned from adolescence to the phenomenon of moods that change according to forces that seem outside the self, women may be more prone to feelings of powerlessness. At the same time, women whose depression worsens during the premenstrual period have lower levels of serotonin than they do postmenstrually, and lower levels than women without PMS.[6]

There has been tremendous controversy about Pre-Menstrual Syndrome as a diagnosis, a controversy that has divided women. Some believe that there is plenty of evidence suggesting that sufficient numbers of women suffer from mood changes, primarily depression but also anxiety, regularly during the menstrual cycle to recognize a constellation of symptoms by calling it an illness (just as has been done with major depression and dysthymia) for which we should look for causes and treatments. Others, afraid that admission of an innate difference between men and women will be used to prove women's inferiority, have strongly resisted the idea. The American Psychiatric Association in compiling the DSM-IV attempted to straddle the fence. First they rejected the commonly recognized name of Pre-Menstrual Syndrome and substituted the awkward and confusing name "Late Luteal Phase Dysphoric Disorder" (the luteal phase being the stage that precedes menstruation; dysphoria referring to a change in mood). Then they put the category in an appendix to the DSM as being a subject worthy of further study rather than a recognized disorder. Presumably further study will have been conducted by the time the next edition of the DSM is released, because the present compromise satisfies no one.

Further buttressing the idea that hormonal changes account for some of the incidence of depression in women are the phenomena of postpartum blues and postpartum depression. Postpartum blues are experienced by most women after child-birth,[7] with transient symptoms of depression peaking around the fifth day after delivery and rapidly decreasing thereafter. Postpartum depression, the equivalent of a major depressive episode, occurs in 10 to 15 percent of new mothers, usually within two weeks after delivery. Though shifts in hormone levels associated with recovery from childbirth are thought to account for much of postpartum depression, the picture is not that simple. Women under greater stress after delivery and women who have a previous psychiatric history are both at greater risk for postpartum depression than are other women.

Still a third factor, other than social role pressure and biology, that is likely to play a role in the incidence of depression among women is their experience of abuse and victimization during development. There is good reason to believe that sexual abuse of female children is much more frequent than anyone would like to admit; in one random sample of adult women, 12 percent reported having experienced serious sexual abuse by a family member before age seventeen, and 26 percent had been abused by someone outside the family by that time.[8] A study conducted by the American Psychological Association's Task Force on Women and Depression found that 37 percent of women reported that, by the time they reached twenty-one, they had had a significant experience of physical or sexual abuse.[9]

The effects of trauma like this can be devastating. A pervasive distrust, a hyperalertness to danger, nightmares, lifelong difficulty sleeping, lifelong difficulty in normal sexual relations, and of course depression—not least, internalizing a sense of helplessness and powerlessness, a passive acceptance of future abuse or discrimination.

So there is plenty of reason to believe that women are, indeed, more depressed than men, and it's easy to understand why this should be the case. But let me, the male writer, say a word about men and depression. Men are five times more likely than women to commit suicide. They are much more likely to become antisocial personalities, or to fall victim to substance abuse, than are women. An interesting new study suggests that socioeconomic stress (poverty, discrimination) results in depression in women, antisocial activity and drug abuse in men.[10] Why is this?

Men are told from birth that they are not supposed to feel. Fear, sadness, helplessness—these are anathema to the male character. Men are trapped inside this supposedly tough outer shell. The number of men I know who have conversations with other men about anything meaningful is pitifully small.

Instead of permitting ourselves to feel the emotional symptoms of depression, we defend against them by acting out (dangerous, self-destructive, or antisocial behavior), by somatization (rushing to the ER with chest pains that turn out to be an anxiety attack), or by trying to treat them with alcohol. Many men feel they are faking it, making it up as they go along, always one misstep away from disaster. They try to reassure themselves by swaggering around the house, but they wonder if women aren't really laughing behind their backs. From where I sit, women's depression is a healthier alternative than any of these; men would actually be a whole lot better off if they could permit themselves to feel depressed. "The majority of men I see in therapy feel they have less power than they are supposed to, are eager to please, and are helpless in the face of those emotions they have been stripped of. . . . Though few women realize it—and feminist literature doesn't convey this—men are both terrified and in awe of them."[11]

Children and Adolescents

Until the 1980s, it was generally thought that children could not become depressed. We depended on a psychological theory that said, essentially: depression is the result of a punitive superego; the superego isn't developed until adolescence; ergo, depression is impossible in children. Now researchers recognize that children, like everyone else, are not immune at all. Because children often do not have the capacity to step back, look at themselves, and recognize that the way they're feeling isn't normal for them, diagnosis and treatment of depression is more difficult than for adults.

Also, the symptom picture of depression in children and adolescents is confusing. Sometimes children will let it be known that they feel hopeless, empty, or overwhelmingly sad—the signs we look for in adults. But more often children cannot express their feelings so directly, and we must interpret their behavior. Irritability is a key indicator. Children may seem easily frustrated, cranky, or moody. They can't be pleased. Boys may simply appear unusually angry or sullen. If this mood is unrelieved for more than a week, and especially if it does not seem to come in response to some real disappointment or loss, most likely the parent should seek help. Other signs of depression in children include changes in appetite or energy level; sleeping a great deal more or less than usual; a drop in school performance; and excessive worrying. Especially troubling is a loss of interest in things that used to give pleasure, as when a child seems not to care any longer for favorite toys or activities. Injuries that may seem accidental may have been the result of carelessness. The child may talk about death or thoughts of punishment.

Untreated, depression can be permanently devastating to children. Relationships within the family are impaired, school performance is affected, and peer relations are disturbed. Depressed children tend to have fewer close friends, and their relationships are not long-lasting. They are shyer and get teased more than nondepressed children. They have difficulty concentrating and are easily distracted and fatigued; they score significantly lower than other children on most standardized tests.[12]

The actual incidence of depression among children is not known. Diagnosis is difficult. Estimates range from a few tenths of a percent to the 15 to 20 percent that is found in adults. One estimate that seems realistic is that 10 percent of all children will suffer a depressive episode before age twelve. It's well recognized now that suicide, usually a result of depression whether diagnosed or not, is on the increase among teens. But thoughts or wishes of death, and self-destructive behavior (often misinterpreted by adults as risky or dangerous play) are increasingly reported by young children.

The idea that a child might think of taking his or her own life is horrifying and repugnant. And while we may be able to entertain the idea in theory, in real life when we run across such a child, perhaps in our own family, our denial kicks in. Every child therapist can tell stories about seemingly caring parents who were unable or unwilling to take the simplest concrete steps—locking up medicines, getting rid of guns—to protect a suicidal child or adolescent. Therapists, teachers, physicians, and others who know the child can get fooled as well, so that though a child or teen may sound seriously depressed to a neutral third party, others can be too close to see the forest for the trees.

I have talked with a surprising number of adults who remember suicide attempts as a child or teen. They were upset and hurt, felt that no one cared and that life wasn't worth living. They took a bottle of pills and went to sleep, expecting never to wake up. Fortunately, they weren't knowledgeable about the lethal dosage, so they woke up the next morning perhaps with nothing more than a bad headache. Because they were convinced that no one cared, they told no one. Things got a little better, and they didn't repeat the attempt. But twenty years later they are in my office, feeling like unlovable failures. They don't connect that feeling to their adolescent suicide attempt because the mind doesn't work that way—repression lets us remember the event without the feelings connected with it—but it's clear that this feeling has been with them for so long it's now part of the self.

When parents become aware of depression in the family, they can often make some adjustments in the way the family interacts to help a child or teen feel better. One teen, after two suicide attempts, finally got angry enough at her parents to tell them their constant fighting made her sick. The parents agreed on some simple behavioral rules—no raised voices, arguments only behind closed doors, arguments to last only fifteen minutes till a time-out—which insulated the daughter from their disagreements. Not surprisingly, with some limits put on their fighting, they also began to get along better.

The suicide rate among adolescents has been rising at a frightening rate, and no one knows why. In the past twenty-five years, while the general incidence of suicide has decreased, the rate for those between fifteen and nineteen has quadrupled.[13] It is generally considered to be the second or third most common cause of death among adolescents, even though it is seriously underreported. Sixty percent of adolescents know someone who has made an attempt. No one has advanced a good theory explaining why teens are taking their own lives in greater numbers, but it's important for everyone to be aware of the problem.

The major risk factors of suicide among young people are not what one might imagine. Instead of the stereotype of a lonely, romantic teen pining away for lack of love, teens who commit suicide have more often been angry, defiant, and in trouble.[14]

Not surprisingly, depression—though it's often not recognized—is the primary risk factor. In younger children and in adolescent boys, it often appears that the child is simply angry or sullen. If this mood lasts more than a week or so with no relief, and if there are other signs of depression—changes in appetite, activity level, sleep pattern; loss of interest in activities that normally give pleasure; social withdrawal; thoughts of death or punishment—it should be taken seriously.

Substance abuse is the second major risk factor. Sometimes teens try alcohol or other drugs to relieve depression. Unfortunately the drugs themselves have a depressant effect and lower inhibitions against self-injurious behavior. Some young people who have never expressed a suicidal thought have taken their own lives when they got drunk to ease the pain of a disappointment or loss. But when they got drunk, they felt worse, not better, and they committed a rash, impulsive act that they wouldn't have carried out sober. Research on adolescent suicide reports that about 45 percent are intoxicated at time of death.[15]

Behavioral problems—getting in trouble in school or with the law, fighting with parents—are the third risk factor for suicide. We tend to think of potential suicides as sensitive, shy people who are overwhelmed by life. We don't see the cocky, obnoxious adolescent as potentially self-destructive, even though his behavior—continually getting in trouble, keeping the world at arm's length—has exactly that effect. I recently reread *The Catcher in the Rye* and was amazed to see Holden Caulfield, whom I had so identified myself with, from my now adult perspective. Though I still felt sympathetic, I was struck by how depressed and self-destructive his behavior seemed. For instance, Holden gets angry at Stradlater, his jock of a roommate, because Stradlater may have seduced a girl Holden liked as a child. Holden's anger is such that he takes a punch at the bigger boy, who wrestles him and pins him:

"Holden. If I letcha up, willya keep your mouth shut?"

"Yes."

He got up off me, and I got up too. My chest hurt like hell from his dirty knees. "You're a dirty stupid sonuvabitch of a moron," I told him. . . . Then he really let one go at me, and the next thing I knew I was on the goddam floor again.[16]

The availability of a gun adds another level of danger for teens who may be thinking of suicide. This makes the consequences of an impulsive act much more lethal. People can survive an overdose or a wrist-cutting when they get medical attention; not often a gunshot wound. Surprisingly, even when a child has made one attempt by other means, parents often fail to remove guns from the home.

The last risk factor is a history of previous attempts. Half of all children who have made one suicide attempt will make another, sometimes as many as two a year, until they succeed.

Other factors that influence suicidal potential include a family history of depression or substance abuse, and a recent traumatic event. Some children who take their own lives are indeed the opposite of the rebellious teen. They are anxious, insecure kids who have a desperate desire to be liked, to fit in, to do well. Their expectations are so high that they demand too much of themselves, so are condemned to constant disappointment. A traumatic event, which can seem minor viewed from an adult perspective, is enough to push them over the edge into a severe depression. Being jilted, failing a test, getting into an accident— they have the sense that their life is a delicate balance, and one failure or disappointment seems to threaten the whole house of cards.

Kurt Cobain, a talented, hugely successful young man, the leader of the rock group Nirvana, killed himself with a shotgun blast in April of 1994. The loss my generation felt with the death of John Lennon, today's teens felt again, but coupled with the confusion and despair that accompany a suicide.

Cobain had a family history of depression; some reports said that three uncles had died by suicide. Aside from the genetic loading for depression, anyone in a family with a history of suicide is haunted by thoughts and images. Suicide may seem more like an acceptable alternative to despair than it does to most people.

He also struggled with substance abuse, heroin and alcohol, and was intoxicated when he died. Many, if not most, suicides take place while the victim is in a toxic state. There is a terrible sense of despair, a momentary impulse, and a death. If not for the intoxicants, the impulse might be ridden out, and a life saved.

Cobain's music was full of depression, which touched a nerve in today's youth. Watch Nirvana's video "Smells Like Teen Spirit" to see a chilling presentation of alienation, futility, and cynicism. What looks like a high school pep rally moves in slow motion, voices muted, colors faded; the cheerleaders dance in self-preoccupation leading soundless cheers. Cobain sings bitterly: "Here we are now. Entertain us."

Anomie is the sense that we are outsiders looking through the window at the real world, which we will never be a part of; or worse, that the real world holds nothing that we want to be a part of. That was a theme in Nirvana's music, and that is a theme for many young people today. There are no heroes; everyone is out for himself. There are no careers; you go to college and end up working at the Gap. There is no family; their parents are caught on a treadmill of work to make ends meet, neglecting what is truly important.

Cobain's death was getting the full treatment from MTV and the popular press; it looked as if he might be considered a martyr fit for canonization, and people who work with teens were concerned about an epidemic of imitators. Then Courtney Love, his wife and the mother of his child, herself a rock star, spoke up, and she was angry. She said Cobain's act was cowardly and self-indulgent. No one else could have said it. But it seemed to quell the fascination with his death.

Depression and Alcohol

Sean was literally driven crazy by his wife's decision to separate. In retrospect, we should have understood that Sean was in an "agitated depression," someone who complains of anxiety symptoms more than depression, but is profoundly depressed and impossible to soothe.

A blue-collar worker, Sean had prided himself on being a good father, but knew he was not a terrific husband. He worked hard and made a good living, but he liked to go to the bars and drink after work. Sometimes he would have too much. He'd come home and his wife would yell at him. More than once he hit her. He was ashamed of this, but didn't stop until it was too late. Finally she moved out, taking their children with her. Sean sobered up and joined AA. He pleaded for her to give him another chance, but she wouldn't consider it.

Sean's therapist didn't know what to do with him. The only thing that mattered to him was getting his wife to reconsider, and that was outside his control. When the therapist tried to talk about ways of being a good father even if a divorce took place, Sean wouldn't hear about it. He showed up for all his sessions but didn't find any relief or comfort. He would pace the office, sweat, yell, and cry with frustration.

One night Sean was picked up by the police, asleep in his car in a park. He had a loaded rifle with him. He told them that he had planned to meet someone who was going to buy the gun, but he fell asleep. The police confiscated the weapon and called his sister, whom he was staying with. He told her the same story, and left for work.

On his way to work he stopped in a gun shop. He asked the clerk to see a shotgun. While the clerk had his back turned, Sean loaded the weapon and shot himself in the head. Without his wife, or without the opportunity to undo the pain he'd caused her, Sean couldn't live.

Sean should have been in a psychiatric hospital or a residential substance abuse program, where he could have been protected from his own impulses. If he'd been on the right medications, even as an outpatient he might have been safer. But he wouldn't accept any of these alternatives. He became so depressed when he stopped drinking that it only makes sense to believe he was depressed to begin with, and had been treating the depression with alcohol.

There is a very clear link between depression and substance abuse, especially alcohol. Some people who are depressed to begin with become alcoholics because of their attraction to alcohol. Some alcoholics, when sobered up, find that they are terribly depressed, more so than is accounted for by the effects of their drinking alone. Certainly people who are prone to depression are likely to treat themselves with alcohol.

Alcohol is perhaps the most effective drug there is. It causes an immediate sense of euphoria, gives confidence, and lowers inhibitions—all of which feel very good to someone with depression. Unfortunately, these effects are only temporary, and the after-effects only reinforce depression. The person feels weak, guilty, and ashamed—and is often in worse trouble because of decisions made or actions taken while intoxicated.

Alcohol is in the same class of drugs as popular tranquilizers like Valium and Xanax, and the general anesthetics—it is a "sedative-hypnotic." These drugs have a depressant effect on the central nervous system. They slow down thinking; they interfere with balance, coordination, and muscular control; and in larger doses they can make us unconscious and interfere with automatic central nervous system functions like breathing. The reason why alcohol is so popular as a recreational drug is that its effect comes in stages. Its initial effect is to depress the inhibitory functions of the brain. It reduces inhibitions and takes away our anxieties; it makes us feel more smart, interesting, and capable; and it permits us to take risks that we otherwise wouldn't. Because of this effect, therapists joke that the superego—the conscience—is the only structure of the mind that is soluble in alcohol.

But these initial desired effects of alcohol use are only temporary; within a few hours of ingestion alcohol also depresses the excitatory functions of the brain. The sedative effects of alcohol take over. We feel sleepy, confused, lethargic, and irritable; we lose motor control, coordination, and balance. With regular use we develop a tolerance for alcohol—it requires larger doses to produce the desired effects—and we develop a dependence on it. We need it, we crave it, we don't feel ourselves without it. At first, the dependence may be only psychological, but eventually the body adapts to alcohol use and will complain—through withdrawal symptoms like anxiety, insomnia, tremors, and hallucinations—when alcohol is stopped.

There is just nothing good to say about heavy alcohol use. Eventually, drinking becomes a life, a self. Recovering alcoholics will say "the bottle was drinking me." The overriding goal in life becomes to drink and to maintain ready access to alcohol; we go to work in order to earn money to drink; we plan our nonwork activities around alcohol consumption. And family and friends get evaluated primarily on the basis of whether they help or hinder drinking. That is why AA succeeds where nothing else does with alcoholics; it offers a new life. The concept of the "recovering alcoholic" is an identity to replace an old one based on alcohol.

For many depressives, alcohol is a constant temptation if not a real problem, and I have no doubt that many alcoholics initially got hooked because drinking seemed to alleviate their depression. Alcohol becomes a self-object for us; a friend who is readily available, whose effect is predictable and reliable. Lacking the ability to soothe ourselves when troubled or energize ourselves when depressed, we turn to alcohol.

William Styron makes no bones about the fact that his first episode of major depression resulted from being forced to suddenly give up drinking:

> Alcohol was an invaluable senior partner of my intellect, besides being a friend whose ministrations I sought daily— sought also, I now see, as a means to calm the anxiety and incipient dread that I had hidden away for so long in the dungeons of my spirit. . . . [But suddenly] I discovered that alcohol in minuscule amounts, even a mouthful of wine, caused me nausea, a desperate and unpleasant wooziness, a sinking sensation and ultimately a distinct revulsion. The comforting friend had abandoned me not gradually and reluctantly, like a true friend might do, but like a shot—and I was left high and certainly dry, and unhelmed. . . . Suddenly vanished, the great ally which for so long had kept my demons at bay was no longer there to prevent those demons from beginning to swarm through the subconscious, and I was emotionally naked, vulnerable as I had never been before.[17]

If you suffer from depression and are successful at drinking moderately (defined as no more than two ounces of alcohol a day no more than three times a week), I won't tell you to stop, but I will say you're an anomaly, because the chances are that if you're depressed and use alcohol at all, it's a problem for you. Those initial disinhibitory effects feel too good; it's like magic for someone who feels anxious and insecure. Most depressed people either don't use alcohol at all, or else struggle with it. Our battle with alcohol becomes one more manifestation of the depression. We get in trouble, we make resolutions to change, we discipline ourselves for a while, then the trouble starts again and we feel confirmed in our sense of ourselves as hopeless failures.

If this picture sounds like you, then my advice is simple and direct: stop drinking and get your depression treated. Check out AA groups in your area; you may find a terrific support system. Some AA meetings are difficult for depressives because they aren't tolerant of feelings or medication, but more and more groups are opening up their attitudes on these issues. Regardless, you have to stop drinking, and you have to face the fact that you will be changing yourself from this point on. You have to challenge the emotional habits of depression that perpetuate its cycle, and you won't get better unless you do.

Part 4

A New Synthesis

20

The Rest of the Story

I RECENTLY PASSED my forty-eighth birthday. No big deal, except that for years I believed I wouldn't live past my thirty-eighth. That was the age my mother was when she took her life, and I was obsessed with the idea that I couldn't outlive her, that whatever drove her over the edge would catch up with me. I've since learned that this is not an uncommon belief with the children of suicides—witness Ted Turner, mentioned earlier.

After my mother died, what I felt, consciously, was anger. I blamed her for being selfish, and I could not believe that she had ever really cared about me. My father and I grew apart; he quickly remarried and I had a new family before I was ready. Rather than let myself feel rejected by my parents, I rejected them. I developed an icy armor. I threw myself into the one thing I knew I could do well, school. I had terrific grades, terrific SATs, was editor of the yearbook. I won a scholarship to a college a thousand miles away from home. I told myself I'd never look back.

But I was unprepared for the fact that there would be lots of people as bright as I at college. It turned out everything I'd accomplished in high school was easy; now that I didn't stand out, things were tough. I got scared. I learned to drink. I became desperate to fit in. My grades were lousy. I wasted four years of college and a few years afterward, scared and depressed. I still had this self-image as a misunderstood genius who was going to write the great American novel, or accomplish something else earth-shaking. But I didn't write or do anything else constructive. My idea of myself as a misunderstood genius was a pitiful attempt not to need anyone. I didn't recognize my real fear, that if I let myself depend on someone again, I could lose them again—and of course it would be my fault, because deep down inside I was truly unlovable. *I started mixing alcohol and pills, the same sleeping pills my mother had used. There were nights when I didn't care if I woke up the next morning.*

Something motivated me to get help. I went to see a therapist a friend recommended. It turned out to be a husband-and-wife team, practicing some of the gimmicky Transactional Analysis–type stuff so popular in the seventies. They passed me back and forth between them and had me join a group they were running. It was pretty hokey, but very helpful. They really helped me realize I needed to change my life—to stop hanging back and embrace living. During this time I changed careers and got married.

I went to graduate school and did pretty well, but I had a problem with stage fright; I couldn't speak up in class. I told one of my professors about it, and also a little about my background. She recommended that I see a colleague of hers, a psychoanalytically trained psychiatrist. I thought I was moving up in the world. I had learned enough in graduate school to look down on the therapy that I had thought had helped me as not scientifically respectable. Also the husband-and-wife team were social workers, and the new guy was a psychiatrist. Despite the fact that I was in training to be a social worker myself, I caught both the profession's own doubts about its own self-worth and its perception of the pecking order in mental health.

Maybe what happened wasn't the psychiatrist's fault. Just

after our first appointment, he came down with a serious illness that laid him up for several months. When he came back, he seemed weak and frail. In his office on the twenty-third floor, he sat between me and the window. I had a full-blown anxiety attack in his office, feeling that something was drawing me out the window. It was devastating, the worst feeling that I ever remembered, and it happened every session after that for three years.

This is what we call an iatrogenic problem—a problem induced by the treatment. Perhaps if the psychiatrist hadn't been sick, if he hadn't presented himself as so gentle and tentative anyway, I would have felt safe. As it was, I couldn't feel comforted in his presence. This was despite the fact that I consciously liked and respected him, and still do. My life on the outside went along pretty well. We had children, and I discovered I was a good father. I did well in graduate school and began to enjoy my work. But every week I would be sweating bullets in his office, convinced I was doomed. My phobia generalized; soon I couldn't go up in any tall buildings, or cross bridges.

Perhaps this helped me by confining my depression, as it were, to this one symptom and letting me get on with my life. Even if this were true, though, it's not how therapy is supposed to work. Besides, these weekly episodes of pure terror were eating away at my self-esteem, making me feel as if there were a demon inside me I couldn't control. It seems incredible to me now that both the psychiatrist and I let this drag on for so long. I hope that now if I were the therapist in this situation, I would say, look, this is crazy. Let's try something different. Let's try some medication, or behavior therapy, or let me refer you to a colleague for a fresh start.

I was thirty-five and still believed time was running out for me, and that I wasn't getting the help I needed. I extricated myself from the situation by getting accepted as an analytic subject at the Chicago Institute for Psychoanalysis—I knew this was something my psychiatrist couldn't argue with. We parted company.

When I met my analyst, I was somewhat disappointed that he wasn't much older than I was—how much could he know? But he was a psychologist, which seemed like maybe a good compromise between psychiatry and social work, and he had already published with some high-powered thinkers in analysis. I rather liked him—he was pretty unstuffy for an analyst, had a quirky sense of humor, and seemed to respect me. I stayed with him for another five years, getting through my thirty-eighth birthday unscathed, with a real sense of relief. We worked on my phobia together, and I felt comforted and supported. I enjoyed the analytic process, and recommend it highly as a growth experience.

Somewhere along the line I learned to understand my mother, to forgive her a little. She knew what her choices were. She had seen her older sister impoverished by divorce, finally forced into another abusive marriage as an economic necessity. Isolated from her family, stuck in a loveless marriage, my mother could see no alternatives. Her suicide was both a result of despair and a gesture of defiance. She was so far down in the well, her vision so distorted, that her choice made sense at the time.

I haven't been symptom-free, but I haven't felt the need for regular treatment. I still have periods of depression. I have a psychiatrist I trust to help me with medication when I need it, and a therapist I know whom I can turn to if I really get strung out. I'm still working on all this; my father, in discussing this book with him, gave me still another perspective on my mother. He reminded me of how much she had loved me, and how guilty she felt about being depressed, the horrible debt that the cost of her treatment had placed upon them. In a sad, twisted way, her suicide was also a self-sacrifice. She saw herself as a burden on us; removing that burden was, in her mind, a gift to us. I'm trying to digest this point of view, and it certainly helps me feel

THE REST OF THE STORY

less anger toward her; but the terrible implicit sadness is some-
thing I can take only in small doses.

Last year my analyst sent me a copy of a paper he was
writing. He used an incident in my analysis to illustrate a point
he wanted to make. In doing so, he had to summarize my
background and treatment. I was knocked for a loop. There was
much in the analysis that I had repressed. I had forgotten all
the times I spent on his couch, in terror and anxiety, trying not
to hear what he had to say. We had gotten past my height
phobia; there were times when I felt very safe with him and
times when I didn't feel safe at all. And seeing my case history
laid out in objective clinical terms, I was overwhelmed with
feeling for my self: pity, but not self-pity in the usual sense; more
the kind of objective empathy we might feel for a stranger. Also,
I could see that, while he had a particular theoretical point of
view about my problems, I had a different one. This wasn't
news. During the analysis we had often disagreed on this sub-
ject, but both felt we were in good agreement as far as the
practical implications for me. But it got me thinking about how
doctrinaire I used to be, and how I seem to have gotten away
from that.

What all this has made me realize is that therapy—and
probably medication—doesn't really work for the reasons pro-
fessionals think it does. My first therapists, with their naive
enthusiasm, helped me greatly using methods that no one takes
seriously now. My second, with all his expertise, did me more
harm than good. My third, the analyst, helped me a great
deal—but I think he did it by treating me like a caring, respect-
ful friend I could lean on, and he thinks he did it by helping
me get in touch with repressed impulses. Peter Kramer and
other psychopharmacologists think that Prozac reduces rejec-
tion sensitivity and enhances self-esteem—but none of them can
say how, or even design an experiment to show exactly what it
does. The therapists at the clinic where I work—from a variety

of training, backgrounds, and disciplines—are very often quite helpful with their clients, but all have different explanations for how therapy works.

So it doesn't matter how you get better, as long as you get better. The wiser, warmer, more experienced therapists can probably help you more reliably, but I think it's like teaching a child how to ride a bicycle. You can explain how to steer and how the pedals work, but you can't explain balance and momentum. You have to hold the bicycle up while the child learns these things for himself.

A good psychotherapy is in essence a creation, a change in the patient's way of being, crafted by the patient and the therapist in a mutual process. For many patients it may be their first creative effort since kindergarten.

A Program for Recovery

DEPRESSION IS a disease and a social problem, an illness to be treated professionally and a failure of adaptation that we must overcome through self-determination. These days, with managed care and medication so predominant, I'm concerned that professional help can't go far enough. Medication and brief treatment don't reduce the likelihood of future depression. The grim truth is that if you have one episode of major depression, you have only a one in two chance of avoiding another; if you have two, your chances of avoiding a third are only 30 percent; and if you have three episodes, your chances of avoiding future depression are only one in ten.[1] But I believe very strongly that a self-directed program of recovery such as I am recommending can reduce those odds and can increase our satisfaction with our selves and our lives.

In this chapter I want to distill our previous discussion into some general principles for recovery, and to comment on how these ideas can be used as the basis for a self-help group. I am concerned that any effort to express the complexities of psychological observations in simple language reduces them to the level of self-evident platitudes. But on the other hand I look at the success of AA, based on twelve steps and twelve traditions, and realize that it is the thought, digestion, meditation, discussion, even arguing over the meaning and application of basic principles that brings their applicability home to individuals. With the caveat, then, that these ideas are meant to serve as the stimulus for work on the reader's part, not to be the summary of wisdom on depression, I will describe what I think are basic principles for a program for recovery from depression.

PRINCIPLE ONE: *Feel Your Feelings*

Depression is an effort to avoid feeling. A great deal of what we depressives assume is our character and personality is the result of years of use of self-destructive defense mechanisms that we have adopted in an effort to insulate us from painful or upsetting emotions. But emotions are important signals to us about life; to try to avoid experiencing them wastes mental energy and deprives us of vital information. Besides, we don't seem to be able to avoid only unpleasant emotions; we miss out on the good things in life too. We numb ourselves; we develop acedia.

There is really nothing to fear about feelings. They are self-limiting. Our most intense joy, our most intense pain, never lasts. Eventually we get distracted, we wear ourselves out, or some new event changes the way we feel. We're like a buoy on the water; waves may knock us over, but we have a balance, a ballast, that means we eventually will return to a stable position. We have to trust that we can ride the waves.

The expression of suppressed feelings, when it's done in the right environment, can lift a depressed mood. A good cry, a healthy argument, an appropriate assertion of our rights, a careful exploration of hidden feelings—these help us feel better. But pick your environment. Make sure that you will have the support and understanding you need.

Remember that there is an important difference between feeling emotions and expressing them. We can, and should, control how we express feelings; in a way, that's what growing up is all about. But we can't control how we experience feelings; the idea that we shouldn't feel the way we do eats away like acid on our self-esteem.

PRINCIPLE TWO: *Nothing Comes Out of the Blue*

When we feel our mood change, there is always a reason; something has happened to make us feel this way. Even when we are sliding into a major depressive episode and we know that the depth of our depression is far out of proportion to the event that caused our change in mood, we can take comfort in the fact that there was an event. We have reasons to feel the way we do; we are not crazy.

If you don't believe this, or if you can't identify the precipitants to your changes in mood, use the Mood Journal regularly. It won't take long for you to begin to penetrate your own defenses and see that, for instance, the depression that took you down for no apparent reason yesterday evening probably has something to do with a difficult conversation with your mother yesterday morning. In the evening, you "forget" about the conversation, but the Mood Journal reminds you.

Sometimes the event is obvious: a loss, a disappointment, a setback. Sometimes the event will be obvious to others; we attempt to deny its importance, but we still feel the hurt. This is where friends, loved ones, and a support system can help. Sometimes the event is a memory, a dream, an association sparked by something we read or heard. This is where a private journal can help.

Knowing what's made us feel bad is the first step toward recovery. When we understand what's causing us distress, remember there are only three choices: Alter, accept, avoid. Try to change the situation, try to avoid the situation in the first place, and if you can't do either, work on accepting it.

PRINCIPLE THREE: *Challenge Depressed Thinking*

Try to keep in mind that your basic assumptions about life and yourself are colored by your disease. You see the world through brown-colored glasses.

You are a pessimist. You expect bad events to be permanent, pervasive, and your fault, while you think good things are temporary, limited in scope, and simply the result of chance, certainly not caused by anything you did. This probably means that you don't prepare adequately, give up too easily, and thus aren't as successful as someone whose thinking isn't dominated by depression.

Most tragically, this depressive thinking is likely to be turned on yourself. You remember all the times you failed and all the times the other guy succeeded; you literally can't remember your successes. You probably think of yourself as different from others: weaker, damaged, shameful. You don't consider that you can't get inside another person's skin: the confidence you envy may be just a front; the skill you wish for is just practice and hard work; the success you covet may be bought at a high price.

These ways of thinking are only bad habits, and they can be changed. But changing any habit is hard work. Use the Daily Record of Dysfunctional Thoughts, or any similar tool, to help you identify your own particular depressed thinking habits. Then learn to argue with yourself. Is there really any reason to hold that particular belief? What does it do to me to believe that way? What if I changed my assumptions? Learn a new habit: challenge every assumption that you make.

PRINCIPLE FOUR: *Establish Priorities*

The more of your time on earth you can spend doing things that will help you get what you really want out of life, the happier you will feel every day; the more time you have to spend doing things that are trivial or unimportant, the more miserable you will feel. But you can't do everything you want. You can't please everyone. You have to make choices.

Take some time to identify what's truly important to you. Take a pencil and paper and list ten things that you feel make living worthwhile. Now rank them in order of importance. Put it aside for a few weeks and make a new list. Compare the two lists, and don't be surprised by some changes. Do this a few times, and you will learn what your core values and goals are. Now try to arrange your life so that you spend some time each day in an activity that moves you closer to your goals or allows you to express your values. You will have to reduce the amount of time you spend procrastinating or in time-wasting activities in order to accomplish this. This will require effort, but it will pay off.

PRINCIPLE FIVE: *Communicate Directly*
We have to give up the wish that our loved ones understand us merely because they love us. If we don't tell people what we want, we can't expect to get it. If we don't tell people how we feel, we can't expect them to understand us. We have to learn to speak in direct, unambiguous language, and we have to learn to match what we say with how we say it. We also have to be responsible for listening carefully to what others say to us. If we don't understand, we have to ask for clarification.

Remember that we depressives tend to give up too easily. We withdraw from conversation when it seems that we can't get our point across. We feel tongue-tied and exasperated. We retreat into feeling misunderstood, put-upon, and self-righteous. Instead, try slowing down. Focus on your feelings and express your feelings as I-statements. Ask the other person for help in making yourself understood: "Please ask me questions."

We have to learn the power of metacommunication, of talking about how we're talking: Do I understand you correctly? Am I making myself clear? You seem to be giving me mixed messages,

A NEW SYNTHESIS

and I don't know how to respond. We tend to think communication is just about the subject of the conversation; on the contrary, all communication is about the relationship between the parties involved. Being direct and open shows respect and caring, and invites the same treatment in return.

PRINCIPLE SIX: *Take Care of Your Self*
We need to learn to enjoy ourselves. Most of us have not experienced much happiness. When occasionally we stumble on it, it scares us. We have to approach it with care.

One way to get used to enjoying ourselves is to work on feeling proud. This is an uncomfortable feeling, but one we can get used to with practice. Take a few minutes each day and jot down in a notebook a list of three things you've done that you feel good about. These may be things you thought you couldn't do, or difficult tasks you had to force yourself to do, or just spontaneous acts of generosity or intimacy. After a week, look through the notebook at all the things you can feel good about. If you start to feel a little proud of yourself, you will probably be a little uncomfortable with that feeling. Never mind all the theorizing about why it's hard for you to feel proud; just ride out the discomfort for a few minutes. You'll see that the discomfort soon recedes a little. With practice, before long you may start feeling pretty good about yourself.

Another way is to pay attention to small pleasures. Most of us depressives are not good at being "in the moment"—instead of paying attention to what's actually going on around us, we're worried about what's going to happen next, or we're feeling bad about what happened before. We can change this habit too. Be aware of how your mind takes you away from the present; when you notice it, bring yourself back. Pay more attention to your senses than your thoughts. Attend to the taste of your food, the sounds in the evening, the colors around you. Do what you can to make things more pleasant for yourself.

312

Find opportunities for flow, the experiences that take us out of our temporal consciousness. Practice activities that are a mild challenge, that occupy our minds and bodies, that require a high degree of concentration, that have clear rules and prompt feedback. Practice concentration, making a deliberate effort to focus your attention on the task at hand. Forget yourself; lose the observing eye that is always evaluating you critically. Even at work, even if you hate your job, you will like yourself better if you find ways to make it challenging and stimulating. If this means you work harder and the boss will be pleased with you, that's just a risk you've got to take.

Learn to relax. Take a course in yoga, or T'ai Chi. Take care of your body, and learn to listen to it. Eat healthy but delicious meals. When we neglect or abuse our bodies, we're only being passive-aggressive with ourselves. We're treating ourselves as if we're unworthy of love.

PRINCIPLE SEVEN: *Take, and Expect, Responsibility*
It may surprise some that I list this as a principle for recovery from depression, because depressives are, if anything, over-responsible. We accept blame for things that are not our fault, and we can feel horribly guilty about trivial events. But if we carefully examine what is our responsibility and what is not, we can free ourselves from much of this depressive guilt. Unfortunately we also have to be willing to accept real guilt, because we do all slip up. But this is the only way to develop self-respect.

We are only responsible for our actions, and our inactions. We are not responsible for how we feel, how we look (within limits), whom we're related to, how smart we are. We're not responsible for the way others feel, except insofar as our actions engendered those feelings. We're not responsible for making others happy. We have to be responsible for making ourselves happy. We're allowed to be selfish, to put ourselves first at times; if we practice continual self-sacrifice, we're not being responsible for our selves. If we don't do it, who will?

We must also expect responsibility from others. If we are hurt by another person's behavior, we need to let them know how they have hurt us; to do less diminishes our self-respect. We can, and should, be forgiving; but there is a line between forgiveness and being taken advantage of. We should expect the hurt not to be repeated. We should be prepared to take action if it is.

PRINCIPLE EIGHT: *Look for Heroes*

When we have no one to look up to, we are impoverished. We live in an age of cynicism and exposé, and we are all lesser for it. But there are people who take risks because of their beliefs, who stand up to oppressors, who can serve as models of *caritas*. Look around your own community. Ask people who they admire—perhaps a teacher, a civic leader, a clergyman, an intellectual figure. Find people for yourself to admire, and strive to be like them. If there are people like this at work in your community, perhaps you can help them in their work.

If there doesn't seem to be anyone around, read biography. You don't have to go back too far in time to find real heroes—Eisenhower, Truman, Franklin and Eleanor Roosevelt. Gandhi and Martin Luther King. My heroes of depression, Lincoln, Churchill, and Freud. These are all people who had faults, who could be petty and human and yet more than human too. When there are people we can admire, we are elevated and enriched through our admiration. We construct our selves on models we derive unconsciously from our experiences with our parents and with popular culture. When our models are people we truly respect, we respect our selves.

PRINCIPLE NINE: *Be Generous*

You can't cure depression by giving all your money away; but if you can cultivate a true generosity of spirit, you can't be depressed. I can't count the number of times I've seen it in my group: a member reaches out to someone in great pain, maybe to tell some of their own story, to show they understand, or maybe just to express their sympathy and support. Often it's the tone as much as the words—somehow an emotional connection is established with someone who is feeling ashamed, alone, and afraid. You can feel the electricity in the air.

The sufferer is comforted, but the person who took a risk and reached out is enriched. She's learned that she herself, just by virtue of being herself, has something valuable to share.

There are probably people close to you who could benefit if you make an unselfish gift of your love, attention, time, respect; whatever it is they need, you have the power to give it. If there's no one like that close to you now, there are opportunities to volunteer in your community.

Charity is big business now. We have United Ways and community trusts and arts councils that vouch for the worthiness of their causes; but you can't get much good feeling about yourself just by writing a check. I think, if you're going to donate money, you ought to get something out of it too. Get to know the people in your charity; get a taste of the problems they're trying to solve; get to feel what it's like to reach out and care.

PRINCIPLE TEN: *Cultivate Intimacy*
Intimacy means laying oneself bare to another, to let the other see you warts and all. It's what we both desire and fear most in relationships. It's more a process than an event or state.

Depressives fear intimacy. We put on masks for the world, because we believe our true selves to be shameful, unworthy. With practice, we can keep our masks up all the time, so no one ever knows what we think we're really like inside. We can fool everybody into thinking we're loyal, honest, generous, and caring when deep inside we are convinced it's an act.

But if you keep up an act like this all your life, who are you fooling? Who is the real you? Is it the one that people love, or is it the secret self inside? I submit that the real you is the self you present to the world; this is the self you are responsible for. The inside self is an artifact of depression, guilt, and shame, no more than a trick of the mind, but one that can dominate our life unless we let people know about it.

If we just open up and let our loved ones know about our secret fears, our doubts, our inadequacies, we can grow through the corrective emotional experience of being loved and accepted despite our guilty secrets; as we do this the gap between our public self and our secret self diminishes; eventually it may disappear altogether so that we are just one congruent person. No secrets, no shame.

PRINCIPLE ELEVEN: *Practice Detachment*
We spend far too much time and effort trying to control things we can't. When we're in a stressful situation and feeling upset, we need to ask ourselves two questions: How much does this really matter in the context of my life, and, What can I realistically do about it? We can find that many things that worry us are really unimportant; we've just gotten caught up in emotional contagion and lost our bearings. We may find that we're trying to change things that we realistically cannot change. If that's the case, the wiser course is to accept the inevitable.

"God grant me the serenity to accept the things I cannot change, the courage to change the things I can, and the wisdom to know the difference." This is the AA serenity prayer. It could serve as well as a mantra for depression. Detachment and serenity are not easy to achieve. They are goals that we must strive for through mental discipline. We have to learn to stop ourselves, to halt the adrenaline rush that makes us feel there is a crisis we must take care of right now. This is where a support group can be helpful. People who know us well can help us learn ourselves.

We're on a roller coaster. The ride will take us up and down, spin us around, and scare us and thrill us. We don't have any steering or brakes and we can't get out. We're better off to look around and enjoy the experience, because we don't get a second ride.

PRINCIPLE TWELVE: *Get Help When You Need It*
Learn to identify the signals that can tell you when you're slipping into depression. These vary from individual to individual. You may have trouble sleeping; you may realize you're having trouble concentrating; you may be cranky or irritable. You may just have a lump in your throat or a knot in your stomach. When you see these signs, get help. Don't tell yourself it will pass. Don't tell yourself you should be tougher. Just going for a one-time visit to your therapist may be enough to arrest your downward slide.

Set up a support system in advance. Develop a relationship with a therapist you can trust who understands depression. Develop a relationship with a psychiatrist who stays informed about the latest developments in medication. Be prepared to take medication for a long time. If it's helping you, don't stop just because you feel it's a sign of weakness; that's your critical, self-destructive self talking. Join, or form, a support group and attend it regularly. Enlist your loved ones in your plans; consider "advance directives" that they should follow if you really get bad.

Remember that being ashamed of needing help is a symptom of your disease. Be smarter than your depression.

Living your life according to these principles will not be easy. It requires a total commitment to change. It means accepting that much of what you take for granted about yourself contributes to your depression, and that you, and no one else, have to devote a lot of time and energy to a continuous self-examination. Then it means that you will have to self-consciously practice new skills to replace your old habits of depression. Learning new skills is not easy, but it can be done. As you are doing this, you are likely to feel anxious and uncomfortable. Remember this is the way you feel when you try anything new; with enough practice the new skills become part of yourself. And you will begin to recover from depression.

It will be easier if you can join a support group. Try to find one in your local community. Ask the local mental health center and the local hospital if they sponsor such groups. Call the local mental health hotline (listed in the front of your phone book). Ask your doctor or clergyman, and check out the community events calendar in your local newspaper. You are not looking for a psychotherapy group, for which you will be charged, but a self-help group for people recovering from depression.

Going to your first meeting will be hard. You will be frightened. More than likely, you will have a good experience. You will meet people you like, who will tell you things about themselves that let you know they can understand you. You should feel that it is safe to talk about yourself there, but you shouldn't feel pressured to do so. But if your first experience isn't good, don't give up. Your depressogenic thinking may have colored your perception. Give any group a few chances before you decide it's not for you.

But if you can't find a group you like, don't be afraid to start one. Chapter 11 has some good advice for how to organize a self-help group. I've laid out these principles of recovery so that they can form the basis of discussion for group meetings. I don't expect everyone to agree with every principle, or for them to be universally applicable to all people with depression. It's the group experience, the process of discussing and digesting ideas like these, that cures. The sharing, support, and confrontation provide us with a safe place to practice the skills we need to undo our depression.

Beyond Recovery

THE READER WHO has come this far understands the complexity of depression. Depression is both a physical process and an emotional process, a disease to be treated and an adaptation to life, an illness within ourselves and a response to the world, a disorder of the body, mind, and spirit all at once.

Maturity and Wisdom

People who are prone to depression seem to need more from other people in order to feel whole, hopeful, and competent. However, they rarely seek what they need from others in a straightforward manner. Instead they distort their needs, presenting them in a variety of self-defeating ways, largely because of their use of immature defense mechanisms, which distort reality. These defenses merely reinforce a depressed position.

Defenses are ways of dealing with conflict between parts of our selves that want different things; defenses serve to keep the conflict out of consciousness. Conflict is always between a wish and a fear, an impulse and the forces in our mind that constrain our impulses. That's why repression is a defense mechanism, even though we feel the uncomfortable emotion; the defense is not against emotion, but against awareness of conflict.

I hope I've made it clear that defense mechanisms are not bad things in and of themselves—they are necessary to life—but some defenses are less healthy than others. Some defenses, like acting out and passive aggression, can mask reality and expose us to real danger or blow up in our faces. Other defenses, like denial and projection, which can dramatically and perhaps permanently interfere with our ability to accept reality, are crippling when compared to others that allow us to perceive reality more correctly. These immature defenses may keep our feelings or impulses out of consciousness, but one of the great cosmic ironies is that we can still feel guilty about feelings we're not aware of. We feel guilty, undeserving, and false without knowing why. That is why I've suggested using the Mood Journal to track the connections between the mood shifts we experience and the external events that cause them. A depressed mood is a response to an external event that has stirred up feelings we try to defend against.

There are alternatives to these immature defenses. These are ways of transmuting the conflict between warring parts of ourselves but don't distort reality so intensely. When we are able to perceive reality more correctly, our actions are much more likely to have the effect we desire. One excellent review and guide to understanding how our defenses work is George Vaillant's *The Wisdom of the Ego*.[1] Vaillant lists five mature defenses:

Altruism involves taking my own needs, correctly perceiving them in others, and achieving some self-gratification by taking care of those needs in others. The paranoid looks at the big houses of the rich and considers himself cheated. The altruist takes care of the poor and considers himself blessed. In so doing he opens himself up to the love and respect of others.

Sublimation takes our out-of-control feelings and allows them to be expressed directly but in a socially acceptable way. Sublimation is the defense of poets, novelists, and playwrights. When O'Neill puts his own tortured family on stage, he is transforming his own interior experience into high art. When I come home from a difficult meeting and watch *The Terminator*, I'm sublimating my rage by vicariously watching someone else act it out.

Suppression is the conscious decision to delay action. There is an awareness of the conflict—an unacceptable desire, a change in reality that must be redressed—but a decision to take no action, to let things cook for a while. We may deliberately decide that waiting is wise, or we may just feel confused and uncertain. But if we can tolerate remaining aware of the conflict—perhaps by buying ourselves some time through intimate conversation about it, through dreaming, through finding other outlets to release the anxiety—we are suppressing.

Anticipation means taking the anxiety over a conflict and dealing with it in advance, a little at a time. It is like inoculating ourselves against a future stress. As in suppression, the conflict is there in consciousness, but we titrate how much of it we'll deal with at any one time. Vaillant refers to Chuck Yeager and other test pilots with "the right stuff": "To have underestimated danger would have been fatal. To have exaggerated danger would have been incapacitating. Thus, they worried in advance, made lists, practiced, and then, appreciating that they had prepared as well as they could, they relaxed. So easy to say, so difficult to do."[2]

Humor is the hardest to define. Somehow mature humor takes the conflict, our dilemma of being caught between the rock of our desires and the hard place of reality, and makes us take a step back out of the picture and see the absurdity of our situation. It doesn't push the conflict, or even the anxiety, out of consciousness; but it defuses it, robs it of some of its energy by letting us see that, even when things are rotten, we might as well enjoy.

The lay reader may object that these are not skills, defenses, or personality styles, these are conscious choices. Religion teaches us altruism. Suppression is just the mature delaying of gratification. Everyone is capable of seeing the humorous side of a situation. But it is not that easy. If we could all choose to suppress our impulses, we wouldn't have jails. If we could all practice true altruism by conscious choice, we wouldn't have need for institutional charity. If we could all anticipate reality, we would floss regularly. We want to believe we can bootstrap ourselves into these abilities, because we want to be able to condemn those who seem to be unable to. But if we're honest with ourselves, we'll acknowledge that it's not that easy.

On the other hand, many of my professional colleagues will object that by suggesting people practice mature defenses or cultivate empathy, I am trying to teach cows to dance. In the therapeutic community there is a general feeling that patients can overcome deep-seated problems only through intensive psychotherapy. In the medical community the perception is that the problematic behavior that accompanies depression is only a result, not a cause, of a chemical imbalance. Both believe that expecting the patient to make much progress through self-conscious attempts to change behavior is futile, if not cruel.

I disagree. The more I learn about people, the more I believe their problems stem from not knowing alternatives rather than from pathology or resistance. It's the old philosophical debate of free will versus determinism. Do we have the power to choose between courses of action, or does it only seem as if we do? Is everything that happens to us preordained, perhaps the logical consequence of a chain of events right back to when the Prime Mover set the universe in motion? I don't mean to duck legitimate scientific questions, but it also seems reasonable to point out that scientists take positions on questions like these not only because of their science but also because of their personal values and beliefs. Meanwhile, the pragmatic answer is that we must behave as if we have the power to control ourselves, because if we don't, we have no hope.

The optimistic observation is that there is such a thing as wisdom. As we grow older, if we allow ourselves to learn from our experiences, we develop a better perspective on what really matters. We grow. We don't lose sleep over details. We learn to value what we have. We learn to let go of what we can't control. We can laugh at the ironies of life a little more easily. Altruism, humor, and the other mature defenses are qualities that life teaches us; we just have to pay attention to the lessons.

A Creative Life

To Vaillant's list of mature defenses I would add one more quality—the capacity for creativity—as essential for recovery from depression.

We tend to think of creativity as something only for artists—"creative types" who write, paint, dance, or sculpt for a living. But a sense of creativity is something we all need in our lives. Creativity is the antithesis of depression. It is a way of saying that what I think and feel matters. Everyone whose work enables them to express themselves or accomplish something meaningful; parents who are devoting themselves to raising their children; those whose leisure activities offer them opportunities for self-expression or for making a difference—all are involved in a creative pursuit.

Depression is not just an illness, but a failure of creativity. We all face the problem of creating meaning in our lives. When we're depressed, we've lost hope for meaning. We all need to make a deliberate effort to make the self fertile; for the depressive, that effort is essential to life. It was almost fifty years ago that Erik Erikson wrote that the developmental challenge of adulthood is generativity versus stagnation.[3] I don't think anyone has since put it more clearly. The challenge is to find ways to grow, produce, create, after we realize that life is short and that we can't do everything we want; the fear is of rotting, growing self-preoccupied and putrescent.

Recently one of my group members spoke of the satisfaction of depression. We all looked at her in surprise; this was not a subject that was on our minds at the time. "I'm serious," she said. "Sometimes I feel entitled to be depressed. I feel like I've suffered a lot of crap in my life, and if anyone deserves to feel sorry for themselves, it's me. Depression feels safe and comfortable. I can wrap it around me like a big old blanket. Keep myself warm at night with all my grievances. I may be lonely but I'm sure self-righteous." I never heard anyone put the attractive side of stagnation any better. Stagnation implies something easy, quiet, and unchallenging. We can stay home, watch TV, and feel sorry for ourselves. It's easier than working our way out of depression. The problem is that stagnation isn't static. Once you start rotting, you don't stop. You may be able to watch a few weeks of TV safely, but any more than that and you will be doing yourself harm. Your self-esteem, ambition, humor, and juices will dry up. Before long you'll have trouble leaving the house at all. You'll stop answering the phone. Pretty soon you'll put your head in the oven.

Because, as Erikson said, our choice is to grow or die. The long-term cure for depression doesn't come from anything other than living right—being productive, generous, caring, other-centered. Happiness is something we achieve through our own effort, not something we can buy or acquire, not something anyone else can give us. It's a by-product of living a certain kind of life that helps us feel good about ourselves. It comes from being fully engaged in life, from paying attention to the present moment, to the process of living.

But living the right kind of life doesn't mean only being dutiful. It implies having some fun along the way. It means learning how to be creative as well as responsible. Creativity requires an element of play. It suggests taking what seems mundane and seeing it from a new perspective, from a child's eyes that have not been trained to see things as they are but instead can see new combinations that lead to new solutions; a new whole is created that is greater than the sum of the parts. It requires an appreciation of humor and paradox. Creativity is also a synthesis of reason and emotion. In visual arts, literature, and music, for instance, the artist creates a product that expresses emotions—it engages the emotions of the audience—through a discipline. We admire the skill and technique, but without emotional engagement we are unmoved. In science and engineering, the creative person is moved by his own emotional engagement in the problem to go beyond the ordinary, to search for unique solutions. He is challenged and stimulated by the problem; solving it becomes an exercise in flow.

Creativity isn't a quality of a personality; most of us rather achieve creativity in a part of our life—our work, our hobby, our family—without becoming necessarily more creative in other parts. "Creativity isn't some kind of a fluid that can ooze in any direction."[4] But the prerequisites of creativity—discipline, playfulness, vision—can be cultivated and can pervade our selves.

Creativity is a mastery of anxiety. There is a recognized process to creativity that starts with hard work. You immerse yourself in the problem or the project. You seek out all the information you can find that might be helpful; the more open you can be to new information, fresh points of view, the more likely you are to come up with new solutions. But doing this creates stress. We hear conflicting ideas, conflicting advice about a subject that is important to us, and we feel frustrated; why isn't there a simple answer? We turn our frustration on ourselves; why can't we find the answer? We seek more and more information until we become overloaded. Our anxiety becomes intolerable, and we put the problem aside.

If we're depressed, that's probably the end of the creative process, because we will self-censor the next phase, during which our unconscious mind works on the problem. If we're not depressed, our unconscious will play with the problem, combining and recombining information in ways that our conscious mind doesn't permit. Eventually, while we're jogging or showering or falling asleep, the pieces fall into place and we have the Aha! experience. The solution is clear and obvious. We forget about all the hard work and anxiety that preceded the solution.

We need to think of ourselves as capable of creativity in all aspects of our lives, not just the artist's studio or the research lab. We can apply the same principles to all the challenges we face—raising our children, making a living, getting along with difficult people. We have to work on the problem, and we have to play with it as well.

Most of us are familiar with the concept of the vicious circle. Most psychotherapy patients are caught in it. One bad event elicits a response that engenders other bad events, eliciting more negative responses, and so on down into the well. The patient who is depressed at her mother's death has trouble concentrating on the job, irritates her boss and gets fired, loses her health insurance and can't get help for the kids when they are sick, and becomes even more depressed as a result. A concept that is not so familiar is the *adaptive spiral.* It's not as dramatic and vivid as the vicious circle but, thankfully for all of us, it happens a lot more often. It's when our response to a single good event makes it more likely that other good things will happen to us. A husband and wife make love and, as a result, the next morning the wife smiles a little more than usual. Her boss notices her cheerful attitude and gives her a special assignment. Pleased with the expression of confidence in her, she continues to feel especially good and eventually earns a promotion.

To feel truly good about ourselves, we must feel challenged. Here is my challenge: consider that your job is your self. You are in charge of rebuilding your self. Take all the help you need, but remember that in the end you are responsible. Remember that if we set our goals too high, we get anxious and discouraged, and if we set our goals too low, we get bored and apathetic. So practice self-constructive behavior at a pace that challenges you. Get to know your own feelings. Question your assumptions. Cultivate detachment and humor. Practice altruism. It doesn't matter that at first you feel self-conscious and awkward. That is how you feel learning anything new. With enough practice, these skills can become part of your self. And the adaptive spiral means that use of these skills can set in motion events that will reward their use, making it easier for us to make them part of our selves.

Appendix A

National organizations that provide advocacy, information, and support about depression and other mental illnesses:

National Depressive and Manic-Depressive Association
730 N. Franklin St., Suite 501
Chicago, IL 60610
800-862-3632

National Foundation for Depressive Illness
P.O. Box 2257
New York, NY 10116-2257
800-248–4344

National Alliance for the Mentally Ill
2101 Wilson Blvd., Suite 302
Arlington, VA 22201
703-524-7600

American Suicide Foundation
(for family members of suicide victims)
800-531-4477

On the Internet:
the newsgroup alt.support.depression

Appendix B

Wakefield Self-Report Questionnaire

Instructions: Read these statements carefully, one at a time, and underline or circle the response that best indicates how you are. It is most important to indicate *how you are now,* not how you were, or how you would hope to be.

A. I feel miserable and sad.
   0. No, not at all
   1. No, not much
   2. Yes, sometimes
   3. Yes, definitely

B. I find it easy to do the things I used to do.
   0. Yes, definitely
   1. Yes, sometimes
   2. No, not much
   3. No, not at all

C. I get very frightened or panicky feelings for apparently no reason at all.
   0. No, not at all
   1. No, not much

2. Yes, sometimes
3. Yes, definitely

D. I have weeping spells, or feel like it.
   0. No, not at all
   1. No, not much
   2. Yes, sometimes
   3. Yes, definitely

E. I still enjoy the things I used to.
   0. Yes, definitely
   1. Yes, sometimes
   2. No, not much
   3. No, not at all

F. I am restless and can't keep still.
   0. No, not at all
   1. No, not much
   2. Yes, sometimes
   3. Yes, definitely

G. I get off to sleep easily without sleeping pills.
   0. Yes, definitely
   1. Yes, sometimes
   2. No, not much
   3. No, not at all

H. I feel anxious when I go out of the house on my own.
   0. No, not at all
   1. No, not much
   2. Yes, sometimes
   3. Yes, definitely

I. I have lost interest in things.
   0. No, not at all
   1. No, not much
   2. Yes, sometimes
   3. Yes, definitely

J. I get tired for no reason.
   0. No, not at all
   1. No, not much
   2. Yes, sometimes
   3. Yes, definitely

K. I am more irritable than usual.
   0. No, not at all
   1. No, not much
   2. Yes, sometimes
   3. Yes, definitely

L. I wake early and then sleep badly for the rest of the night.
   0. No, not at all.
   1. No, not much
   2. Yes, sometimes
   3. Yes, definitely

Scoring: Most depressed people tend to score above 14, although high scores may be caused by physical illnesses or temporary stressors. Scores lower than 15 may still warrant consultation if subjective distress is substantial. Repeating the test in two weeks may be helpful; a rising score is cause for concern.

Notes

Chapter 1.

1. Gerald Klerman, "Evidence for Increases in the Rate of Depression in North America and Western Europe during Recent Decades," in H. Hippius, G. Klerman, and N. Mattusek (eds.), *New Results in Depression Research* (Berlin: Springer Verlag, 1986).

2. See Martin E. Seligman, *What You Can Change and What You Can't* (New York: Fawcett, 1995), and David A. Karp, *Speaking of Sadness: Depression, Disconnection, and the Meanings of Illness* (New York: Oxford, 1996).

3. Daniel Goleman, "A Rising Cost of Modernity: Depression," *New York Times,* Dec. 8, 1992; "The Changing Rate of Major Depression," editorial, *Journal of the American Medical Association* 268(21): pp. 3098–3105 (1992).

4. U.S. Department of Health and Human Services, Public Health Service, Agency for Health Care Policy and Research, *Clinical Practice Guideline: Depression in Primary Care,* vol. 1, *Detection and Diagnosis* (U.S. Government Printing Office, Washington, D.C., 1993).

5. Paul E. Greenberg, Laura E. Stiglin, Stan N. Finkelstein, and Ernst R. Berndt, "The Economic Burden of Depression in 1990," *Journal of Clinical Psychiatry* 54(11): pp. 405–424 (1993).

6. Fascinating new research has shown that, at least for obsessive-compulsive disorder, psychotherapy produces changes in brain functioning that

are similar to the effects of medication. PET scans of the brains of individuals suffering from OCD and treated with cognitive-behavioral therapy showed changes in the links between brain structures associated with OCD and changes in the caudate nucleus, an area of unusual activity in patients with OCD. These findings suggest that researchers are beginning to be able to trace the neurological pathways by which therapy—or perhaps any important life experience—affects personality. See J. M. Schwartz, et al., "Systematic Changes in Cerebral Glucose Metabolic Rate after Successful Behavior Modification Treatment of Obsessive-Compulsive Disorder," *Archives of General Psychiatry* 53(2): pp. 109–113 (1996).

7. Alice Miller, *The Drama of the Gifted Child [Prisoners of Childhood]* (New York: Basic Books, 1981).

8. William Styron, *Darkness Visible: A Memoir of Madness* (New York: Random House, 1990).

9. Agency for Health Care Policy and Research, *Depression in Primary Care,* vol. 1, *Detection and Diagnosis.*

10. Gerald Klerman and Myrna Weissman, "Increasing Rates of Depression," *Journal of the American Medical Association* 261(15): pp. 2229–2235 (1989).

11. Gerald Klerman, et al., "Birth-Cohort Trends in Rates of Major Depressive Disorder Among Relatives of Patients with Affective Disorder," *Archives of General Psychiatry* 42(7): pp. 689–693 (1985).

12. Daniel Goleman, "Depression in the Old Can Be Deadly, but the Symptoms Are Often Missed," *New York Times,* Sept. 6, 1995, C10.

13. J. A. Egeland and J. N. Sussex, "Suicide and Family Loading for Affective Disorders," *Journal of the American Medical Association* 254(7): pp. 915–918 (1985). David B. Cohen, *Out of the Blue: Depression and Human Nature* (New York: Norton, 1994).

14. Cohen, *Out of the Blue.*

15. Jane Brody, "Personal Health: Myriad Masks Hide an Epidemic of Depression," *New York Times,* Sept. 30, 1992. Anonymous, "NMHA Survey Finds Many Americans Are Poorly Informed About Depression, Slow to Seek Help," *Hospital and Community Psychiatry* 43(3): pp. 292–293 (1992).

16. Karp, *Speaking of Sadness,* p. 57.

Chapter 2.

1. American Psychiatric Association, *Diagnostic and Statistical Manual of Mental Disorders* (DSM-IV) (Washington, D.C.: APA, 1994).

2. Agency for Health Care Policy and Research, *Depression in Primary Care,* vol. 1, *Detection and Diagnosis.*

3. See *Time's* profile on Turner (Jan. 6, 1992).

Chapter 3.

1. Thomas Kuhn, *The Structure of Scientific Revolutions,* 2nd ed., enlarged (Chicago: University of Chicago Press, 1970).

2. Respectively, the White House aide who recently took his own life; the young mother who was convicted of drowning her two sons after having convinced the world they had been abducted by a stranger; and the former chief justice of the State of New York, recently released after serving eighteen months for the bizarre blackmail scheme he acted out against his estranged girlfriend.

3. Milton F. Shore, "Narrowing Prevention," *Readings: A Journal of Reviews and Commentary in Mental Health* (Sept. 1994), pp. 13–17.

4. An interesting new study from Israel shows that schizophrenia seems to have a strong genetic link, but that depression (in women) and substance abuse and violence (in men) are more responsive to social stresses. See Bruce P. Dohrenwend, Itzhak Levav, Patrick E. Shrout, Sharon Schwartz, Guedalia Naveh, Bruce G. Link, Andrew E. Skodol, and Ann Stueve, "Socioeconomic Status and Psychiatric Disorders: The Causation-Selection Issue," *Science* 255(5047): pp. 946–951 (1992).

5. Karp, *Speaking of Sadness.* Karp is quoting an anonymous prepublication review of his own book.

6. Researchers who investigate incidence like to treat the different diagnoses of depression as hard science, but other researchers are continually investigating the confusion and overlap in practical applications of the diagnoses. An important recent contribution is John Z. Sadler, Osborne P. Wiggins, and Michael A. Schwartz, *Philosophical Perspectives on Psychiatric Diagnostic Classification* (Baltimore: Johns Hopkins, 1994). Also, Eileen P. Rubinson, M.S.W., and Gregory M. Asnis, M.D., "Major Depression: Masks, Misconceptions, and Nosologic Ambiguities," *Psychiatric Annals,* pp. 360–364 (July 1989).

7. This section draws greatly on Peter Kramer's elegant summation of a complex field of research in *Listening to Prozac* (New York: Viking, 1993).

8. Harry F. Harlow and Robert Zimmerman, "Affectional Responses in the Infant Monkey," *Science* 130: pp. 421–432 (1959).

9. Stephen J. Suomi, "Primate Separation Models of Affective Disorder," in John Madden IV, ed., *Neurobiology of Learning, Emotion, and Affect* (New York: Raven Press, 1991), pp. 195–214.

10. Peter D. Kramer, M.D., "Politics and Prozac," *Commonwealth*, Nov. 17, 1993.

11. Miller, *The Drama of the Gifted Child*.

12. For an excellent, readable review of what is now known about the child's development and attachment to the parents, see Robert Karen, *Becoming Attached* (New York: Warner, 1994).

Chapter 4.

1. Heinz Kohut, *The Analysis of the Self* (New York: International Universities Press, 1971), and *The Restoration of the Self* (New York: International Universities Press, 1977). Kohut is difficult reading even for the veteran of psychoanalytic journals. A more readable exposition of his basic ideas is in Ernest Wolf, *Treating the Self* (New York: Guilford, 1988).

2. Miller, *Drama of the Gifted Child*, p. 57.

3. Joe Palombo, who used this metaphor, didn't warn us about how the parent feels later on, when the child rides off into the distance without a backward glance.

4. Samuel Slipp, *Object Relations: A Dynamic Bridge Between Individual and Family Treatment* (New York: Jason Aronson, 1984), p. 181.

5. Anonymous respondent, quoted in Karp, *Speaking of Sadness*, p. 111.

Chapter 5.

1. Jerome Frank, *Persuasion and Healing: A Comparative Study of Psychotherapy*, rev. ed. (New York: Schocken Books, 1974).

Chapter 6.

1. George E. Vaillant, *The Wisdom of the Ego* (Cambridge: Harvard University Press, 1993).

2. Beverley Raphael, *The Anatomy of Bereavement* (Northvale, N.J.: Jason Aronson, 1994), p. 402.

3. Judith Viorst, *Necessary Losses* (New York: Simon and Schuster, 1986), p. 238.

4. Raphael, *The Anatomy of Bereavement*, p. 403.

5. Gerald M. Klerman, M.D., Myrna Weissman, Ph.D., Bruce J. Rounsaville, M.D., and Eve S. Chevron, M.S., *Interpersonal Psychotherapy of Depression* (New York: Basic Books, 1984). The other problem areas are interpersonal role disputes, role transitions, and interpersonal deficits.

6. A very helpful resource on anger is Carol Tavris, *Anger: The Misunderstood Emotion,* rev. ed. (New York: Simon and Schuster, 1989).

7. Michael Fellman, *Citizen Sherman* (New York: Random House, 1995), pp. 105–106.

8. Geoffrey C. Ward, *The Civil War: An Illustrated History* (New York: Knopf, 1990).

9. Shelby Foote, *The Civil War: A Narrative,* Part 3, *Red River to Appomattox* (New York: Random House, 1974), p. 996.

10. Robertson Davies, "The Deadliest Sin of All," in *One Half of Robertson Davies* (New York: Viking, 1977), pp. 62–68. Martin E. Seligman (*What You Can Change and What You Can't*) deserves credit for emphasizing this concept and discovering this essay. Wallace says the term survives in common speech in Appalachia as *acidie* (by folk etymology a sour mood). Edwin R. Wallace, "Psychiatry and Its Nosology," in John Z. Sadler, et al., *Philosophical Perspectives on Psychiatric Diagnostic Classification.*

11. Martin E. Seligman, *Learned Optimism* (New York: Pocket Books, 1990).

12. Mihaly Csikszentmihalyi, *The Evolving Self* (New York: HarperCollins, 1993).

13. One very helpful book on journal writing is Christina Baldwin, *One to One: Self-Understanding Through Journal Writing* (New York: Evans, 1991).

Chapter 7.

1. Aaron T. Beck, A. J. Rush, B. F. Shaw, and G. Emery, *Cognitive Therapy of Depression* (New York: Guilford Press, 1979), pp. 130–131.

2. Hyrum W. Smith, *The Ten Natural Laws of Successful Time and Life Management* (New York: Warner, 1994).

3. There is now a lot of literature on time management, personal efficiency, and self-improvement, which can be helpful in recovering from depression. Steven Covey's books (*The Seven Habits of Highly Effective People,* etc.) are not bad, though I enjoyed more Hyrum Smith's *The Ten Natural Laws of Successful Time and Life Management.* With both of these, you have to put aside any prejudice you might have against Babbitry and boosterism. Stephanie Winston's books (*Getting Organized,* etc.) are very practical and helpful. Martin E. Seligman has made a good contribution with *What You Can Change and What You Can't.* None of these is the answer if you're really depressed; they are to help you as you recover.

4. Jane B. Burka, Ph.D., and Lenora M. Yuen, Ph.D., *Procrastination: Why You Do It, What to Do About It* (Reading, Mass.: Addison-Wesley, 1983).

5. David Burns, M.D., *The Feeling Good Handbook* (New York: Plume Books, 1990), pp. 182–202.

6. Vaillant, *The Wisdom of the Ego,* p. 52.

7. Edmund J. Bourne, *The Anxiety and Phobia Workbook* (Oakland, Calif.: New Harbinger, 1990); Robert E. Alberti and Michael Emmons, *Your Perfect Right* (San Luis Obispo, Calif.: Impact Press, 1974); Sharon and Gordon Bower, *Asserting Yourself* (Reading, Mass.: Addison-Wesley, 1976); Manuel J. Smith, *When I Say No, I Feel Guilty* (New York: Dial Press, 1975).

8. Herbert Benson, M.D., with Miriam Z. Klipper, *The Relaxation Response* (New York: Morrow, 1975).

9. Two resources with much helpful information about relaxation, habit control, and self-care are Mary Ellen Copeland, *The Depression Workbook* (Oakland, Calif.: New Harbinger, 1992), and Bourne, *The Anxiety and Phobia Workbook.*

Chapter 8.

1. Harold A. Sackheim, Ph.D., and Barbara L. Steif, M.A., "Neuropsychology of Depression and Mania," in *Depression and Mania,* edited by Anastasios Georgotas, M.D., and Robert Cancro, M.D. (New York:

Elsevier Science Publishing, 1988). Quoted in Colette Dowling, *You Mean I Don't Have to Feel This Way?* (New York: Bantam, 1991), p. 63.

2. Interesting new research suggests that the cognitive theorists have been a little hard on depressives. It now turns out that depressed people tend to be more accurate judges of themselves than "normal" people are. Given a performance test, then asked to rate their performance, people who are depressed tend to agree with objective observers. People who are not depressed tend to rate their performance more highly than objective observers do. This supports the idea that depressed people are "sadder but wiser"—they see themselves and the world more accurately than other people, who may be using rose-colored glasses. On the other hand, the same research shows that people who are depressed are indeed harder on themselves in that they tend to overestimate the performance of others. Thus they view themselves more accurately than nondepressed people, but they view others less accurately. See, for example, Lauren B. Alloy, "Depressive Realism: Sadder but Wiser?" *Harvard Mental Health Letter,* April 1995, pp. 4–5.

3. Beck, et al., *Cognitive Therapy of Depression.*

4. The reader who is interested in learning more about this way of understanding depression should look into Beck, et al., *Cognitive Therapy of Depression,* and Burns, *The Feeling Good Handbook.*

5. Seligman, *Learned Optimism.*

6. Of course, to blame others consistently and unrealistically is no healthier than to blame ourselves all the time. Ideally, we want to perceive the world clearly and objectively. But all of us have some tendency to generalize in predictable patterns.

7. Albert Ellis, *Reason and Emotion in Psychotherapy* (New York: Birch Lane Press, 1994).

8. Jon Kabat-Zinn, *Full Catastrophe Living* (New York: Delta, 1990).

9. Beck, et al., *Cognitive Therapy of Depression.*

Chapter 9.

1. Karp, *Speaking of Sadness,* p. 28.

2. Kramer, in *Listening to Prozac,* pp. 87–107, has a thoughtful discussion

of this subject, summarizing the work of Donald F. Klein, a research psychiatrist.

3. Kramer, *Listening to Prozac.*

4. I saw a wonderful illustration of this in, of all places, *The Magnificent Seven.* Chris (Yul Brynner) is trying to convince Frank, the greedy one, that there is no gold in the village. Frank, assuming that everyone else is as greedy as he is, thinks that Chris is just putting on an act for the benefit of the villagers. "Don't understand me so fast," says Chris.

5. Clara G. Livsey, M.D., *The Marriage Maintenance Manual* (New York: Dial Press, 1982).

Chapter 10.

1. John Bradshaw, *Healing the Shame That Binds You* (Deerfield Beach, Fla.: Health Communications, 1988).

2. Robert Karen, "Shame," *The Atlantic,* Feb. 1992, pp. 40–70.

3. "NMHA Survey Finds Many Americans Are Poorly Informed About Depression, Slow to Seek Help," *Hospital and Community Psychiatry* 43(3): pp. 292–293 (1992).

4. Charles L. Whitfield, *Boundaries and Relationships* (Deerfield Beach, Fla.: Health Communications, 1993).

5. Maggie Scarf, *Intimate Partners: Patterns in Love and Marriage* (New York: Random House, 1987), and *Intimate Worlds: Life Inside the Family* (New York: Random House, 1995). Two of the most reliable and readable books available on the struggle for intimacy and the need for autonomy.

6. Thomas F. Fogarty, M.D., "The Distancer and the Pursuer," *The Family* 7(1): pp. 11–16 (1979).

7. Susan Nolen-Hoeksma, "Sex Differences in Control of Depression," in Daniel Wegner and James Pennebaker, *Handbook of Mental Control* (Englewood Cliffs, N.J.: Prentice-Hall, 1993).

8. Tavris, *Anger: The Misunderstood Emotion.*

9. Kramer, *Listening to Prozac,* ch. 1.

Chapter 11.

1. Kramer, "Politics and Prozac."

2. Sidney J. Blatt, et al., "Characteristics of Effective Therapists," *Journal of Consulting and Clinical Psychology* 64(6): pp. 1276–1284 (1996).
3. Beck, et al., *Cognitive Therapy of Depression*.
4. Klerman, et al., *Interpersonal Psychotherapy of Depression*.
5. Kramer, *Listening to Prozac*.
6. Michael W. Miller, "Listening to Eli Lilly: Prozac Hysteria Has Gone Too Far," *Wall Street Journal*, March 31, 1994, B1.
7. Geoffrey Cowley, "The Culture of Prozac," *Newsweek*, Feb. 7, 1994, pp. 41–43.
8. Copeland, *The Depression Workbook*.
9. Burns, *The Feeling Good Handbook*.

Chapter 12.

1. Ernest Wolf, *Treating the Self*, p. 102.

Chapter 13.

1. Csikszentmihalyi, *Flow*, p. 158 et seq.
2. Ibid., p. 159.
3. M. Scott Peck, *The Road Less Traveled* (New York: Simon and Schuster, 1978).

Chapter 14.

1. Deborah Tannen, Ph.D., *You Just Don't Understand* (New York: Ballantine Books, 1990).

Chapter 15.

1. See Scarf, *Intimate Partners*.
2. Eric Berne, *Games People Play* (New York: Ballantine, 1985).

Chapter 16.

1. Mary Sykes Wylie, "Swallowed Alive," *Family Therapy Networker*, Sept./Oct., 1994.
2. Ibid., p. 22.
3. G. Pirooz Sholevar, M.D., and Linda Schwoeri, *The Transmission of De-*

pression in Families and Children: Assessment and Intervention
(Northvale, N.J.: Jason Aronson, 1994).

4. Jane E. Brody, "Sorrow's Web: Depressed Mother and Difficult Child,"
   New York Times, Nov. 2, 1994, C12.

5. Laura M. Pappano, "The Connection Gap: Why Americans Feel So
   Alone." Paper presented at conference, Loneliness in America, Taun-
   ton, Mass., April 11, 1997.

Chapter 17.

1. Neil Kalter, "Long-Term Effects of Divorce on Children: A Developmental Vulnerability Model." *American Journal of Orthopsychiatry*
   57(4): pp. 587–600 (1987).

2. Judith S. Wallerstein and Sandra Blakeslee, *Second Chances: Men,
   Women, and Children a Decade after Divorce* (New York: Ticknor &
   Fields, 1989).

Chapter 18.

1. Phil Ochs, "There but for Fortune," © 1963, Appleseed Music, Inc.

2. Klerman and Weissman, "Increasing Rates of Depression."

3. Mary Sykes Wylie, "Whatever Happened to Community Mental
   Health?" *Family Therapy Networker*, July/August 1992, p. 22.

4. John Berendt, "Phil Ochs Ain't Marchin' Anymore," *Esquire*, August
   1976, p. 132.

5. Ibid., p. 136.

6. Michael Schumacher, *There but for Fortune: The Life of Phil Ochs*
   (New York: Hyperion, 1996).

Chapter 19.

1. Myrna M. Weissman and Mark Olfson, "Depression in Women: Implications for Health Care Research," *Science* 269(5225): pp. 799–801 (1995).

2. Phyllis Chesler, *Women and Madness* (New York: Doubleday, 1972).

3. Maggie Scarf, *Unfinished Business: Pressure Points in the Lives of
   Women* (New York: Ballantine, 1980).

4. Carol Gilligan, *In a Different Voice: Psychological Theory and Women's
   Development* (Cambridge: Harvard University Press, 1982).

5. Colette Dowling, *You Mean I Don't Have to Feel This Way?*

6. Ibid., p. 75.

7. Weissman and Olfson, "Depression in Women," p. 800.

8. D. E. H. Russell, *Sexual Exploitation* (Beverly Hills, Calif.: Sage Library of Social Research, 1984).

9. Ellen McGrath, et al., *Women and Depression: Risk Factors and Treatment Issues* (Washington, D.C.: American Psychological Association, 1990).

10. Bruce P. Dohrenwend, et al. "Socioeconomic Status and Psychiatric Disorders: The Causation-Selection Issue."

11. Frank Pittman, *Man Enough: Fathers, Sons, and the Search for Masculinity* (New York: Putnam, 1993).

12. Joaquim Puig-Antich, M.D., and Burt Weston, "The Diagnosis and Treatment of Major Depressive Disorder in Childhood," *Annual Review of Medicine* 34: pp. 231–245 (1983).

13. Cohen, *Out of the Blue.*

14. Jane Brody, "Suicide Myths Cloud Efforts to Save Children," *New York Times,* June 16, 1992, C1.

15. Harry M. Hoberman and Barry D. Garfinkel, "Completed Suicide in Children and Adolescents," *Journal of the American Academy of Child and Adolescent Psychiatry* 27(6): pp. 689–695 (1988).

16. J. D. Salinger, *The Catcher in the Rye* (New York: Little, Brown, 1951).

17. Styron, *Darkness Visible,* pp. 40–43.

Chapter 21.

1. Agency for Health Care Policy and Research, *Depression in Primary Care,* vol. 1, *Detection and Diagnosis,* p. 73.

Chapter 22.

1. Vaillant, *The Wisdom of the Ego.*

2. Ibid., p. 72.

3. Erik H. Erikson, *Childhood and Society,* 2nd ed. (New York: Norton, 1963).

4. Howard Gardner, quoted in Daniel Goleman, Paul Kaufman, and Michael Ray, *The Creative Spirit* (New York: Plume Books, 1993).

Recommended Reading

ALBERTI, R. E., AND M. L. EMMONS. *Your Perfect Right: A Guide to Assertive Living.* California: Impact, 1990. Paper, $9.95.

BAER, JEAN. *How to Be an Assertive (Not Aggressive) Woman in Life, in Love, and on the Job.* New York: NAL-Dutton, 1991. Paper, $5.99.

BARLOW, DAVID H. *Anxiety and Its Disorders.* New York: Guilford, 1988. Hardback, $67.95. The most comprehensive professional explication of anxiety causes and treatments.

BARLOW, DAVID, AND RONALD RAPEC. *Mastering Stress: A Lifestyle Approach.* New York: American Health Publishers, 1991. Paper, $18.95.

BASS, ELLEN, AND LAURA DAVIS. *The Courage to Heal: A Guide for Women Survivors of Child Sexual Abuse.* New York: Harper Perennial, 1993. Paper, $8.00.

BEATTIE, MELODY. *Codependent No More: How to Stop Controlling Others and Start Caring for Yourself.* New York: Harper/Hazelden, 1987. Paper, $10.00.

BECK, AARON T. *Love Is Never Enough: How Couples Can Overcome Misunderstandings, Resolve Conflicts, and Solve Relationship Problems through Cognitive Therapy.* New York: HarperCollins, 1989. Paper, $12.00.

BENSON, HERBERT. *The Relaxation Response.* New York: Outlet, 1993. Paper, $7.99. Techniques from meditation applied to help relaxation in everyday life.

BLACK, CLAUDIA. *It Will Never Happen to Me.* New York: Ballantine,

1987. Paper, $5.95. One of the first books to explain codependency, and a classic.

BLOOMFIELD, HAROLD H., M.D., AND PETER MCWILLIAMS. *How to Heal Depression.* Los Angeles: Prelude, 1994. Hardback, $14.95. Self-help, directive, very good advice.

BOURNE, EDMUND J. *The Anxiety and Phobia Workbook.* Oakland, Calif.: New Harbinger, 1990. Paper, $13.95. Very detailed, practical information; lots of helpful exercises to practice alone or use in a group.

BOWER, S. A., AND G. H. BOWER. *Asserting Yourself: A Practical Guide for Positive Change.* Reading, Mass.: Addison-Wesley, 1991. Paper, $12.95.

BRIGGS, DOROTHY. *Celebrate Yourself: Enhance Your Own Self-Esteem.* New York: Doubleday, 1986. Paper, $9.95.

———. *Your Child's Self-Esteem: The Key to His Life.* New York: Doubleday, 1975. Paper, $10.95.

BURKA, JANE B., PH.D., AND LENORA M. YUEN, PH.D. *Procrastination: Why You Do It, What to Do About It.* Reading, Mass.: Addison-Wesley, 1990. Paper, $6.95. A very thorough, thoughtful treatment of this subject.

BURNS, DAVID, M.D. *Feeling Good.* New York: Avon, 1992. Paper, $5.99. Cognitive treatment of depression in a self-help framework.

———. *The Feeling Good Handbook: Using the New Mood Therapy in Everyday Life.* New York: NAL-Dutton, 1990. Paper, $14.00.

CHARLESWORTH, EDWARD A., AND RONALD G. NATHAN. *Stress Management.* New York: Ballantine, 1985. Paper, $5.99.

COLGROVE, MELBA, HAROLD H. BLOOMFIELD, AND PETER MCWILLIAMS. *How to Survive the Loss of a Love.* New York: Bantam, 1991. Paper, $12.00.

COPELAND, MARY ELLEN. *The Depression Workbook.* Oakland, Calif.: New Harbinger, 1992. Paper, $17.95. This is real self-help, a long compendium of exercises and advice meant to be used as an individual workbook.

COYNE, JAMES C., ed. *Essential Papers on Depression.* New York: New York University Press, 1986. Hardback, $25.00. Professional review of theories.

CRONKITE, KATHY. *On the Edge of Darkness: Conversations about Conquering Depression.* New York: Dell, 1994. Paper, $12.95. Celebrities and others describe their experiences. Very well written, with good dramatic examples that will lend you courage and inspiration.

CSIKSZENTMIHALYI, MIHALY. *Flow.* New York: Harper & Row, 1990. Paper, $13.95. Psychological research of peak experiences—how to access a creative state of mind—very readable, very helpful with depression.

CURRAN, DOLORES. *Stress and the Healthy Family.* New York: HarperCollins, 1993. Paper, $5.50.

DAVIS, MARTHA, E. R. ESHELMAN, AND M. MCKAY. *The Relaxation and Stress Reduction Workbook.* New York: New Harbinger, 1988. Paper, $13.95.

DODSON, FITZHUGH. *How to Discipline with Love.* New York: NAL-Dutton, 1987. Paper, $5.99. Dodson's books are minor classics.

———. *How to Father.* New York: NAL-Dutton, 1992. Paper, $5.99.

———. *How to Parent.* New York: NAL-Dutton, 1988. Paper, $5.99.

DOWLING, COLETTE. *You Mean I Don't Have to Feel This Way? New Help for Depression, Anxiety, and Addiction.* New York: Bantam, 1991. Paper, $11.95. Very readable, persuasive, helpful. Describes her own family experience well.

DREIKURS, RUDOLF, AND LAWRENCE ZUCKERMAN. *Children the Challenge.* New York: NAL-Dutton, 1991. Paper, $10.00.

DUNNE, EDWARD J., JOHN L. MCINTOSH, AND KAREN DUNNE-MAXIM. *Suicide and Its Aftermath: Understanding and Counseling the Survivors.* New York: Norton, 1987.

ELKIN, MICHAEL. *Families Under the Influence: Changing Alcoholic Patterns.* New York: Norton, 1990. Paper, $9.95.

ELLIS, ALBERT, AND ROBERT HARPER. *A New Guide to Rational Living.* Los Angeles: Wilshire, 1975. Paper, $7.00. Ellis's rational-emotive therapy, a useful forerunner to cognitive therapy for those who feel ready to face their problems.

FABER, ADELE, AND ELAINE MAZLICH. *How to Talk So Kids Will Listen and Listen So Kids Will Talk.* New York: Avon, 1982. Paper, $14.00. Very good concrete advice about communicating with children.

FIEVE, RONALD R., M.D. *Moodswing,* rev. ed. New York: Morrow, 1989. Hardback, $22.95. This book has been a standard since 1975. Last updated in 1989, so doesn't refer to Prozac and its congeners. Emphasis on bipolar disorder.

FIORE, NEIL A. *The Now Habit: Overcoming Procrastination through*

Quality Work and Guilt-Free Play. New York: J. P. Tarcher, 1989. Paper, $8.95.

FRANKL, VICTOR. *Man's Search for Meaning: An Introduction to Logotherapy.* Boston: Beacon, 1992. Paper, $15.00. Frankl, an Auschwitz survivor, addresses the meaning of life in a very moving book.

GRAVITZ, HERBERT L., AND JULIE D. BOWDEN. *Recovery: A Guide for Adult Children of Alcoholics.* New York: Fireside, 1987. Paper, $7.95.

HYATT, CAROLE, AND LINDA GOTTLIEB. *When Smart People Fail.* New York: Penguin, 1993. Paper, $12.00. An analysis of self-destructive behavior and the effects of disappointment on self-esteem.

JAMES, JOHN W., AND FRANK CHERRY. *The Grief Recovery Handbook.* New York: Harper Perennial, 1989. Paper, $10.00.

JAMISON, KAY REDFIELD. *An Unquiet Mind.* New York: Knopf, 1995. Hardback, $22.00. A respected researcher reveals her own struggle with bipolar disorder. Well written and interesting.

JOHNSON, VERNON. *I'll Quit Tomorrow.* New York: Harper, 1990. Paper, $10.00.

KARP, DAVID. *Speaking of Sadness.* New York: Oxford University Press, 1996. Hardback, $25.00. Karp is a sociologist and a sufferer from depression. His book is a fascinating analysis about the social effects and meaning of depression in contemporary American society.

KLEIN, DONALD F., M.D., AND PAUL H. WENDER, M.D. *Understanding Depression: A Complete Guide to Its Diagnosis and Treatment.* New York: Oxford University Press, 1993. Paper, $7.95. Klein is a leading researcher in the pharmacological treatment of depression, and presents it here as a brain disease. This is a comprehensive and useful review, surprisingly readable.

KRAMER, PETER, M.D. *Listening to Prozac.* New York: Viking Penguin, 1993. Paper, $22.50. A fascinating book about chemistry and character, also a sensitive and thorough discussion of depression.

KÜBLER-ROSS, ELIZABETH. *Death: The Final Stage of Growth.* New York: Touchstone, 1986. Paper, $9.00. The most accessible book from the originator of current understanding on death and dying.

KUSHNER, HAROLD S. *When Bad Things Happen to Good People.* New York: Avon, 1983. Paper, $4.99. Very readable and comforting.

LERNER, HARRIET GOLDHOR, PH.D. *The Dance of Anger: A*

Woman's Guide to Changing the Patterns of Intimate Relationships.
New York: HarperCollins, 1989. Paper, $12.00.

LESHAN, EDA. *Learning to Say Good-bye: When a Child's Parent Dies.*
New York: Avon, 1988. Paper, $8.00.

MANNING, MARTHA. *Undercurrents.* San Francisco: Harper, 1994. Paper, $12.00. A therapist's diary of two years' struggle with depression, leading to ECT.

MCCOY, KATHLEEN. *Crisis-Proof Your Teenager: How to Recognize, Prevent, and Deal with Risky Adolescent Behavior.* New York: NAL-Dutton, 1991. Paper, $4.99.

———. *Understanding Your Teenager's Depression.* New York: NAL-Dutton, 1985. Paper, $4.95.

MCGRATH, ELLEN, PH.D. *When Feeling Bad Is Good.* New York: Bantam, 1992. Hardback, $22.50. A feminist view of depression in women, stressing that it is often a response to an unhealthy society, and suggesting more adaptive responses. Good concrete advice and clear case illustrations.

MILAM, JAMES, AND KATHERINE KETCHAM. *Under the Influence: A Guide to the Myths and Realities of Alcoholism.* New York: Bantam, 1984. Paper, $5.50.

MILLER, ALICE. *The Drama of the Gifted Child (Prisoners of Childhood).* New York: Basic, 1981. Paper, $11.50. Misleading title: it really concerns the creation of depression in the child.

MILLER, LYLE, AND ALMA DELL SMITH. *The Stress Solution.* New York: Pocket Books, 1993. Paper, $22.00.

MOORE, THOMAS. *Care of the Soul.* New York: HarperCollins, 1992. Hardback, $25.00. Coming to terms with the differing needs of parts of our selves, especially the spiritual side.

NEUMAN, FREDERIC. *Fighting Fear: The Eight-Week Program for Treating Your Own Phobias.* New York: Bantam, 1986. Paper, $3.95.

NORWOOD, ROBIN. *Women Who Love Too Much.* New York: Pocket Books, 1989. Paper, $6.99.

OSHERSON, SAMUEL. *Finding Our Fathers: How a Man's Life Is Shaped by His Relationship with His Father.* New York: Fawcett Columbine, 1987. Paper, $10.00.

———. *Wrestling with Love: How a Man Struggles with Intimacy.* New York: Fawcett Columbine, 1993. Paper, $10.00.

PAPOLOS, DEMITRI F., AND JANICE PAPOLOS. *Overcoming De-*

pression. New York: HarperCollins, 1992. Paper, $13.00. Despite the title, this book focuses on explaining depression and how to get help, not on recovery. Good, very practical advice.

PECK, M. SCOTT. *The Road Less Traveled.* New York: Simon and Schuster, 1978. Paper, $12.00. A wise, classic book, very helpful for the depressive in recovery.

PEURIFOY, RENEAU Z. *Anxiety, Phobias, and Panic: Taking Charge and Conquering Fear.* New York: Life Skills, 1992. Paper, $12.95.

PITTMAN, FRANK S., M.D. *Man Enough: Fathers, Sons, and the Search for Masculinity.* New York: Putnam, 1993. Hardback: $22.95. Highly recommended.

SCARF, MAGGIE. *Unfinished Business: Pressure Points in the Lives of Women.* New York: Ballantine, 1980. Paper, $4.95. Depression through a woman's life cycle. Well written and readable.

———. *Intimate Partners: Patterns in Love and Marriage.* New York: Ballantine, 1988. Paper, $5.95. This is a very helpful and accessible book that popularizes much of what family therapy understands about love and marriage.

SELIGMAN, MARTIN E. *Learned Optimism.* New York: Pocket Books, 1992. Paper, $10.00. An excellent resource, surprisingly interesting, personal, and readable.

———. *What You Can Change and What You Can't: The Complete Guide to Successful Self-Improvement.* New York: Fawcett, 1995. Paper, $12.00. A thorough review of the state of current knowledge about self-modification, from alcoholism through sexual dysfunction.

SHOLEVAR, G. PIROOZ, AND LINDA SCHWOERI, eds. *The Transmission of Depression in Families and Children: Assessment and Intervention.* Northvale, N.J.: Jason Aronson, 1994. Hardback, $40.00.

SMITH, HYRUM W. *The Ten Natural Laws of Successful Time and Life Management.* New York: Warner, 1994.

SMITH, MANUEL. *When I Say No, I Feel Guilty.* New York: Bantam, 1985. Paper, $5.99.

STAUDACHER, CAROL. *Beyond Grief: A Guide for Recovering from the Death of a Loved One.* New York: Active Parenting, 1987. Paper, $10.95.

STYRON, WILLIAM. *Darkness Visible: A Memoir of Madness.* New York: Random House, 1990. Paper, $8.00. Styron's account of his struggle with depression at the height of his fame.

TANNEN, DEBORAH, PH.D. *You Just Don't Understand: Women and Men in Conversation.* New York: Ballantine, 1991. Paper, $12.00.

TAVRIS, CAROL. *Anger: The Misunderstood Emotion.* New York: Touchstone, 1989. Paper, $11.00.

THOMPSON, TRACY. *The Beast.* New York: Putnam, 1995. Hardback, $23.95. Journalist's account of descent into and recovery from major depression.

THORNE, JULIA, AND LARRY ROTHSTEIN. *You Are Not Alone: Words of Experience and Hope for the Journey Through Depression.* New York: Harper Perennial, 1993. Paper, $10.00. Inspirational self-help, reflections, and meditations.

WILSON, R. REID. *Don't Panic: Taking Control of Anxiety Attacks.* New York: HarperCollins, 1987. Paper, $12.00.

WINSTON, STEPHANIE. *Getting Organized: The Easy Way to Put Your Life in Order.* New York: Warner, 1991. Paper, $10.95. Reducing chaos in your life.

WOITITZ, JANET GERINGER. *Adult Children of Alcoholics.* New York: Health Communications, 1990. Paper, $8.95.

WOLF, ANTHONY E., PH.D. *Get Out of My Life, But First Could You Drive Me and Cheryl to the Mall? A Parent's Guide to the New Teenager.* New York: Noonday Press, 1991. Paper, $10.80.

ZIMBARDO, PHILIP. *Shyness: What It Is, What to Do About It.* New York: Addison-Wesley, 1977. Paper, $12.00. A classic of self-modification.

Index

disease, as, 20
experience of, 29–33
familiar feeling as, 21
functional autonomy and, 58, 59
hallmark of, 30
ideal-hungry, 77–81
major, 36–38
mirror-hungry, 81–85
monkey, 59–61
precipitant for depressive episode,
   65
recognition of, 31, 32
self-defeating nature of, 72–77
symptoms, 30
warning signals, 32, 33
Depression Workbook, The
   (Copeland), 206
Depressive disorder not otherwise
   specified (DDNOS), 41, 42
Depressive neurosis, 38
Depressogenic assumptions, 146
Desyrel, 198
Detachment, 181–183, 316
Diagnosing depression, 34–49
   adjustment disorder, 46, 47
   bipolar disorder, 42–46
   depressive disorder not otherwise
      specified, 41, 42
   dysthymic disorder, 38–41
   major depression, 36–38
   mood disorder due to general medi-
      cal condition, 47
   phenomenological approach, 35, 36
   seasonal affective disorder, 47–49
Dichotomous thinking, 144
Dickinson, Emily, 48
Disputation, 150
Distant relationship, 241
Divided allegiances, 259
Divorce, 228, 242, 243, 257–271
   children's positive adjustment to,
      268, 269
   contest, as a, 271

depression and, 270, 271
effect on adults, 269, 270
effect on children, 258–269
paternal support for college, 267
statistics, 257
visitation, 266, 267
Dowling, Colette, 283
DSM-IV, 34–36, 285
Dysthymic disorder (dysthymia), 38–41

Effective psychotherapy, 90, 91. *See
   also* Psychotherapy
Effexor, 198
Elavil, 196
Electroconvulsive therapy (ECT), 203
Ellis, Albert, 150
Emotional divorce, 241
Emotions, 91, 92, 95–120, 308
   anger, 110–115
   expression of feelings, 118–120
   grief, 107–110
   journal, 119, 120
   joy/pride, 115–117
   learning to feel, 99, 100
   mood changes, 103, 104
   Mood Journal, 104–106
Employment. *See* Work
Enjoyable activities, 222–224, 312, 313
Epidemiologic studies, 282
Erikson, Erik, 323
Ewing, Thomas, 113
Excessive responsibility, 144
Experience of depression, 29–33
Explanatory style, 149, 150
Expression of feelings, 118–120

Falling in love, 227, 228
Falling out of love, 239
False front, 85
Families, 245–256. *See also* Children
Family support, 206–210
Family therapy/therapists, 62, 157,
   175, 240, 245

Program for recovery *(continued)*
    feelings, 308
    generosity (charity), 314, 315
    heroes, 314
    intimacy, 315
    mood changes, 309
    prioritization, 310, 311
    responsibility, 313
    seek help, 317, 318
    support group, 317
    thinking, 309, 310
Progressive muscle relaxation, 140
Projection, 101, 162, 163, 236, 320
Projective identification, 162
Prozac, 156, 157, 182, 188, 198–202,
    305
Pseudoadults, 40
Psychoanalysis, 103
Psychotherapy, 56, 90, 91, 191–195
Ptolemaic system, 50, 51

Reaction formation, 98
Recognition of depression, 31, 32
Recovery movement, 176, 177, 227
Recreation, 142
Rejection sensitivity, 156
Relationships, 93, 155–171. *See also*
    Love, Marriage
    ambiguous communication, 160–162
    compromise, 164
    metacommunication, 158, 159
    projection/projective identification,
        162–165
    rejection sensitivity, 156–158
    stress/crises, 165–171
    withdrawal, 165
Relaxation, 139–142, 313
Relaxation Response, The (Benson),
    139
Repeating back, 164
Repression, 102, 103, 319
Resistance, 96

Responsibility, 177, 313
Revolving door treatment, 273, 274
Rhesus monkeys, 59, 60
Rivers, Joan, 139
Roosevelt, Eleanor, 26

Scarf, Maggie, 283
Seasonal affective disorder, 47–49
Second Chances (Wallerstein), 264
Selective abstraction, 144
Selective serotonin reuptake inhibi-
    tors (SSRIs), 198–202
Self, 93, 172–189
    body, 183–185
    boundaries, 175–180
    detachment, 181–183
    guilt/shame, 172–175
    play, 185–187
    self care, 187–189
Self care, 187–189
Self-constructive behavior, 72
Self-destructive behavior, 132–137
Self-esteem movement, 123
Self-help, 203–206
Self-object, 73
Self psychology, 64, 70, 73, 74, 157
Self-reference, 144
Seligman, Martin, 148–151
Serzone, 198
Sex, 141
Shame, 173–175
Sherman, William Tecumseh, 112–
    115
Shock therapy, 203
Sinequan, 196
Sixties, 272
Skills of depression, 78
Skinner, B. F., 148
Sleeper effect, 265
Sloth, 115
Smith, Susan, 53
Social problems, 272–280